PRAISE FOR *THE MOSCOW RULES*

"If there was ever a single book which could sum up the dangers, heroism, inventiveness, and intrepidity of the intelligence officers of the CIA it is *The Moscow Rules*. It is from the very first words a personal history of two of the nation's bravest intelligence officers, whose mundane day-to-day activities spell out an intense, gripping spy thriller from the darkest moments of the Cold War. This final homage to one of the nation's bravest patriots will be an instant best-seller. It is the real-life spy thriller one can't put down."

—Malcolm Nance, *New York Time*s best-selling author of
The Plot to Destroy Democracy

"Intriguing true stories of the techniques of CIA spying on the dangerous front line of the Cold War."

—Dame Stella Rimington, former director of MI5

THE
MOSCOW
RULES

THE MOSCOW RULES

THE SECRET CIA TACTICS THAT HELPED AMERICA WIN THE COLD WAR

ANTONIO J. MENDEZ AND
JONNA MENDEZ
WITH **MATT BAGLIO**

PUBLICAFFAIRS

New York

PublicAffairs
Hachette Book Group
1290 Avenue of the Americas, New York, NY 10104
www.publicaffairsbooks.com
@Public_Affairs

Printed in the United States of America

First Edition: May 2019

Published by PublicAffairs, an imprint of Perseus Books, LLC, a subsidiary of
Hachette Book Group, Inc. The PublicAffairs name and logo is a trademark of the
Hachette Book Group.

The Hachette Speakers Bureau provides a wide range of authors for speaking
events. To find out more, go to www.hachettespeakersbureau.com or call (866)
376-6591.

The publisher is not responsible for websites (or their content) that are not owned
by the publisher.

Print book interior design by Amnet Systems.

Library of Congress Cataloging-in-Publication Data

Names: Mendez, Antonio J., author. | Mendez, Jonna, author.
Title: The Moscow rules : the secret CIA tactics that helped America win the
    Cold War / Antonio J. Mendez and Jonna Mendez ; with Matt Baglio.
Description: First edition. | New York : PublicAffairs, 2019. | Includes
    bibliographical references and index.
Identifiers: LCCN 2018057371 (print) | LCCN 2018058591 (ebook) | ISBN
    9781541762176 (ebook) | ISBN 9781541762190 (hardcover)
Subjects: LCSH: United States. Central Intelligence Agency—History—20th
    century. | Intelligence service—United States—Methodology. | Espionage,
    American—Soviet Union—History. | Cold War.
Classification: LCC JK468.I6 (ebook) | LCC JK468.I6 .M464 2019 (print) | DDC
    327.127304709/045—dc23
LC record available at https://lccn.loc.gov/2018057371

ISBNs: 978-1-5417-6219-0 (hardcover), 978-1-5417-6217-6 (ebook)

LSC-C

10 9 8 7 6 5 4 3 2 1

This book is dedicated to the CIA officers who supported the Agency's activities in the Soviet Union during the Cold War. These men and women served under unusually harsh conditions and were subjected to pervasive surveillance techniques for the duration of their tours in Moscow. They were heroic in their efforts to obtain the intelligence that our policy makers needed in order to make informed foreign policy decisions. It was the CIA's Office of Technical Service who provided close support to those officers, and this book endeavors to lift the veil on their efforts, which were heroic in their own right.

CONTENTS

Photo section appears between pages 76 and 77

MOSCOW RULES

- Murphy is right.
- Never go against your gut.
- Always listen to your gut; it is your operational antenna.
- Everyone is potentially under opposition control.
- Don't look back; you are never completely alone. Use your gut.
- Go with the flow; use the terrain.
- Take the natural break of traffic.
- Maintain a natural pace.
- Establish a distinctive and dynamic profile and pattern.
- Stay consistent over time.
- Vary your pattern, and stay within your profile.
- Be nonthreatening; keep them relaxed. Mesmerize!
- Lull them into a sense of complacency.
- Know the opposition and their terrain intimately.
- Build in opportunity, but use it sparingly.
- Don't harass the opposition.
- Make sure they can anticipate your destination.
- Pick the time and the place for action.
- Any operation can be aborted; if it feels wrong, then it is wrong.
- Keep your options open.
- If your gut says to act, overwhelm their senses.
- Use misdirection, illusion, and deception.
- Hide small operative motions in larger nonthreatening motions.
- Float like a butterfly; sting like a bee.

- When free, in obscura (IO), immediately change direction and leave the area.
- Break your trail, and blend into the local scene.
- Execute a surveillance-detection run designed to draw them out over time.
- Once is an accident, twice is a coincidence, but three times is an enemy action.
- Avoid static lookouts; stay away from choke points where they can reacquire you.
- Select an IO or meeting site so you can overlook the scene.
- Keep any asset separated from you by time and distance until it is time.
- If the asset has surveillance, then the operation has gone bad.
- Only approach the site when you are sure it is clean.
- After the IO meeting or act is done, close the loop at a logical cover destination.
- Be aware of surveillance's time tolerance so they aren't forced to raise an alert.
- If an alert is issued, they must pay a price, and so must you.
- Let them believe they lost you; act innocent.
- There is no limit to a human being's ability to rationalize the truth.
- Technology will always let you down.
- Never fall in love with your agent.
- Betrayal may come from within.

AUTHORS' NOTE

This book contains stories from two overlapping careers in the CIA that, combined, spanned fifty-two years. For reasons of clarity, we've chosen to write most of our stories from Tony's perspective, but we have also included some narratives that can only be told from Jonna's point of view. In those cases, we've told those stories, her stories, in third person. Throughout the book, first-person pronouns such as "I" and "me" refer to Tony.

INTRODUCTION

"Don't harass the opposition."

It was still dark in Moscow on the morning of June 6, 2016. Sunrise would not come until 3:48 a.m. at this northern latitude. The temperature was cool, hovering around fifty degrees Fahrenheit. The YouTube video does not show these parameters, but they set the scene: early morning, nighttime, and chilly.

The images are grainy but clear enough to make out the incident. Point of view is a security camera focused on the facade of a building. A well-lit glass doorway occupies the center of the frame. Lower right on the screen, a bright-yellow taxi emerges and pulls up to that doorway. A male figure steps out. In silhouette, we can see that the passenger is wearing a knit cap, pulled down low, and a light jacket over street clothes, but his face is obscured. He does not stop to pay the driver; he must have done so as they approached his destination. He takes three steps toward the doorway when a uniformed figure explodes out of a guard booth to the right of the frame. Moving blindingly fast, like an animated figure out of a cartoon, the guard attacks him and slams him to the ground.

This is all in the first four seconds of a one-minute video. What's happening is that the Federal Security Service (FSB), the successor to the KGB, is attacking a US citizen who is trying to enter the American embassy, located in the Presnensky District in Moscow's city center.

The American is an officer assigned to the US embassy. Blindsided, he is thrown to the ground, pinned on his back. The Russian throws punches at him from above, almost as if the two were engaged in a World Wrestling Entertainment street brawl. Amazingly, while the Russian flays away at him, the American manages to kick and slide his way toward the two glass doors separating him from the safety of his embassy: US sovereign territory. After twenty seconds, it's clear that the American is making progress, although the Russian is still raining blows on him.

Five seconds later, the officer is close enough to reach back and just touch the right-hand portion of the glass door.

The door must have an electronic sensor on it, because it opens almost instantly. The Russian struggles to maintain control, and yet the American is somehow able to swing one leg up and through the opening. A second later, the American lifts his other leg through the door and begins shoving back against the frame, pushing the two of them deeper into the American embassy foyer. They are clearly on American soil now. However, the Russian doesn't let up and continues to pummel the American with blows. The screen goes black.

It is not clear at what point in the attack the American's collarbone was broken, but he was evacuated out of Moscow the following day to receive urgent medical treatment.

This unprecedented physical attack on an accredited American diplomat violated all the protocols governing relations between Western countries. But the larger context was even more alarming. In the months leading up to the incident, American diplomats in Moscow had been aggressively targeted by the Russian security services on numerous occasions. US officials had their cars vandalized, their homes broken into, and their children followed home from school. Russian agents reportedly even broke in and killed the dog of a US Defense attaché in the city. The US State Department was so alarmed that it called the Russian ambassador, Sergey Kislyak, to launch a formal complaint.[1]

All this paled in comparison to the subsequent hacking and information war launched by the Russian secret services in an attempt to manipulate the 2016 US presidential election. A declassified intelligence assessment published on January 6, 2017, determined that Russia used a multifaceted approach involving paid social-media users, or "trolls," as well as cyberoperations against targets like the Democratic National Committee in order to influence the election. In addition, Russia's state-run media outlets served up made-up stories designed to misinform and contributed to the influence campaign by offering a platform for the Kremlin on an international stage. Even more alarming, though, was the conclusion by the US intelligence community that this operation was the "new normal" in a concerted effort on the part of Russia to undermine the US-led liberal-democratic order.[2]

In response, President Obama decided to expel thirty-five Russian diplomats and to close two compounds used by the Russian government inside the United States. In addition, Obama imposed sanctions on two of Russia's intelligence agencies, including the military intelligence organization known as the *Glavnoye Razedyvatelnoye Upravlenie*, or GRU. Both of these moves made observers wonder if the United States and Russia might be entering into a new Cold War.

It was thought by some political pundits that the election of Donald Trump might be able to thaw the growing tension between Washington and the Kremlin. Throughout his campaign, Trump seemed to go out of his way to praise Putin at every opportunity, and even now, he is still reluctant to admit that Russia played any kind of role in trying to disrupt the 2016 presidential election. However, even President Trump was forced to act when Russian security agents were accused of poisoning a former Russian double agent, Sergei Skripal, in Britain on March 5, 2018. In a similar move to President Obama's, the Trump administration expelled nearly sixty Russian diplomats and ordered the Russian consulate in Seattle to be closed.[3] Russia was quick to hit back, expelling sixty US diplomats and closing the American consulate in St. Petersburg.

While some call these developments "unprecedented," as a former Central Intelligence Agency officer who spent time in Moscow during the Cold War, I am reminded of the adage that history tends to repeat itself.

During the summer of 1986, the United States and the Soviet Union went through a very similar tit-for-tat affair, known as the PNG War, which was touched off when the Federal Bureau of Investigation (FBI) arrested Soviet physicist Gennady Zakharov on charges of espionage. The Soviets responded by arresting US journalist Nicholas Daniloff, and in retaliation, the US government expelled twenty-five Soviet diplomats. The Soviets followed in kind, and then, in a coup de grâce, the Russians removed all 183 Foreign National employees from Moscow and Leningrad, plus another 77 personal maids, teachers, and private staff. Almost overnight, the American embassy in Moscow became the only US diplomatic mission in a foreign country with no Foreign Service National employees.

There have been other flare-ups over the years. The truth is that our two countries have always had a tense relationship. However, after the fall of the Soviet Union, the consensus among experts was that Russia's ability to influence world events was finished. Their infrastructure was crumbling; their economy was in ruins; and their political leadership was in disarray. Yet somehow Russia has been able to claw its way back onto the world stage.

It's anyone's guess what this might mean for the balance of power going forward, but America's clandestine services have never been more relevant to the security of our nation. For this reason, I think there are important lessons to be learned from the past. If this really is going to be the start of a new Cold War, then it seems only logical to examine the operations that played such a vital role in helping America to defeat the Soviet Union in the first place.

Throughout the Cold War, roughly from 1955 to 1988, the CIA and KGB faced off on just about every continent. Nowhere was this battle more acute than on the streets of Moscow. During the Cold War, Moscow was categorized as a "denied area." According to Thomas Allen and Norman Polmar's *The Encyclopedia of Espionage*, a denied area is "a country with such strict internal security that foreign intelligence agents dare not contact informants in person." It is an apt description. The Soviet capital was teeming with KGB surveillance.

In the end, the harsh conditions in Moscow as well as the paranoid nature of the society itself forced the CIA to refine its tactics and develop a fresh point of view in order to combat the KGB's Seventh Directorate, which was responsible for surveillance. This new approach—including not only a new set of techniques but also a host of new technologies and disguise methods as well as the recruitment of a new type of case officer—would come to be known as the "Moscow Rules," and it would revolutionize clandestine operations for years to come.

CHAPTER 1

"If the asset has surveillance,
then the operation has gone bad."

On the morning of November 2, 1962, the wife of Hugh Montgomery, the CIA's deputy chief in Moscow, answered a telephone call. On the other end, the caller remained silent for ten seconds and hung up. When Montgomery's wife told him what happened, he immediately realized the implications and began to make arrangements. The silent call was part of a prearranged signal from a Soviet spy named Oleg Penkovsky. Penkovsky had been missing for several months, and the CIA feared the worst. Now, out of the blue, the spy had resurfaced to signal that the Soviets were about to start World War III.[1]

Code-named HERO, Penkovsky was a colonel in the GRU, Soviet military intelligence. He also held a senior position at the State Committee for Coordination of Scientific Research Work, a government body that oversaw technology exchanges with the West. Both positions provided him with invaluable access to Russian military and technological capabilities.

Penkovsky first tried to contact the CIA in the winter of 1960 by handing a letter to a couple of American tourists in Red Square. After similar attempts the letter made its way into the hands of the CIA, which grew instantly suspicious. The letter was too vague. In it, Penkovsky wrote that he had important information on numerous subjects that would surely be of interest to the American government. However, he had refused to identify himself, and the chief of Moscow Station feared the whole thing might be a KGB trap. Penkovsky finally handed another letter to a British businessman, who then shared it with British Secret Intelligence Service (MI6). In this letter, Penkovsky included enough details to allow his identity to be confirmed, and the Brits and Americans decided to work together. This was at a time when an indifferent American public's knowledge of espionage was primarily derived from watching James Bond movies or reading the recent John le Carré best seller *The Spy Who Came in from the Cold*. Reality, it would seem, was trumping fiction.

Penkovsky was a dedicated and motivated spy. He hated the KGB and was disillusioned with the Soviet regime, which had repeatedly overlooked him for promotion.

Over the next seventeen months, he would become one of the most productive Soviet assets the CIA had ever run in Moscow. Their first face-to-face meeting with the Russian spy took place in a hotel room in London, where Penkovsky handed over an envelope stuffed with secret documents that included diagrams of Soviet missiles and launchers. On two subsequent visits to London and another to Paris, he delivered more than a hundred rolls of exposed film, along with nearly twelve hundred pages of handwritten notes and diagrams. In all, he provided the CIA with so much classified information that thirty translators and analysts were hired to work on the material full time.

Washington made Penkovsky's intelligence a top priority. It was hand delivered to the president and assigned two code names, IRONBARK and CHICKADEE, to make it appear as if the material came from more than one source. The information touched on a variety of sensitive topics, including Soviet intentions during the Berlin blockade as well as the technical capabilities of nuclear missiles that the Russians sent to Cuba in the fall of 1962. In fact, it can be argued that Penkovsky's intelligence played a key role in helping President Kennedy stand up to the Soviet premier, Nikita Khrushchev, during the Cuban missile crisis. The American president knew not only the exact type of missile the Russians had placed in Cuba but also that Khrushchev was overstating the capability of the Soviet nuclear arsenal. Kennedy knew it was unlikely that the Soviets would go to war with the United States, and when he called Khrushchev's bluff, the Soviet leader backed down.[2]

For his role in helping the United States navigate the Cuban missile crisis, Penkovsky would be dubbed the Spy Who Saved the World and acknowledged as one of the CIA's most important assets of the early Cold War era.[3]

In the beginning, there were no rules. The Penkovsky operation went relatively smoothly while the spy was allowed to travel abroad, where it was much easier for him to slip away and meet up with his CIA handlers. Things changed, however, in the fall of 1961, when his foreign travel was curtailed. The CIA in the 1960s was woefully unprepared to run such a sensitive operation out of the US embassy in Moscow, and so arrangements had been made with MI6 to handle the case jointly. The British assigned Janet Chisholm, the wife of the MI6 station chief, to serve as a go-between for the Russian agent, and over a three-month period, she met with Penkovsky almost a dozen times.

In the summer of 1962, the CIA finally sent a trained case officer, Rodney Carlson, to link up with Penkovsky in Moscow, but Carlson and Penkovsky would never meet. By September, the Russian spy had disappeared. Had something gone wrong? Penkovsky had always been one to take risks, sometimes daring to snap photographs of sensitive materials when Soviet officials had only just stepped away from their desks. Perhaps he'd been in an accident or become ill. Due to the sensitive nature of the operation, Montgomery decided to wait rather than risk attempting contact. Then, on the morning of November 2, Montgomery's wife lifted the telephone receiver and heard ten seconds of silence: Penkovsky had resurfaced.

Because of the heavy surveillance in Moscow, the established way of communicating with Penkovsky was a dead drop. The location for the drop was a radiator tucked under the stairs inside the entrance to an apartment building on Pushkinskaya Street. However, in the event that the spy had critical time-sensitive information—namely, that Russia was about to attack the United States—Penkovsky was to dial a series of telephone numbers, remain silent for a specified amount of time, and then hang up.[4]

After the silent call to the Montgomery residence, consensus at the US embassy was that the warning was a false alarm. It's true that in November 1962, Soviet nuclear missiles were still in Cuba. But tensions had abated, and the crisis had passed. It seemed unlikely the Soviets would suddenly launch a preemptive strike after backing down. So then why had Penkovsky placed the call? With so much at stake, a case officer named Richard Jacob was sent to see if Penkovsky had loaded the dead drop site with a new message. But when Jacob entered the dingy hallway and approached the radiator, a team of KGB officers sprang from the shadows and grabbed him. It then became clear that the KGB had placed the call and set a trap. How the Russians had known the location of the dead drop and the procedure for the silent phone call was also clear: Penkovsky must have told them.

Confirmation of Penkovsky's arrest arrived in the December 12 issue of the Russian newspaper *Pravda*. The article reported that the spy had been apprehended in late October, a full week before the silent call. Throughout his time in Moscow, Penkovsky had met with Janet Chisholm multiple times and passed small packages of chocolates to her, ostensibly for her three children but with exposed photographic film inside. It was unclear when and how he had been compromised, but the KGB likely had witnessed one of these exchanges and become suspicious. Or possibly George Blake, a British spy recently exposed as a double agent, had tipped them off.

Whatever the source of their suspicions, the KGB had drilled a hole in the ceiling of Penkovsky's study and installed a camera. They had also hidden a camera on his windowsill and stationed an officer in a building across the river. Finally, a search of Penkovsky's apartment unearthed a cache of espionage-related equipment, including a Panasonic radio used as a one-way voice link (OWVL) to send coded messages, a one-time pad (OTP) used to compose ciphers, and other encryption devices.

After grabbing him at the dead drop, the KGB held Jacob for a few hours, photographed him, and sent him back to the US embassy. Because he was an officer with diplomatic immunity, the Russians could do nothing to him. However, now that he had been identified, Jacob was declared persona non grata (PNG'd), and his days in

Moscow were effectively over. He was put on a flight the following morning. Meanwhile, Oleg Penkovsky wasn't so lucky. After a brief trial, the Soviets executed him on May 17, 1963.

The capture and killing of Oleg Penkovsky was a decisive moment in the history of the CIA as well as in the history of relations between the United States and Russia. In some ways, we still live in the wake of those events today.

On his own, Penkovsky had cracked the security system of the world's most paranoid government and left it virtually in pieces. At that point, he was the highest-ranking Soviet officer to spy for the United States, and in the aftermath of his arrest, some three hundred Soviet intelligence officers were immediately recalled to Moscow from overseas.

Penkovsky's avowed goal had been to prevent a nuclear war between the United States and the Soviet Union, and in that, he succeeded. The technical information he provided about the Soviet missiles deployed to Cuba in 1962 allowed the United States not only to track the missiles but also to gauge their operational readiness. As a result, at the time of his meeting with Khrushchev, Kennedy knew that the Soviets needed several days to make the missiles operational, time that allowed him to achieve a diplomatic solution.[5]

In the wake of Penkovsky's death, the CIA was forced to take stock and examine what had gone wrong. Although the Agency had had numerous successes recruiting agents and spies throughout the world, the Soviet capital was a different story. In describing the difficulties of working in Moscow, former CIA director Richard Helms said that it would probably have been easier to run an agent on the planet Mars.[6]

Moscow has always been an ominous destination for an intelligence officer. From the days of Catherine the Great through the rule of Vladimir Putin, no other espionage environment has rivaled it. As a metropolis in the same category as New York and Paris, Moscow has a distinct urban character, a mystique that hangs over the place like a fog. A visitor never mistakes the fact that they are in the Russian capital, and if that visitor happens to be a CIA officer, well, Moscow is a very special place indeed.

During the Cold War, American officials were routinely restricted in their ability to travel outside the city, but similar rules applied to Soviets in America. In fact, in Washington, DC, for many years, it was part of a CIA officer's duties to report the presence of a car with Soviet diplomatic plates anywhere in the metropolitan area— at a shopping mall, at a Redskins game, or, most importantly, outside the city. This did not exactly replicate the attention our officers received in Moscow, but it served the same purpose. All CIA reports of Soviet sightings were funneled to the FBI, the agency responsible for keeping track of Russians in the United States, whether in Washington, DC, or at their consulates in San Francisco or New York. The Russian footprint was and is wide and extends from Washington, DC, to New York to San Francisco to Seattle and Houston.

In Moscow, on the other hand, American diplomatic cars typically came under close vehicular surveillance the instant they passed through the embassy gates. In fact, there was a militiaman at that gate whose duty it was to call out the American cars as they drove past. Surveillance teams waiting outside the compound then swung into action, tailing the American vehicle until it returned to the embassy.

These surveillance teams, both on foot and in cars, were deployed by the dreaded Second Chief Directorate (SCD), an enemy that seemed superhuman, and the Seventh Directorate–Surveillance, which supported the SCD. Together they formed a veritable army, vastly outnumbering US agents on the streets of Moscow. According to former KGB general Oleg Kalugin, during the 1970s, there were more than fifty thousand KGB officers in Moscow alone.[7]

Today the SCD has morphed into the shadowy FSB, the breeding ground of Putinism. The majority of Russians now in important positions of power are alumni of the FSB and its predecessor organizations.

Because the Soviets had no way of knowing which Americans belonged to the CIA, they kept a close watch on everyone. The KGB had immense resources at their disposal, and thanks to the paranoid nature of the Soviet regime, they had essentially carte blanche when it came to operational rules. Files were kept on most foreigners, phones were tapped, and patterns studied. If a subject deviated from a daily schedule or in any way acted suspiciously, the KGB closed in immediately. Any conspicuous maneuver (driving the wrong way down a one-way street, for instance) resulted in being bumper-locked, by a KGB Volga, unable to move. These heavy-handed methods applied to the US embassy as well.

Shortly after the United States recognized the Soviet Union and established diplomatic relations in 1933, plans for a US embassy got underway. Stalin himself offered American ambassador William C. Bullitt a site in the Lenin Hills overlooking the Moscow River. America, however, was having none of it. We didn't want to be outside the city, on its periphery; we wanted to be in the middle of the middle, in the center of things. The American delegation moved temporarily into an area near Red Square, and in 1953, they were offered a property on Ulitsa Chaikovskogo, a site known as the Existing Office Building (EOB).

No matter what it was called, the EOB was quickly revealed to be inadequate in every way and insecure to boot. The site had been constructed in such a way that the Soviets could conduct surveillance from every angle: from adjoining buildings that provided views of windows, the courtyard, and gates; from the militiamen who guarded those gates; from surveillance teams housed in warming rooms ringing the embassy, waiting for targets to emerge; and finally from inside the EOB itself, where information could be gathered by a multitude of electronic bugs, taps, and intercepts.

The EOB was a ten-story Soviet-style apartment building. Old and crowded, it was a firetrap. Typical of buildings made during that period, it had narrow corridors and small rooms. Conditions were considered unsafe. The walls were filled with straw; the electrical wiring was shoddy and out of date, and the building was packed with Soviet nationals, most of whom reported directly to the KGB. It quickly became apparent that the EOB was unsuitable as an embassy, and in the 1960s, talks about a new office building (NOB) began. Who could have imagined then that the construction of a new US embassy in Moscow would take thirty years—a lifetime if you were among those American diplomats and their administrative staff who would toil for decades in conditions that were almost indescribably severe?

These conditions created a sense that the EOB, the structure itself, was the enemy. In 1963, we learned from a Soviet defector that the embassy was riddled with microphones and sophisticated listening devices, some of which had been embedded in the very foundations of the building.

Many State Department and CIA employees lived in residential apartments connected to the embassy compound. These apartments were bugged with live audio feeds. The offices in the embassy section of the complex were also bugged. Meanwhile, at the CIA station, a claustrophobia-inducing space fondly known as the Yellow Submarine, just in case, we were not above silently passing notes to each other at the water fountain.

In the early 1960s, the United States verified that windows in the Moscow embassy were being bombarded with low-intensity microwaves, a technique used to capture audio signals. Later, waves whose duration and intensity posed greater health hazards penetrated the upper floors of the central wing of the embassy— home to the ambassador's office and intelligence offices. These were directional microwave beams—ultra- and superhigh frequency radio waves—coming from transmitters near the embassy. They were clearly related to intelligence work—either to jam our radio waves or collect classified data.[8]

We would discover keyloggers in some of the embassy's IBM Selectric typewriters and hidden cameras in Xerox machines. Even the local Foreign Service Nationals (FSNs), who did everything from running the switchboard to cleaning the building, staffing the cafeteria, and dispatching the vehicles, were all assumed to be on the KGB payroll. American citizens were clearly the target, and the EOB itself was the spearhead in the attack.

The Soviets were never ones to respect boundaries. If you were an American in Moscow, you might return from a vacation to find your apartment door off its hinges. You would then be admonished—perhaps someone had smelled smoke—and reminded to not lock your doors when you went away so that your apartment could be accessed without knocking the door down.

On more than one occasion, CIA officers or spouses came home to find that an article of clothing had mysteriously disappeared from their wardrobe only to reappear the following day, after the KGB had had a chance to sew a microphone into the lining.

The lone secure area in the US embassy was a clear plastic-walled structure elevated above the floor on transparent Plexiglas blocks. Known as the Bubble, it was the one room in Moscow where a person could discuss sensitive information without being overheard by the KGB.

In the face of such an overwhelming challenge, many in Washington felt that the Agency wasted its time even thinking about trying to recruit and handle agents in the Soviet capital. The decade of the 1960s was a frustrating time for CIA case officers: hemmed in by the KGB's Seventh Directorate on one side, they felt hamstrung by overcautious supervisors on the other. Little was accomplished.

Blocked from gathering intelligence on the ground, the United States was forced to rely on technological platforms such as the CIA's U-2 spy plane; signals intelligence or SIGINT, signals intercepted for intelligence; and spy satellites—although in 1960, when Gary Powers's U-2 was shot down during a reconnaissance flight, it appeared that even Soviet skies were closed to us. The US government, however, wanted information on the plans and intentions of our enemy, and if the Penkovsky operation had proven anything, it was the value of human intelligence, or HUMINT, covert intelligence gathered by agents.

Penkovsky had smuggled schematics and images of weapons systems in development. He had shared information gleaned from top-secret military journals that described cutting-edge Soviet tactics—information no satellite could capture. The breadth of the Russian spy's intelligence was encyclopedic and included everything from the exact planned dimensions of the Berlin Wall, to the name of the new Soviet intelligence resident in London, to the defects in a new military helicopter and thousands more pieces of vital information.[9]

Penkovsky had lived near the apex of a tightly centralized society that allowed him to see clearly up and down the chain of command.[10] The range of his access has been matched by only a handful of spies in the history of US espionage.

More than anything, Penkovsky's tremendous value showed that the Agency could not abandon its operations in Moscow. But if the CIA was ever going to neutralize the stranglehold that the KGB's Seventh Directorate had on Moscow, then it was going to need a new set of tactics, a new approach. A new generation of men and women would need to be trained specifically for posting to the Soviet capital, new techniques perfected, and new technologies and disguise scenarios created that would enable case officers to "go black" and evade the ever-present KGB surveillance teams. Over time, a particular phrase would come to symbolize this new approach: the Moscow Rules.

George Smiley, a fictional character in the espionage thrillers of John le Carré, was the first to invoke the term "Moscow Rules." A British intelligence officer before becoming an author, le Carré demonstrated from his early writings—notably *The Spy Who Came in from the Cold*—that he knew what he was talking about. His ease with the intelligence lexicon was part of the clarity with which he wrote about espionage operations. A similar expression, albeit less elegant, comes from Mario Puzo's extraordinary novel *The Godfather*, in which Sonny Corleone announces the family is "going to the mattresses," Mafia slang for all-out war against their archenemies. The Moscow Rules echo that sentiment, the spirit of preparing to engage in an epic battle, which fairly sums up the CIA's intentions in Moscow during the Cold War.

Originally a set of operational guidelines, the Moscow Rules became symbolic of a much-larger effort on the part of the CIA to counter the threat of the KGB's Seventh Directorate. As an intelligence officer for twenty-five years, I gained an understanding of them firsthand. Although I did not invent the rules, I helped to refine them as an active participant at CIA headquarters in Langley, Virginia, experience I took to Moscow in 1976, remaining involved for many years after that. Operating on the hostile streets of Moscow during the height of the Cold War was the highlight of my career with the CIA.

CHAPTER 2

"Use misdirection, illusion, and deception."

I never set out to become a spy. I grew up in the hardscrabble back roads of Eureka, Nevada, as far away from the world of international intrigue as one could imagine. When I was about eight years old, my mom gave me watercolors after noticing that I liked to draw on used brown paper bags; she told me I was going to be an artist. Perhaps she saw in me something that I had yet to realize myself, but in the end, her premonition turned out to be true. I also had a natural fascination with magic from an early age. I discovered and studied a 1905 book of do-it-yourself wonders called *The Boy Mechanic*. I found out later that I was in good company; although just a grouping of tricks and illusions, that book was the inspiration for many would-be magicians. I had an early fascination with the clandestine and was deceitful enough to carry out some rudimentary sleight-of-hand operations, such as selling yesterday's newspapers on the train that thundered to a stop once a day in Eureka. Who can say, perhaps my career in the smoke and mirrors of intelligence operations was preordained, and I didn't even know it.

I attended the University of Colorado at Boulder for a year before leaving and looking for a job that would support my family. My father, John G. Mendez, had died in a mining accident when I was only three years old, and my mother had been left to raise four kids on her own. It was around this time that I also met my future wife, Karen Smith, and as the two of us began to plan our future, it was clear that I didn't have the luxury of going to college. I needed money. I transformed my love of art into a successful graphics business and began working for Martin Marietta, then an aerospace and defense company, as a tool designer and artist illustrator. But painting was always my passion, and I envisioned seeing my work hanging on the walls of a New York gallery someday. Then one afternoon three years later, I saw an ad in the *Denver Post* asking for artists to work overseas with the US military; after that, my life was never the same. As I was to learn when I went in for the interview, it wasn't the US military that was looking for artists: it was the CIA. I was twenty-five years old.

I was brought on board because of my talent for fine art. But at Martin Marietta, I had also developed an ability to capture incredibly fine detail by making life-size drawings of wiring harnesses and junction boxes on the Titan IIIC booster rockets. This precision and attention to detail was going to play a major part in my career at the CIA, but I didn't yet appreciate how these skills would be applied.

I started out my new career in 1965 in the artist's bullpen, surrounded by other artists with similar backgrounds and capabilities. We were hired because of our hand-eye skills and, in some instances, because of our creativity, but our imaginations were firmly bounded by the parameters of the CIA's technical requirements. We were not making fine art; we were typically re-creating things, copying things—documents, to be specific.

We were counterfeiters, creating both fake documents and fake identities.

As an artist, I worked within a tightly controlled set of rules: Never improvise. Don't get creative. Copy it, but do not try to improve it. Don't issue it unless it is good enough for you to use yourself. Would you cross a hostile international border using the document you just forged? My initial exposure to the CIA's rules for operational activities was extensive and taught me that my work could be the difference between life and death.

My heart rate got a workout throughout my career. We frequently held in our hands the wherewithal to send a man or woman to prison; to have one of our agents executed because of a simple error on our part; to cause a child to be raised an orphan, a wife to become a widow. It truly was life and death, and from the first day, I was never able to forget that fact. That human connection inspired my work and caused me to stay until midnight on weekends, come in on holidays, and travel halfway around the world on a moment's notice.

★   ★   ★

The graphics department was located in the Technical Services Division (TSD), part of the Directorate of Operations (DO), the operational element of the CIA. Later, in 1973, the TSD would be renamed the Office of Technical Services (OTS). We were the gadget makers who provided the tools for the field officers to carry out their missions, not unlike the character Q (Quartermaster) from the James Bond films. However, unlike Q, who never left the lab, CIA technical officers spent considerable time in the field, working with our case-officer colleagues and their foreign agents.

The Office of Technical Services rose out of the research and development (R&D) branch of the famed Office of Strategic Services (OSS). Headed by a chemist, Stanley Lovell, it would take a few years for OTS to find its footing. However, by the early 1960s, we had expanded from fewer than fifty employees to several hundred. If an operation required a specific piece of hardware, such as a wiretap or a small concealed camera or a set of modified documents, then it would be up to one of our techs to provide it and, if it didn't exist, to create it. Culled from a variety of backgrounds, the technical officers who made up the ranks of OTS shared a deep sense of purpose and professionalism. We were also adventurous and willing to push the envelope.

We were cut from a different cloth than our Ivy League colleagues in the Directorate of Plans—the case officers. While the first waves of CIA officers were recruited from prestigious American universities and social-register families, we technical officers were typically young scientists: chemists, mechanical and electrical engineers, physicists, and another group devoted to esoteric specialties like inks, batteries, and hot air balloons. We had a global responsibility and a worldwide presence. Travel was a major part of our duties, and you never knew when walking through the doors in the morning where you might end up that night. Cairo? Havana? Moscow?

We had a joke at OTS that if we weren't trying to save the country, we would probably have been out there somewhere in the heartland robbing banks.

Most of us spent our entire careers in OTS. It was not just a job; it felt more like a calling. Our retirees had an unfortunate history of dropping dead in the first months of retirement. Their work was their life, and without it, they were unmoored. They died. I always said that our work was like drinking from a fire hose and retiring was like jumping from a moving train.

Throughout the decades following the war, we had one foremost target: the Soviet Union. They presented the newly formed OSS and then the CIA with a bull's-eye target from which we never swerved. They were always our preeminent adversaries, and while the Soviet Union has become Russia, that has not changed to this day. They knew us then and know us today as the Main Enemy.

★   ★   ★

Moscow is a city of constant rebirth, a city that has survived Napoleon and Stalin and hopefully will survive Putin. The crowded streets and clogged subway are testament to its current resurgence. On the other hand, the gargantuan cathedral of Christ the Savior, built in the 1800s to celebrate the expulsion of Napoleon, was demolished by Stalin, smashed like a pile of Legos, in 1931. Eventually, the Moscow subway stations were beneficiaries of the marble from the demolished church. More recently, the punk band Pussy Riot took to the altar of the rebuilt cathedral and was arrested for flouting Putin's autocratic rule. Rebirth and resurgence indeed.

This is a great way to think of the Moscow Rules as well: birth and resurgence.

In the 1960s, the CIA did not have the operational methodology, clandestine hardware, or personnel to run secure operations inside the USSR. There would be years of backbreaking effort, begun after Penkovsky's heartbreaking execution, before the advantages of CIA technology and operational tradecraft, also known as the Moscow Rules, would reach a tipping point and start to shift the balance in favor of the West.

The Directorate of Operations was working on street tradecraft for its case-officer cadre, devising methodologies that ranged from creating opportunities for sleight-of-hand techniques to using the local terrain to mask its activities. The Office of Technical Services, on the other hand, was busy crafting and refining the technology that would allow the CIA's foreign assets to collect and pass their intelligence to us, to communicate the data, in more secure ways.

All of this would start paying off in the 1970s, but in the aftermath of Penkovsky, the enormous force of the KGB's omnipotent surveillance would almost shut down agent operations in Moscow.

Two important categories of work arose before us. First was the tradecraft, the street craft that would allow our officers to operate under the pressure of the twenty-four-hours-a-day, seven-days-a-week surveillance teams that accompanied them everywhere. Second, and equally important, would be the technology that would go hand in hand with officers on the street and in cars.

Developed over time, the Moscow Rules became a set of behaviors used to manipulate hostile surveillance, with the goal of making them think that you were doing something you were not; that you were there when you were absent; and that if they could not locate you, they had lost you, not that you had escaped. The fault, of course, was theirs. Then, when they were almost ready to report their "mistake," we would arrange for them to "find" you. You would magically appear, and the surveillance team would breathe a sigh of relief. *There is no limit to a human being's ability to rationalize the truth.* This, incidentally, became one of the most important rules.

My area of the Office of Technical Service provided many narrowly specific tools for this most difficult of challenges. Our disguise technology, for instance, grew in response to situations that would arise only in Moscow, such as needing to replicate our own officers as a direct result of the übersurveillance they had to withstand. No other city in the world at that time required us to take such elaborate precautions with our officers on the street.

★   ★   ★

The Moscow Rules were born in a vacuum, or that's how it seemed to those early pioneers at the CIA who wanted to try to push back against the KGB onslaught in the wake of Penkovsky's arrest. It was considered madness, impossible, in large part because the paranoia of one man had sucked all the air out of the room.

When James Jesus Angleton became chief of counterintelligence in the early 1950s, the CIA was like a toddler just taking its first steps. President Harry Truman had only just signed the National Security Act of 1947, which had officially given birth to the CIA, and the Agency was understaffed and underfunded. It was also trying desperately to crawl out from under the shadow of the OSS, America's intelligence agency during World War II. Run by the charismatic Major General William "Wild Bill" Donavan, the OSS had been involved in several off-the-wall schemes during the war, including parachuting saboteurs behind enemy lines, engineering especially creative sabotage weapons, and creating devices like the stinger, a small .22-caliber pistol that could be disguised as a cigarette.[1]

Angleton had actually served on the counterintelligence staff in the OSS as a corporal after being drafted by the army in 1943. During that time, he'd been stationed in London but had been given the task of conducting operations in the Italian theater. He had a reputation for being a bit of an eccentric. He wore a heavy cape with a high collar, like a cartoon spy, and could often be found crawling around on the floor of his office searching for listening devices.[2] But he was a stellar worker who just also happened to be very well connected thanks to his Ivy League pedigree; it would take him only six months to be promoted from corporal to second lieutenant, and then, as the war began to wind down in the fall of 1944, he was made commander of counterintelligence operations inside all of Italy.

As the chief of the CIA's counterintelligence staff, Angleton wielded an immense amount of power, made more so by the fact that he had cultivated close personal friendships with both Allen Dulles, the director of the CIA (DCI) during the 1950s, and Richard Helms, who would serve as DCI from 1966 until 1973. As a result, he was given unparalleled leeway outside the normal chain of command and ran his department as if it were his own personal fiefdom. And thanks to his position, he had an all-access pass to the most critical operations that the CIA ran at the time.[3]

Secretive and suspicious, Angleton devoted himself to anything he set his mind on, whether it be his counterintelligence work or his other two passions: growing orchids and crafting fly-fishing lures. He also cultivated an air of mystery, which made him an intimidating presence in an organization that prided itself on having access to secret information. If you were part of his inner circle, then you were in the know; if not, it was best to keep your head down and hope that his owlish spectacles never turned in your direction.

Primarily, Angleton's job was to assess the validity of the information being collected by our foreign assets, while, at the same time, he was to be on the lookout for foreign agents trying to infiltrate the CIA. It was an important role, especially given the aggressive nature of the KGB. After all, how can an intelligence agency collect information if it can't trust its sources? However, there is a danger in going too far, in believing that all the secrets being obtained are suspect or that everyone willing to offer information is a double agent. This is where Angleton began to lose his way.

A tall and gaunt man who wore thick-rimmed glasses that gave him the appearance of an undertaker, Angleton was a compulsive individual who spent the majority of his day cloistered in his office with the drapes drawn, poring over cable traffic and operational reports while smoking one cigarette after the other. He felt that the Soviet's closed society and totalitarian style of government gave it an advantage when it came to deception operations.[4] After all, the KGB had been running these types of operations for nearly forty years, all the way back to the end of the Bolshevik Revolution.

During that time, the KGB, then known as the Cheka, had spent the majority of its time trying to entrap royalist émigrés who were plotting to overthrow the nascent Soviet Union. In one such operation, known as the Trust, the Cheka even set up a fake royalist organization in order to ferret out anyone who might harbor sympathies toward the royalists' cause. The operation, which ran from 1921 until 1926, was successful in luring several prominent royalists back to Russia, where they were promptly arrested and put to death.[5]

Given such a history, it's understandable that the CIA's first counterintelligence chief might wish to err on the side of caution. But Angleton took it one step further and became convinced that the KGB was running a massive penetration operation to establish a mole inside the CIA, which came to be known as the Monster Plot.

The idea for the Monster Plot seems to have come from a former Soviet KGB officer, Anatoly Golitsyn, who had defected in 1961. Golitsyn told the counterintelligence chief that the KGB had devised a sinister plan to infiltrate the CIA with a veritable army of double agents.[6] Golitsyn's reason for doing this might simply have been to ensure his continued relevance, even after he had already provided the CIA with whatever secrets he had to share.[7] Either way, this information played into Angleton's tendency to see danger around every corner, and it wasn't long before his paranoia began to infiltrate the Soviet and East European (SE) Division, responsible for running operations inside the

Soviet Union, with disastrous ramifications, ruining the careers of several CIA officers and leading to the deaths of several Soviet agents. The result was a complete shutdown of all operations against the Soviet Union throughout the decade of the 1960s.

It is worth noting that when Penkovsky volunteered in December 1960, Angleton was already convinced that the KGB was having success in running deception operations against us. As has been well documented, Penkovsky provided voluminous intelligence to the US government and is still considered a benchmark agent. But over time, Angleton came to have doubts, believing that even Penkovsky was a provocation sent by the KGB to flummox American and British intelligence.[8]

It's for this reason that years later at a conference on "US Intelligence and the End of the Cold War," Paul Redmond, a senior SE Division officer, said, "The KGB referred to Angleton as one of their better assets, not in the sense of being an agent but of being a big help to them."

By 1971, it was apparent to CIA director Richard Helms that something had to change, and so he decided to shake things up by appointing David Blee to chief of the SE Division. Blee's major career highlights consisted of chief-of-station assignments in Asia and Africa and then running the CIA's Near East Division. When he was told about his new assignment, it seems that Blee tried to turn the job down, claiming that he didn't have any experience working on Soviet operations. Helms, however, told him that this was exactly why he'd been chosen.[9] The Soviet Division needed a fresh set of eyes and someone who had not been influenced by Angleton and his counterintelligence staff.

Not surprisingly, Angleton was less than thrilled by Blee's appointment. The counterintelligence chief would continue in his position until he was finally removed in 1974, and he made sure that Blee knew of his disapproval. Blee, for his part, chose a path of least resistance, never directly challenging Angleton while at the same time moving forward with what he thought needed to be done.

It was clear to Blee that the SE Division had become mired in Angleton's paranoia, and he set about making wholesale changes, replacing older and more entrenched managers with younger and more aggressive case officers who were unafraid to take on the Soviet Union. One such officer was Burton Gerber, a tall, soft-spoken, and lanky midwesterner who had spent his formative years in Eastern Europe, where he witnessed firsthand the difficulties of trying to run agents in denied areas like East Berlin. Open, creative, and intellectually engaging, Gerber was part of a new wave of case officers who had begun to join the Agency during the 1950s. Often graduates of state universities and military academies, these hardworking and self-motivated officers brought an increased sense of determination and professionalism to the Agency, in contrast with the earlier preparatory-school elitism that had permeated the ranks of the OSS.

Gerber was out of the country when most of Angleton's Monster Plot had played out during the 1960s, but when he returned to headquarters in 1971, he came face-to-face with the toxic environment the counterintelligence chief had created. Angleton had been so worried that any new recruit might be a Soviet plant that case officers had stopped bothering to recruit at all. And even if they did believe that a potential agent might be legitimate, there was no way for them to challenge Angleton without coming under suspicion themselves.

In other words, it was safer to simply turn everybody away. Gerber saw this as a self-defeating position. What was the point of having an intelligence agency if they couldn't recruit agents? If the ultimate goal of the CIA was to try to penetrate into the Soviet Union in order to understand the plans and capabilities of our chief adversary, how was the Agency supposed to accomplish this mission if they were told it was too risky to even try?

On his own initiative, Gerber decided to go back and review in exacting detail all the cases where the Soviets had approached the Agency during the previous fifteen years. The information was then compiled into a report, which indicated that the CIA had most likely turned away countless legitimate assets and lost immeasurable intelligence, all because of Angleton's paranoid script.[10] According to Gerber's analysis, it made no sense for the

CIA to be afraid to talk to the Soviets. There were always going to be dangles, spies who were actually double agents, but shutting down operations, as Angleton had done, over the prospect that something might go wrong was the height of folly. Instead, the only way to counter the aggressive tactics of the Soviets was to counter them with bold moves of our own.

Gerber's report spelled out his belief that Angleton had over-reacted and that the majority of Soviet volunteers were legitim-ate. And even if the Soviets tried a dangle, there were still many ways in which the Agency could test them. Furthermore, Gerber discovered no evidence that the KGB had ever used one of its genuine officers as a dangle. It would seem that the Kremlin just didn't trust them enough. This meant that if a KGB officer was offering to work for our side, it was probably a good idea to take him or her seriously.[11]

In essence, Gerber had developed the first set of rules govern-ing operations in the Soviet Union, which came to be known as the Gerber rules. These new rules served as a pivotal point in SE Division, turning Angleton's convoluted thinking on its ear.

★   ★   ★

Another young CIA officer who had a massive impact on chang-ing the rules in Moscow was Haviland Smith. Prior to joining the CIA in 1956, Smith had served in the US Army as a Russian-language intercept officer. A gifted linguist who attended Dart-mouth and then later the University of London, where he had majored in Russian studies, Smith was first posted to Prague, where he hit upon a novel idea. Using his experience from his days in the army, Smith was able to tune in to the radio frequency of the Czech surveillance teams in order to discover whether or not he was being followed.

The rudimentary technology of the day didn't allow him to learn this in real time—only after he had returned to the station to analyze the recording.[12] If the tape showed that he had been in the clear when making a dead drop, then he could be relatively certain that the operation would be a success. If not, then Smith would know to contact the agent and tell him or her to abort the mission. More often than not, though, Smith discovered that he was almost always under surveillance, which led to another breakthrough.

Smith discovered that the Czech surveillance teams tended to stick to a strict methodology. In other words, like all communist state-run organizations, they were unimaginative and predictable, which Smith realized could be used against them.

In order to test out his theory, Smith became as drab as possible—a slow-moving, predictable, and cautious American diplomat who would be of little interest to those tasked with keeping tabs on him. He went to the same places each week on the same day. He went to the market, he took his dog to the vet, and he went out to the same restaurants and quite possibly ordered the same dish every time. He became boring, what we call a "little gray man." Then, once he had his surveillance team lulled into a zone of comfort where they would begin anticipating his next destination, he began experimenting with their training and their reactions.

Smith discovered, for instance, that if his car made two right turns in succession, with minimal space between them, he just might find himself out of sight of the vehicle trailing him. From the moment he disappeared from view until the moment they rounded the second corner, he had a brief opportunity to perform an operational act. He could toss a dead drop from his car window or even hand an envelope to an agent waiting in the shadows, anticipating his arrival. Smith's discovery of this hidden opportunity became known as "working in the gap."

Crucially, this scheme depended on Smith being boring all the rest of the time. Vanishing from view would look suspicious if he seemed to be trying to elude surveillance, but if he kept heading for his usual destination, his observers would blame themselves for the error—not him. *Let them believe they lost you; act innocent.*

For that reason, the gaps had to be kept short. Originally timed at less than fifteen seconds, eventually a gap could be expanded to several minutes if the case officer planned it successfully. In spite of its disarmingly modest name, the gap was one of the most powerful tools that the CIA developed for use against the suffocating surveillance that they experienced in places like Moscow.

Another technique Smith began perfecting was called the "brush pass." Throughout the early days of the CIA, the most secure way to communicate with an agent in denied areas was by using dead drops. A dead drop would simply mean that the CIA officer would leave a package behind for the agent to then pick up a few hours later. These packages would, of course, be disguised to look like everyday objects so that a curious bystander wouldn't pick them up. During a dead drop, the case officer and the spy were never in the same place at the same time, thus avoiding suspicion in cities where foreigners were under almost constant surveillance. After all, in places like Moscow, just being seen in close proximity to an American would be enough to draw the attention of the KGB. Now imagine if the Soviet citizen in question happened to be a high-ranking scientist working on a secret military project.

The dead drop wasn't without its flaws, however. They were incredibly complicated operations to coordinate, involving multiple signals and communications plans as well as concealment devices that would often take months to put together. Another problem was that it required that the package be left out in the open, where a trailing surveillance team might snatch it up. In the case of the CIA officer, this might not be that big a deal, since the package wouldn't contain anything that could be traced back to him or her. However, the same could not be said for the spy, who might be including incriminating information or photographs of secret documents. For this reason, Smith envisioned a technique that would utilize the sleight of hand of a magician, allowing the case officer to brush past the spy, who could then place the material directly into his or her hand.[13]

Smith did not create the technique; he borrowed it from a book that the CIA had commissioned in 1953 from a world-renowned magician named John Mulholland. Before my arrival in OTS, our office expressed an interest in the use of sleight-of-hand magic as a potential tool for our operations officers. Dr. Sidney Gottlieb, our office director, contacted Mulholland to put together a manual for use by nonmagicians describing close-up magic that might be useful to a case officer in the field.

Initially, the requirement was to allow our officers to be able to clandestinely place a tablet or powder into a drink without alerting suspicion. This sleight of hand was a common skill used by professional magicians, and Mulholland had no problem putting the handbook together. It was so well received that the CIA made a second request, asking him to produce a book on recognition signals. Mulholland complied, and this new book detailed techniques for communicating information surreptitiously, as magicians clearly were able to do, without being observed.

These two volumes demonstrated the CIA's respect for and interest in using the tools of the professional magic industry to further the goals of gathering information. Magic and intelligence work would appear on the surface to be an unlikely combination, but as the partnership between the dark arts and the Agency evolved, the craft of magic and the CIA's need for clandestine operations locked together like the last two pieces of a jigsaw puzzle. Just like the British, America had a long history of supporting the magic industry on stage. Headquartered in Los Angeles and more specifically on the edge of Hollywood, this community was a heretofore-untapped resource. And once we had our foot in the door, it led to even more interesting connections in the areas of special effects and disguise.

But I am getting ahead of myself. Mulholland's first book was originally intended to teach case officers about the various sleight-of-hand techniques that a magician uses to fool his or her audience. Mulholland was careful to outline that the key to success was in deciding when and where and how to act.

When done well, the brush pass is almost invisible. There were many variations, but basically both officers would move by each other. One could be stationary, the other walking. Or both could be moving. They could carry a variety of materials—umbrellas, briefcases, books, or shopping bags—but those objects would only mask the transfer. Another important aspect of the trick that Mulholland stipulated was that "the larger motion would hide the smaller motion." For instance, if you looked at your watch with one hand, it would be easier to pass a package into a colleague's hand with the other without being noticed.

This brush pass technique formed a transition from face-to-face meetings between case officers and foreign agents to the more secure impersonal communications that all agents working in denied areas would use. While there was personal contact between agent and case officer, the brush pass minimized the time they were in proximity with each other. And, as with all good sleight-of-hand performances, it relied heavily on the point of view of the surveillants, or audience. The site chosen for the brush pass (i.e., the stage) only worked with surveillance trailing the agent. If the surveillants could get out in front of the agent, they might possibly see the transfer of material. Choosing the stage and knowing the audience were incredibly important.

Smith would later demonstrate the technique in Washington, DC, in order to win over a skeptical Helms, who thought it sounded incredibly risky. At the time, Smith had been asked to train an intelligence source from Czechoslovakia who was nervous about using dead drops for fear that the Czech police might discover the material and trace it back to him. Smith described to him the concept of the brush pass, which the agent agreed sounded like a much better option. Helms, however, was absolutely against it and torpedoed the idea.[14]

As it turned out, the agent was sent back to Czechoslovakia, but since he hadn't been given permission to use the brush pass, he refused to hand over any material. Finally, in 1965, after a full year had gone by, Smith was furious at the loss of potential intelligence and once again approached Helms about getting clearance to use the technique.[15]

This time Helms agreed to a demonstration and sent his deputy, Thomas Karamessines, to witness it. The demonstration took place in the lobby of the swank Mayflower Hotel in downtown

Washington, DC. Smith stood just inside the entrance, waiting. Then one of our OTS technical officers, who had prepared the package to be passed, entered the Mayflower Hotel through the magnificent main doors. The two men briefly passed by each other. The tech used his raincoat as a distraction, moving it from one hand to the other, and handed Smith a small package at the same time. They headed off in opposite directions.

The larger motion was the transfer of the raincoat from left to right. The smaller motion consisted of the brush pass, in which the technical officer handed off the package. All of it was done for the benefit of the audience, namely Tom Karamessines, who completely missed the exchange. The act was invisible.

Afterward, Karamessines dutifully reported back to Helms what he had seen (or not seen), and as a result, the technique was approved for use the very next day. The Czech agent would go on to use the method to great success and hand over hundreds of rolls of film the following year.[16]

Essentially what Smith had done was to prove that there were no such things as denied areas; it was simply a question of methods. If the right techniques were used, anything was possible.

CHAPTER 3

"Execute a surveillance-detection run designed to draw
them out over time."

Jonna stood perfectly still just inside the bathroom door of the
restaurant, taking a few deep breaths before stepping onto
the mezzanine. Her heart was pounding, and she could feel her
pulse in her ears. From this vantage, she could see the expanse
of the brilliantly lit restaurant with its two-story windows and
spectacular view of the Potomac River. And everyone in the room
could see her. There was a surveillance team around this restaurant, inside and out, sweeping the area, looking for her. It was the
FBI's best team, the Gs, the team that tracked the Soviets in our
nation's capital, and this afternoon they were tracking her.

This morning had begun at Union Station, where a PBS camera crew had outfitted Jonna and me with concealed audio and
video devices. I had a camera in my tie, and Jonna's camera was
in a fanny pack. Both of us were wearing concealed microphones
as well. Today's exercise was going to be filmed as part of a PBS
series on espionage, and our exercise against the FBI's Gs was to
be a centerpiece of the episode. Just like in our real-life exercises,
there was no way to anticipate who would win this battle. But our
goal was to set up a meeting between Jonna and a fake terrorist
at a predetermined site in Georgetown and to pass a document
to the terrorist without being detected by the Gs. Their goal was
to witness the meeting.

I was making my way independently through this part of the
city, an area we both knew particularly well. This is where we

trained our CIA colleagues in some of our more esoteric equipment and techniques. It was also where we trained the CIA officers who were heading off to work in denied areas, such as Moscow. Usually the last bit of training they would get before boarding their flight, the exercise was one more opportunity to see if they could detect surveillance in the benign environment of Washington, DC. And it was also an opportunity to test new and novel methods of becoming invisible when necessary.

Thinking we would give the Gs a chance to organize themselves before the real game began, we had stopped at a bookstore along the way, just past the Palm Restaurant. Jonna browsed the shelves, and I bought a magazine. Sure enough, two of the Gs came in with us. They were discreet, two young women who came in separately. But we could see them. And they could see us.

When Jonna and I entered the Four Seasons hotel on M Street in Georgetown, we also entered what we called the Zone. We had told the FBI that we would stay in that area, roughly from the Potomac River to P Street and between Thirty-Seventh Street and Wisconsin Avenue. That defined the parameters of the Zone, helping to install guardrails on the geography of this exercise. A surveillance team is usually not responsible for knowing the whole city, but they should be intimately familiar with their piece of the turf.

Jonna and I had a plan, and it began in the hotel lobby. We called it a mini-starburst. I leaned over and gave her a kiss on the cheek, whispering, "Go get 'em, Jonna." Then I went into the gift shop while she walked down a flight of stairs. We loved this hotel because of the labyrinth of hallways and external doors. Jonna dropped down yet another level and would exit to the outside through a small door from one of the ballrooms. I didn't think the Gs had gone with her, because when the two of us split up, the Gs had to make a snap decision on whom to follow. Who was carrying the football? Most of them would stay with me. We expected the Gs to focus on the male officer. (They had very few professional women at the FBI at the time.) As a result, she would be able to leave the hotel by the side door that took her down to the sandy towpath running along the C&O Canal.

Now she stepped through the bathroom door and walked slowly down the open stairway to the ground floor. When she had entered the bathroom, she was wearing heels and a wrap-around skirt, horn-rimmed glasses, and a black tank top and was carrying an umbrella. When she left the restroom, she had on long black pants, flat black shoes, a blue denim shirt, and a curly gray wig. She was carrying a small plastic bag with a Clydes of Georgetown logo, carrying the pieces of her clothing that she had removed.

We had recruited a friendly accomplice, a dog walker in Georgetown we had come across while scouting our path earlier in the week, who was happy to play a part in our little exercise. She was waiting farther down the path with two dogs, and when Jonna walked up, she handed her the leash for a large black standard poodle named Louie. Off Jonna and Louie went, two women with their dogs, strolling slowly down the river, as walking too fast draws the eye and the Gs were probably getting a little nervous at this point. So was Jonna. Even though this was only a training exercise, once you are in the moment, it becomes very real. They'd had no problem following me, as we had planned, but once they discovered that they had lost Jonna, I knew they would be retracing their steps outside of the hotel, realizing that she had disappeared and trying to reacquire her. But, as it turned out, they were a little late.

Jonna had one more stop to make. Handing the poodle back to its walker, she stepped into a convoluted apartment complex along the river with multiple levels and intricate turns. Jonna and I had explored this site the week before and thought it offered perfect cover for her last deception. She stepped into a niche in the wall, slipped off her wig and put it in the bag, pulled out a baseball cap to put over her short blonde hair, removed her earrings, and put on a pair of wire-rimmed men's spectacles. Then she pulled another bag out of the first one and put the Clydes bag in that. The frosting on the cake was the gray mustache glued to her wrist, ready to be removed and applied to her upper lip with just a couple of gentle pats.

All this took about ten seconds, after she had practiced it a number of times in front of a mirror. The last touch was to take a small handful of gravel out of her pocket and put it in one of her shoes and to take a cigar and a lighter out of the other pocket. She lit the cigar. When Jonna stepped out of the apartment complex, she was a little gray man, walking slowly with a slight limp, smoking a cigar, carrying a plastic bag. She was headed for Dean & DeLuca, where she was to meet the terrorist and hand off documents. Jonna could not know for sure at this point whether the Gs were with her, but her gut told her that she was without surveillance; she was black.

As she approached Dean & DeLuca, Jonna knew that the PBS camera crew would already be set up there to film the final scene, as prearranged. She knew exactly where they would be: shooting the scene through the glass window of the store, looking into the café. A cluster of tall grass and hydrangeas screened them from view. The terrorist she was to meet was already there. Jonna could see her through the window: young, female, with long dark hair—she looked like a college student. As Jonna approached, her heart was pounding again, going a hundred miles a minute. She saw no evidence of FBI surveillance. It felt like she was black, like she had lost them, so she went into the café and approached her target, sweat slowly trickling down her back. Jonna sat down across from the terrorist, took a puff on the cigar, and slid the folded document across the table, where it was palmed and slipped into a bag.

From the back of the room, the PBS producer stood up, nodded to Jonna, and walked outside to talk to the camera crew. Then she came back in and asked if Jonna could go outside and do the whole ending again—approaching the café, scanning for surveillance, entering, and handing the document to the agent. As it turned out, Jonna's disguise was so effective that the PBS crew, who had been looking for her, had completely missed the money shot. She had to do it over. The scene that ran in the finished episode was essentially a retake.

I headed to a bar just down the street in Georgetown for an after-action debrief with Jonna and the Gs. When Jonna approached, the Gs looked up as an old man sat down at their table and then laughed as Jonna removed her gray moustache. A bit later, one looked down at her foot.

"You're bleeding!" he said.

"It's nothing," she told him. "Just something in my shoe.

★   ★   ★

Around the same time that Helms was cleaning house and turning things around inside the SE Division during the early 1970s, the Agency began to rethink how it assigned case officers to Moscow. Since the Soviet Union was such a difficult environment to operate in, conventional wisdom required that the job should fall to our most experienced officers. But wouldn't the KGB expect that? And what about the overwhelming surveillance that our case officers would face on the streets of Moscow? Those with more experience tended to come from other postings and as such had more baggage; they were easier to identify. In a place like Moscow, that would make their job harder, not easier. For this reason, the CIA decided to turn to a younger and newer generation for assignments to denied areas. Not only were they hungry, but they would also have less of a history. Known as Pipeliners, these young new case officers would soon come to form an important component of the Moscow Rules.

Pipeliners tended to be the best and brightest that the Agency had to offer. For a young CIA officer, bagging an assignment to Moscow Station was like being chosen to receive the Heisman Trophy for a college football player. At the same time, it offered an obvious conundrum, in that the Agency was basically proposing to send inexperienced and relatively green individuals into the most hostile environment an intelligence officer would ever have to face. The Moscow Rules, as they evolved, became like a set of road signs for these officers, guiding them along a treacherous highway that would normally be considered out of bounds for such untested officers.

The Internal Operations Course (IOC) was a grueling six-month course that Milt Bearden, a former chief of SE Division at the CIA, liked to compare to the US Navy's Top Gun school for fighter pilots.[1] Run by experienced CIA case officers, including at one point a stern ex-marine named Jack Platt, the IOC put the young Pipeliners through their paces and taught them how to execute a host of covert operations, including photographing a potential signal site while driving, servicing a dead drop, and performing a car toss—all without being detected by the KGB.

The more realistic the scenario, the better, which is why the instructors would set up elaborate training exercises on the streets of Washington, DC, like the one above, in which the trainees would have to outsmart the FBI's famed counterintelligence unit in the hopes of carrying out their clandestine act unseen. The training was grueling and the washout rate high. The FBI even went so far as to stage and conduct a realistic drug bust and arrest with the local police in order to test the officer's ability to stand up under what seemed to be very real pressure. Many of them broke, believing that the police had arrested them by mistake.

Officers trained with a partner, either a colleague who would be serving with them in the foreign location or, ideally, a non-Agency spouse. Often the spouses, who tended to be less rigid in their thinking and more open to role playing, less scripted perhaps, proved the more adroit of the two, an awkward situation at the beginning of a tough assignment. We would note which of the couple was the more skilled driver, the better photographer or sketcher, and the more composed under duress, and we would assign operational duties accordingly.

At this point, it is worth pausing for a moment to consider the qualities that make a good case officer. Being selected for an assignment to Moscow was a career high point, one most of the operations officers would compete for. After all, the Soviets were our number one target, just as the CIA was considered to be the KGB's main enemy. It was a head-to-head battle, and only the cleverest, the most intelligent, and the most persistent would win. Life and death were in the mix, not to mention an officer's reputation. The stakes were as high as they got.

CIA case officers were larger-than-life characters. Many qualities were desired in our Directorate of Operations colleagues. Some could be taught if the applicant didn't bring them. We could teach tactical and analytical skills. We could teach languages. We could immerse officers in area studies to an extent that they knew the layout of the terrain before ever setting foot in the country. We could give them classes on the significant cases that had preceded them, and we could show them how the various personalities in the Soviet hierarchy affected their operations. You only have to look at Vladimir Putin today to understand how his history with the KGB influences his actions on the world stage. He is brash but measured, aggressive but careful, and an expert at manipulating public opinion.

We could, in other words, mold and sculpt a young officer into the intelligence-collecting soldier we needed to send into the fray. But there were other attributes that could not be taught. Personality. Ego. Competitiveness. Curiosity. Charisma. Self-assurance. They needed to be adventuresome problem solvers. These were the hallmarks of a CIA case officer, the traits that could not be taught but could be scouted for. It also helped if they were gregarious, outgoing, and amiable. After all, it was their job to recruit foreign agents, and it would only help if the person they were recruiting found them to be approachable.

At the same time, the nature of the work required them to become and often remain practically invisible, to be able to get black and to stay in the background. The more successful their operations, the more necessary it was that they recede into the shadows. There would hopefully be no headlines, no attaboys, no applause. In terms of recognition, the most they could hope for would be a commendation from the CIA, but this was done most often in a closed ceremony with only those with a need-to-know in attendance. And after the ceremony, the commendation would be taken back and inserted into the officer's secret 201 file, which was the main personnel file for an officer's entire career.

We would take these outsize characters, shoehorn them into an impossibly hostile environment, give them an assignment that was heavily weighted against success from its inception, and ask them to navigate the most dangerous environment we could provide. Anonymously. These case officers were and are the life-blood of the CIA.

★   ★   ★

After Penkovsky, it was determined that face-to-face meetings with Soviet agents in Moscow were no longer on the table. Our Office of Technical Service began to draw up an enhanced program for enabling impersonal communications between our case-officer colleagues and our foreign assets. The lack of technology, or advanced tradecraft, had to be chalked up to the fact that the CIA did not yet have the wherewithal to support a clandestine intelligence operation inside the borders of the Soviet Union.

But that was about to change; the KGB and its sophisticated surveillance machine were up against a newly formed and highly motivated technical foe. Haviland Smith's efforts in the 1960s on working in the gap and delivering material via brush passes were already paying off. We began to work down the list of capabilities we would like to develop next and started to broaden the concept of impersonal communications, now that it was the name of the game in Moscow's urban environment. It would include not only encrypted electronic communications, dead drops, and a new generation of subminiature cameras, along with one-way voice links, but also the use of disguise and its various techniques in order to deliver requirements to the foreign agent.

Throughout their time at the IOC, our Pipeliners would be required to master a variety of technical equipment that OTS had built specifically for use in Moscow, such as encrypted electronic communication systems and burst transmission devices, proprietary disguises, and even a pop-up dummy known as the Jack-in-the-Box, or JIB. The inexperience of the field officers put a lot of pressure on us old hands to play our part and get them ready.

By 1978, I had formed an auxiliary CIA team that trained DO operations officers preparing for assignment to Moscow. The Special Surveillance Team, or SST, was ad hoc; an after-hours exercise, it offered no pay to our officers and no official recognition that they had participated. Fueled by operational zeal and professional exuberance, the SST was composed of technical officers, many of them engineers, physicists, chemists, forensics specialists, and graphic artists who would never have feet on the ground in an actual CIA overseas operation.

Many had no denied-area operational background; the scientists, übernerds, rarely stepped outside their R&D laboratories, but they were motivated, bright, and vigorous and had volunteered to work extra hours in addition to their regular job. The skills they would develop and their understanding of street operations would be of incalculable value in their future endeavors, informing their interpretation of operational requirements levied upon them. As a team, we could simulate those operations in Washington and give our soon-departing Pipeliners some final training after they graduated from SE Division's IOC.

The team had been steeped in all the data we could muster about the KGB in Moscow because we were asking them to emulate the KGB's surveillance techniques here in Washington, DC. They had been briefed by many of the case officers who had served in Moscow, including Jack Downing, the chief of the Soviet Branch during the late 1970s, whom I had met when he was the deputy chief of station in Moscow in 1976 and I was conducting their disguise survey. As a result of Jack's experience and unique ideas, we had reinvented some of the Moscow Rules while I was there.

There were also a good number of professional women on our Special Surveillance Team, some engineers, some from the art department, others from admin.

Jerry, a chemist who had an engineer's penchant for organizational excellence, led the SST. We had a dedicated car and one van. We had magnetic signs that we used on the vehicles. My favorite was the Tony's Pizza sign with a faux address and a faux phone number. (I took that sign home with me when I retired.) The van was loaded with electronics and filled with surveillance and disguise materials. Jerry, a typical male, drove, and the women handled the material and technology.

Marilyn and Patricia basically ran the command center, which was in the van. It was loaded with communication equipment. Each of our officers was issued a Motorola phone, but before any electronic communications could be used, everybody had to master hand signals. These were the primary mode of communication, because the phones would fail. Invariably. And always at the worst times. The hand signals allowed the team to be cohesive and communicate their intentions without electronics, even when driving into a dead zone. There were code names that we used in our communications, along with numeric codes for direction of the team. They came up with the code OZ for our headquarters building out on the George Washington Parkway in Langley. It was named OZ because of the green-glass shielding that covered the building's exterior, protecting it from all sorts of electronic penetrations. The wizard was understood to occupy the seventh-floor executive offices.

Pat was the team's mother. Heavyset and middle-aged, she directed our troops like the mother of five she was. She brooked no nonsense and tolerated no goofing off. But she was also the one who always showed up with six dozen chocolate chip cookies for her colleagues. Marilyn, on the other hand, was shrewd, never missing a beat. When a team member dressed as a homeless guy had been rounded up during a particularly cold evening by another van handing out warm meals, she sent him back repeatedly to collect more fried chicken for his colleagues. Together they made a wonderful whole.

In the van with Marilyn and Pat would be an assortment of disguise materials and accessories. We had a baby carriage; we always had at least one dog on a leash and an assortment of skateboards, bicycles, and clothing changes. On occasion, our female colleagues would even bring along their children, their babies. Who would suspect a woman with a baby on her hip of being a surveillant? Our surveillance team members were made aware early on of rudimentary team rules: If the target made you once, you could stay in the exercise with a change. If twice, you were out of the exercise. There were no third sightings.

Andrea was a lean, tanned blonde, and her favorite guise was the bike-messenger look, complete with a helmet, sunglasses, and a pouch full of mail. She was fearless on two wheels, cutting in and out of traffic for the sheer fun of it. Valerie, our electrical engineer, blonde and very fit, styled herself as a runner. In DC, where wearing sneakers on the street with a business suit was considered normal, she would actually sit down on a park bench and change out of work garb to reveal her running clothes and set off down the path with her business clothes in a backpack. Susan, tall and black and somehow both beautiful like Iman and almost invisible, liked to push the baby carriage. The dogs were up for grabs. Who is suspicious of somebody walking his or her dog?

The team was lethal, almost invisible, and disciplined. Marilyn and Pat deployed their "feet," our team members on foot, and called in the vehicles if our target suddenly jumped in a taxi or got on a bus. They were also responsible for the maps with the plastic overlays.

All SST members carried a laminated card explaining that they were part of a street exercise for the US government. It contained the phone number of the CIA duty officer, without actually noting the CIA sponsorship. We realized we needed these cards one night after a cop stopped our van—our Mother Ship, as we called it—as it raced down a street in Georgetown while the target was getting away. The women talked their way out of the ticket, even earning encouragement from the traffic cop to "Go get 'em," but we made sure everybody carried that card after that.

Our goal with the SST was to shock the Pipeliners after they came out of the IOC and before they boarded the plane for Russia. We all knew that if they could not see their surveillance in Russia, there was a good chance that they would lead them to the agents in place working for us. And they would be arrested and executed. It was a life-or-death proposition, and no matter how well the Pipeliners had done in the IOC, we were able to show them that surveillance can be so stealthy that it is almost invisible. Or maybe totally invisible.

★   ★   ★

"COURTYARD! COURTYARD!"

Phil was yelling into the shroud of his Motorola transceiver surveillance radio as he broke into a full sprint. Good-looking with a mop of dark hair and intelligent eyes, Phil was a brazen but bright junior technical operations officer in OTS. He had a master's degree in forensic chemistry and was recruited into the Agency through the student co-op program at the Rochester Institute of Technology.

Phil would have a very successful career in OTS, with one major detour along the way. Years later, he would be visiting the CIA station in the US embassy in Beirut in 1983 on the day when the embassy was hit by a car bomb. Phil, who had just arrived in Beirut that morning, excused himself and headed to the men's restroom. While he was in the restroom, the bomb detonated, and Phil was the only CIA survivor. He spent months recovering afterward. What saved him, he was told, were the rebar and the pipes that served as extra support for the restroom where he lay, trapped. The station was totally crushed, along with all the occupants. But this was years in the future, his future, and today, in the present, he was a valuable member of the SST and currently caught up in a street simulation exercise.

At this highly charged moment, Phil was rising to the chase. He had just emerged into a parking lot. Suddenly he had line of sight to me as I made the turn into a walkway, a block and a half ahead of him. He and two others were the only members of the team left in the exercise. Phil was on point, and the two others were paralleling me on the streets of the city blocks on my right and my left.

The twenty or thirty other members of the team, less quick and less resilient, had been eroded away by attrition as I followed one of the well-established cover patterns I had developed over the past four months during many noontime outings.

I was dressed conservatively as a businessman in a dark-blue raincoat with no hat. A white shirt and tie were visible at the collar, and dark business trousers and dark leather shoes were worn below. I had a mustache but was otherwise clean-shaven. I was carrying no bags or packages. Dana and Beth accompanied me this time, as was often our pattern, and they, too, were dressed appropriately for professionals at the office and in what passed in Washington, DC, as high style: conservative business suits with skirts just at the knee and sturdy low heels.

We set out walking from the office up Twenty-Third Street several blocks to the Foggy Bottom Metro. We took the Metro to L'Enfant Plaza shopping mall, switching trains at Metro Center, lunched at the hotel above it, reentered the Metro, made a change at Metro Center, and ended up at Farragut North Station. That, of course, was just the warm-up. We began to walk on a stair-step pattern—diagonally across the grid formed by the several city blocks heading west and south back in the direction of the office. Since we took advantage of the light changes and walked at a brisk pace, zigzagging in a general direction toward our goal, anyone pursuing us and still in the game would be hard-pressed to overtake us by car or on foot and to anticipate us by getting out in front of us. The SST had identified several potential operational sites on our usual noontime routes and had assigned them code words. COURTYARD was one of those sites.

As soon as I made the turn up the sidewalk on the other side of Lisner Auditorium in the middle of George Washington University campus, Phil knew that this courtyard was the destination. The remaining team members were in full sprint and converging on the courtyard from three sides.

I headed up the sidewalk at a brisk pace, while Beth and Dana slowed down to a relaxed stroll, falling back about ten paces as a way of holding the point back as well. The point was also known as the eye, the team member at the tip of the surveillance team, closest to the target. The team could not come barreling past them; that would be a breach of discipline that the KGB would never countenance. I was looking straight ahead. Oddly, out of the corner of my eye, I noticed a man sitting on a park bench at the end of the walk holding his briefcase by the handle and standing it upright in his lap. It was odd because he was somewhat out of place in the courtyard now crowded with students, and he seemed to be the only one even vaguely interested in my arrival.

Focus on the details.

I made a hard left around a small brick building, unbuttoning my raincoat and then putting my left hand in the left pocket of the raincoat. Now, with both hands in front of my body and on the way up to my nose and eyes, consistent with my forward motion, I continued walking in front of the small building. Nobody noticed that I had just changed my appearance by reversing my coat and donning a disguise.

I began putting the final touches on the disguise as I approached an opening on my left, a narrow walkway between two small brick buildings facing the courtyard. The disguise was simple but effective. I made a left into the passageway as Dana and Beth continued on by. The team flowed by behind them. Malcolm came barreling in from the right into the courtyard from a passage behind the auditorium and stopped abruptly just before he ran into the women. Phil emerged from around the corner and dropped in behind the women as Ian appeared from another passageway on their left.

Everyone was in the courtyard except for me. My heart was beating, and adrenaline was flowing. I could hear my heartbeat; that throbbing sensation was taking over, and I was totally immersed in the exercise. *Just like the real thing*, I thought, *just like that teachable moment that we always try to provide for the Pipeliners.* Being on the hunt was one thing; being the one hunted was quite another. Right now the blood was flowing, and I was no longer teaching the team; they were teaching me. I decided to go to ground.

I crossed the street and stepped through the opening in a tall hedge, disappearing down a sidewalk that led to a large garden area. I settled onto the grassy lawn and blended in with the students. In a few minutes, the team, determining that I was no longer with them, summoned as many of the other members as they could and began to sweep back through the area, trying to reacquire me, just as the KGB would do. Lying on the grass among the students, I stayed hidden in plain sight and watched the watchers as they moved by, feeling the rush of being invisible.

★   ★   ★

Martha Peterson would come to represent a number of firsts for Moscow Station. Not only would she shatter the glass ceiling by being the first-ever female case officer sent to Moscow, but she would represent a new evolution in the rules by being the CIA's first "in the black" officer.

In her case, "black" meant that she was under such a unique cover that we hoped to make her completely invisible to the Soviet Foreign Ministry. The idea was that she would have absolutely no overt connection to the CIA station during her overseas posting. She would not socialize with any of the CIA officers there or with their families. She would not mix with them at the Marine House TGIF parties, famous around the world. Marti was to comport herself as just another State Department admin officer. Since we knew that the KGB did not use women operatives in their work, we figured that the KGB would probably identify Marti as a clerk or a secretary. Their misogynistic view of women left her free to operate without detection. Or so we believed.

Pretty, blonde, and single, Marti had one duty to perform in Moscow, one official chore, and it was of the highest importance. She was given the files on her assignment while still in Washington. A sensitive Russian agent, code-named TRIGON, was being transferred from South America back to Moscow, and it was expected that he would attempt to reestablish contact at any moment. Marti's job was to be ready to be his clandestine contact when he reappeared and to manage his impersonal communications with Moscow Station.

The CIA had recruited TRIGON, whose real name was Aleksandr Dmitryevich Ogorodnik, two years earlier in Columbia. At the time, the thirty-eight-year-old Russian was serving as economics officer in Bogota. Ogorodnik was considered a rising star among the Soviet diplomats; however, it soon became apparent that he also had a darker side. Though married, he was having an affair with a local Spanish woman, and through her, he had expressed his disillusionment with the Soviet system of government.

The local station chief used the woman to get to Ogorodnik, who readily agreed to come over to the other side. He was a handsome man and had a love for Western fashion and fast cars. He asked to be paid for his services but agreed to let the US government keep the money in escrow so he wouldn't draw attention to himself, although he did use some of it to buy emerald jewelry for his mother and other items that couldn't be found inside the Soviet Union, like contact lenses. Ogorodnik seemed to be a bit of an idealist and expressed hopes that his actions might somehow make a positive impact on his home country. In many ways, he seemed relieved that the CIA had found him. For the first time, he felt that he was finally going to live his life on his own terms.[2]

His zeal pushed him hard and made him an incredibly productive agent. He took risks and was a fast learner, mastering a host of new spy equipment, including the CIA's first subminiature camera, in order to photograph hundreds of secret documents that came straight out of the Soviet embassy's diplomatic pouch. An OTS technical officer was given several weeks to provide Ogorodnik with intensive tradecraft training, renting a room at the Bogota Hilton for the duration.

At the end of that tutelage, he was serendipitously able to photograph a top-secret policy paper while he was under observation in a secure vault inside the KGB *referentura*—essentially a vault within the Soviet embassy that housed the most sensitive documents—something that had never been done before. Head-quarters was impressed.[3] Ogorodnik provided the United States with intelligence on several aspects of the Soviet's intentions in South America, especially their attempts to infiltrate and influ-ence the local governments throughout the region.

The CIA was able to convince Ogorodnik to return to the Soviet Union to work for us. In return, his mistress and child would receive financial support, and then, at a time and place to be determined, the CIA would assist him in defecting. In order to seal the deal, the CIA decided to fly Jack Downing into Bogota to meet with him face-to-face.[4] Jack was scheduled to be the next deputy chief in Moscow, and he reassured Ogorodnik that every precaution would be taken to protect his identity. And in the event that Ogorodnik felt his life might be in danger, the CIA wouldn't hesitate to exfiltrate him out of the country.

Ogorodnik realized that if he really wanted to change the Soviet system, he could only do that by returning to Moscow. However, he did have one stipulation. He told Jack that he wanted to have a suicide pill, or "L-pill," so that if he was ever caught, he could go out on his own terms and die like a man.[5] The Agency has always tended to shy away from issuing L-pills whenever possible, as the stresses of running a double life can often lead an agent to become paranoid and feel that the enemy is closing in. Our case officers' goal is to keep agents safe, not give them the tools to end their own lives. When Ogorodnik refused to continue spying unless he was given an L-pill, the CIA eventually told him that they would work on getting him one.

Ogorodnik finally returned to Moscow in the fall of 1974. A secret communications plan had been hidden among his belong-ings, instructing him on how he should go about reestablishing contact with Jack, but the date for this meeting had been sched-uled for several months in the future. The KGB often forced returning diplomats to undergo a security investigation for fear that the CIA might compromise them while serving abroad. As a result, Jack had told Ogorodnik to try to settle in and keep a low profile.

All that remained was to reestablish contact. It was a tall order, given that up until that point, the CIA had never actually run an operation on the streets of Moscow before. It was a do-or-die moment if there ever was one. Had the Agency learned anything in the decade since the days of Penkovsky? If the CIA couldn't run an agent in Moscow, that would only give fuel to the people in headquarters who felt that technological platforms like the U-2 spy plane were a much safer and more reliable way to collect intelligence on our enemy than human intelligence. But TRIGON had been able to photograph a top-secret policy paper inside a secure vault, something a spy satellite could never have done. For those diligent individuals who had been pulling all-nighters in the hopes of proving the naysayers wrong, this was their moment. This was the moment to show that the Moscow Rules were ready. And Marti Peterson, the first female case officer ever stationed to the Soviet capital, was going to be the one to do it.

Marti's career in the CIA was certainly not preordained. Her husband, John, had served in Laos as a CIA paramilitary officer, and Marti had gone along to be with him in 1971. The two of them had been in the country a little over a year when tragedy struck: John was killed in a helicopter accident while advising Laotian troops. After John's death, Marti stayed with her parents in Fort Lauderdale while she tried to put her life back together. A man at the DMV processing her driver's license application had asked her whether she was single or married. She looked at him eye to eye and said, "Widow." He said, "You're too young."[6]

Marti could have gone back to her civilian life; she had been a teacher in a number of categories: college students, the blind, and the National Teacher Corps in New Mexico. She had even tried to teach English to the Lao while in Pakse. In wrapping up her husband's affairs at the CIA, she was encouraged to apply to the Agency and specifically to the Career Training Program.

Marti did not realize that the fast-track training program for officer development was filled almost exclusively with male trainees. In fact, when she tried to apply, she was initially offered a secretarial position, even though she spoke three languages, had traveled extensively, and had work experience with the Agency in Laos as a contract employee. Gender trumped qualifications evidently. Offended, she persevered, and eventually it paid off when a supervisor who knew John decided to see what he could do and pulled some strings to get her into the elite program. And so in 1973, just a year after losing her husband, her career in CIA operations began.

Marti took the IOC without the benefit of a partner, a unique student in an already-elite course. Learning to make a car toss, literally throwing a dead drop from the driver's seat of a vehicle, was a particularly tricky undertaking. It required a one-way street for the toss and a series of turns leading up to the site. Marti remembers a training episode while in the IOC that had her driving up the spiraling ramp at Parkington Shopping Center's parking garage in Virginia and then down the reverse spiral ramp to exit. She attempted a car toss that should have pierced the center of the spiral and landed one or two floors below. She miscalculated her aim slightly, and the package sailed all the way to the bottom of the ramp, making it easy for the trailing surveillance team to find it.

With another officer in the car, the toss would have easily gone out the passenger window. But because of her status as a deep cover officer, Marti would never have a partner to share her operational chores with. She would never have somebody else driving the car so that she could photograph sites or sketch them. She would never have a sidekick to look for repeats on the license plates or the presence of windshield wipers or the inverted dusty V on the front of the vehicles, all of which were clues for a KGB car. She would never have a backup, someone to drop her off, or someone to pick her up. There was nobody to help her gauge the gap in surveillance and whether it was safe to lay down a drop or pick one up. She would have to figure all of this out on her own.[7]

In one sense, Marti's first few months in the Soviet capital during the fall of 1975 were not that much different from Ogorodnik's. Upon landing at Moscow's Sheremetyevo Airport, she spent the winter building her deep cover and acclimating herself to the city, taking long drives in her tan Soviet-made Zhiguli. Her main goal was to find out if she had any surveillance, which would dictate how useful she might be to the station. However, she was careful not to be too aggressive about it. She'd been taught at the IOC that she shouldn't do anything suspicious, like trying to map out the entire city in the first week.

So instead Marti decided to set up a pattern that would make her blend in with the other single women at the embassy. She lived in a foreigners' compound located a few miles away from the embassy. The Soviets had basically fenced in an apartment block, even posting a militiaman in a guard shack at the gate. The residents, mostly diplomatic personnel from the various embassies as well as some foreign businessmen, took to calling the compounds "diplomatic ghettos." It was a not-so-subtle way for the Soviets to keep tabs on foreigners and ensure that they would essentially be walled off from the local citizens.

In many respects, her cover job was a lonely existence. Marti was careful never to be seen with any CIA personnel outside of the station, but she found it hard to connect to the other Americans at the embassy who had no idea that she was working for the Agency. There was also the question of her role as the first female operations officer assigned to the station. Like many women of her generation, she was not a feminist. She intended to prove her worth pragmatically, by working harder and doing the job better than her male colleagues. However, there was no denying that there were a few misogynistic hurdles placed in her way.

After several months of carefully studying the city, Marti concluded that the KGB had not been following her, but more than a few of the male case officers found this hard to believe. Instead, they thought that she couldn't detect the surveillance teams, and so a test was set up. She was told to pass by a certain storefront window while on one of her surveillance-detection runs (SDRs) so that a station officer standing behind the window could observe to see if there was a KGB surveillance team following her. As it turned out, she was right. Her cover had worked to perfection, and the KGB had no idea that she was actually working for the CIA. The time had come for her to perform her first operational act.

Human espionage, by definition, presumes the passage of information—intelligence—between two individuals. In a classic espionage case, there must be an assumption that your foreign agent, or asset, is not under surveillance. If he or she is, then you do not have an intelligence operation. It's that simple. This was why it was so much easier for the CIA to run operations outside the Soviet Union, where the foreign agents had much greater freedom of movement. In fact, throughout his posting in Bogota, Ogorodnik was typically able to meet up with his CIA handlers, a case officer and an OTS officer, in a hotel room rented for that specific reason.

Such a scenario was deemed impossible on the streets of Moscow, where the average foreigner was either boxed in by KGB surveillance teams or spied on by citizen informers including hotel floor monitors, militia guardsmen, telephone operators, translators, or just about anyone who might interact with a foreigner on a daily basis. The simple act of making a dinner reservation required that an American diplomat first contact a Soviet fixer at the embassy so that they could obtain a reservation paper that had been stamped for approval by the Soviet government.

As one might imagine, under these circumstances, renting a safe house was out of the question. This meant that the only real way to run an agent in Moscow was through impersonal communication. In other words, the case officer and the agent had to be separated by both time and distance. It was a slow and painstaking process, and far from perfect. But it was the only way that we could protect the foreign asset who was working with us.

Since Ogorodnik had been told to lie low after returning to Moscow, the first element of his communications plan simply required that he make an appearance so that we would know that he had made the transition safely and that the KGB were none the wiser. He was asked to stand inside a post office on the Arbat, a main shopping street, at a certain date and time and to face the street, at which point Jack and his wife would stroll by.[8] The second signal came a few weeks later when a case officer spotted Ogorodnik's car parked at a prearranged signal site known as PARKPLATZ. The location of PARKPLATZ was within the normal route of Ogorodnik's daily commute, meaning that the KGB wouldn't necessarily suspect that anything was out of the ordinary to see his car parked in the neighborhood.

Both these signs were good news. However, in the months following, Ogorodnik seemed to fall off the map. He failed to leave a mark at a designated location signifying that he was ready to pick up a dead drop package. When the CIA went ahead and delivered the package anyway, the Russian didn't retrieve it. Several more months would pass until eventually the CIA was able to reestablish contact in December 1975, when Jack picked up a crushed triangular milk carton that Ogorodnik had left at a prearranged site. Ogorodnik had included a note inside the package, explaining why he'd been so hard to contact. As it turned out, he'd been ill for several months and laid up in a hospital, and during the winter, he often put his car up on blocks, which was why he hadn't been able to signal the CIA using PARKPLATZ.[9] However, he reiterated that he was in good spirits and indicated that he had passed the KGB security checks.

The best piece of news, though, was that he had been transferred to the Global Affairs Department in the Ministry of Foreign Affairs (MFA), which would give him access to secret cables for all Soviet embassies worldwide. He would see all incoming and outgoing classified Soviet foreign-policy plans and objectives. He also handed over top-secret Soviet diplomatic documents that gave the United States unprecedented insights into Moscow's negotiating positions during SALT, the strategic-arms limitations talks of the 1970s.[10]

Marti's first operational act came the following January when she was asked to leave a package for Ogorodnik at a site called STENA, which had been cased the previous summer. The dead drop had been crafted to look like a smashed cigarette package, but despite its diminutive size, it still contained a miniature camera, cassettes, and a roll of special thirty-five-millimeter film with miniature writing.

Initially the idea had been to do a rolling car toss; however, the snowbanks were so high that Marti was instructed to place the package at the base of the lamppost on foot. Marti's training now took over, as she spent several hours driving alone through the streets of Moscow in her Soviet-built Zhiguli in order to ensure that she wasn't being followed. She had carefully planned out her route, crisscrossing through neighborhoods and industrial areas until she parked her car near the subway entrance and hurried inside.

Marti had no way of knowing if a man sitting across from her on the subway happened to be an off-duty surveillance officer, but she had taken precautions anyway. She had chosen her outfit carefully in order to try to blend in with the local populace: an ugly gray tweed coat made in Finland and a dark knit cap pulled down low to cover the highlights in her hair, which could easily identify her as a foreigner. She rode the train for several stops before finally emerging onto a residential street. She'd been told to make the drop no later than 9:00 p.m., but she was running about a half hour late. The danger was that she might still be in the area when Ogorodnik made his appearance.

The snowbank was higher than she had anticipated, which caused a bit of a problem. The camera was so delicate that she couldn't risk throwing it into the hole, so she had to come up with another means of placing it at the base of the lamppost. Thinking fast, Marti leaned against the snowbank and pretended to simultaneously blow her nose and adjust her boot, which gave her a chance to put down the crushed cigarette package without being seen.[11]

Unfortunately, as with the earlier drop, Ogorodnik failed to pick up the package, and Marti was forced to return to the site an hour later to retrieve it. By the time she returned home, it was well after midnight. She was cold and tired and worried about what might have gone wrong.

Marti would be sent out again in June to deliver a second package, this time to a site in a wooded area known as LES. The dead drop had been designed to look like a hollowed-out log and contained within it the all-important L-pill that our techs had concealed inside an expensive-looking fountain pen. The pen had been constructed in such a way that it would still work. In the event that Ogorodnik chose to use it, he would only have to bite down on the end to crush the glass capsule and release the cyanide. Death would come instantaneously.

Due to the nature of the contents, the CIA had also included a simple note to reassure Ogorodnik that the Agency was committed to maintaining his safety and had put in place an exfiltration plan, a rescue scenario, in case he ever felt that his life was in danger. Last, the tech who had put together the contents of the log wrapped a warning notice around the contents. Written in Russian, the notice was a precaution in case a Soviet citizen discovered the log. It said that the contents were incredibly dangerous and should simply be thrown into the river.

As she had done on the previous dead drop, Marti took a circuitous route through the city to ensure that she was free from surveillance. Ogorodnik had been told in a previous communications package that this was to be a timed exchange, which meant that he would pick up the drop that had been left for him and simultaneously put down one of his own in the same spot. It was a risky strategy, in that it required pinpoint timing, something that was hard to coordinate when there was no direct way to quickly communicate with Ogorodnik to tell him about any last-minute changes. But it also limited the amount of time that the materials would be left out in the open and thereby lessened the chance that they might fall into the wrong hands.

Marti emerged from the subway a little before 9:00 p.m. and made her way toward the woods. Despite the lateness of the hour, it felt more like late afternoon, as there was almost no sunset at this northern latitude in the summer. Relieved, Marti saw that the pathway into the park's wooded area disappeared into dark shadows. There was a bus stop across the street from the entrance to the park, but she seemed to be completely alone. Still, Marti couldn't take any chances. In Moscow, it was always best to simply assume that you were being watched at all times. For this reason, she walked at a natural pace, not hurrying or doing anything that might draw any undue attention.

She had been outfitted with a new device, a small receiver attached to her bra that rested in the crook of her arm. Totally concealed, the device, known as the SRR-100, had been created by our techs to monitor the radio transmissions of the surveillance teams. State of the art for its day, the SRR-100 communicated to an earpiece via an induction loop, which Marti wore around her neck. At the time, the device was still in its rudimentary stages, but if any surveillance team was in the area, the earpiece would pick up on the squelches of their radio transmissions. It offered an extra level of security that gave Marti the confidence to carry on.

She had hidden the hollowed-out log inside her purse, but once Marti entered the shadows of the park, she removed it from her bag and tucked the log under the crook of her arm. The location of the drop was a lamppost just inside the park. As Marti neared the lamppost, she lifted her arm slightly and let the log slide gently to the ground, then turned and walked away. To anyone watching, it would have looked like she had simply made a wrong turn and was retracing her steps. Her training told her to always keep moving and to never look back, and that is exactly what she did.

When Marti came back to the woods an hour later, just after 10:00 p.m., she found that the log was gone and an old soiled, smashed milk carton had been left in its place. The carton had been smeared with a disgusting-looking material that resembled yellowish vomit, in order to discourage anyone else from touching it. *A nice bit of tradecraft,* Marti thought, one that Ogorodnik had invented on his own. She hesitated before touching it herself—it was that effective. Marti's heart raced as she picked the carton up and carefully placed it inside of a plastic bag hidden in her purse. As far as she could tell, nobody was around to see the exchange.[12]

The next portion of the plan called for Marti to make a mark with lipstick on the side of a nearby bus shelter so that Ogorodnik would know that the package had been retrieved. But caught up in the adrenaline of the moment, rather than leave a thin red line like she was supposed to, she pressed too hard, creating a huge blob on the side of the shelter. Frustrated with herself for this minor slipup, she was nonetheless elated that the operation had been a success.

The following day, the station was buzzing with excitement as the package was opened and the contents examined. The tech explained to Marti that the sickening material on the outside of the package was a form of a mustard plaster that was often used in the Soviet Union during that era for chest congestion. Inside the package, Ogorodnik had included several rolls of thirty-five-millimeter film containing images of documents marked with the highest security clearance. Headquarters was thrilled. The Moscow Station had pulled off a major success and was quickly commended for a job well done.

But even as the station was celebrating, there was cause for concern. The TRIGON operation had been going on now for the better part of a year, during which the Russian had essentially been completely on his own. Perhaps it was the fact that TRIGON had finally received an L-pill, but some worried that the spy might do something to endanger his life. TRIGON had told the Agency that he planned to use the pill only as a last resort. But how would he know? It wasn't uncommon for agents under extreme duress to feel that the walls were closing in and to begin seeing enemies where there weren't any. Now that Ogorodnik had come through, people were worried that he might become fatalistic. As the station couldn't meet the agent in person, there was no way of knowing for sure.

As the days passed, Marti found herself wondering about Ogorodnik and the stresses that he must be going through. She tried to put herself in his shoes. How could somebody go out and risk his or her life on a day-to-day basis and not be able to share that with anybody? She knew from her own experience that the only place she felt truly at home in Moscow was in the CIA station, where she could commiserate with her colleagues. But who did Ogorodnik have?

While he'd been in Bogota, he'd been able to meet with Jack, another case officer, and the technical officer who trained him in person. There had been camaraderie, which had allowed for the men to congratulate the Russian spy and help buoy his spirits. But here in the Soviet Union, he had nothing like that. In the absence of such a connection, she worried that he might lose his will to carry on.[13] Even though our case officers are told not to form attachments with the agents they run, it's not an easy rule to follow. There are risks, and it's normal to feel concern for their well-being. Our job is to keep the agents safe while collecting their information. Full stop.

It seemed that Jack had also been having similar thoughts. Jack was the one who had actually gone to meet with Ogorodnik in Bogota, and in many ways, he felt responsible for the Russian spy. The two had become friends, and yet, apart from a few impersonal notes in the dead drops, there had been no way for Jack to really express his gratitude for what the spy had done. He recalled with fondness how they had been able to meet in Bogota. If only there were a way that he could meet with the spy in Moscow, then Jack could personally thank him for what he had done, look him in the eye, and reassure him that his work was making a difference.

Jack wanted Ogorodnik to know that his reporting was going to the president and senior US policy makers.[14] The only other operation that had involved face-to-face meetings in Moscow was Penkovsky, and that had led to the spy's arrest and execution. To make matters worse, as Jack was scheduled to leave at the end of the summer, the KGB might be expecting him to make a bold move. But the more he thought about it, the more he realized it had to happen. The rules of the game were flexible and transactional; the ground beneath their feet was always shifting, and CIA tradecraft had to be able to move with it. It was time for the Moscow Rules to evolve once again.

CHAPTER 4

"Pick the time and the place for action."

Jack Downing was as hardworking and innovative as they come, a tough ex-marine and Harvard graduate who had served in Vietnam before joining the clandestine service. He was also a talented linguist, testing at high proficiency in both Russian and Chinese. Originally from Texas, the forty-three-year-old looked like he had been plucked right out of central casting. However, despite his Hollywood good looks, Jack came across as uncomplicated, a man who was focused on the mission at all times. He was unflappable. No matter what the task, his calm and steady approach always got results.

That didn't mean that he didn't take risks from time to time. Maybe it was the ex-marine in him, but Jack was always pushing boundaries, and in Moscow, that meant testing the KGB surveillance teams. A jogger, Jack would often go for a morning run, testing the watchers to see if they could keep up. It's quite possible that they thought he was out of his mind, but he relished the challenge. Eventually, after so many morning runs, they began to anticipate his route, and he got them to back off enough that he could use it to his advantage by creating a gap, which is how he was able to pick up Ogorodnik's first drop in the fall of 1975.

Like all good leaders, Jack was constantly looking for ways to improve our operational capabilities. And as it turned out, even before the TRIGON operation had begun to heat up, he happened to stumble upon a concept that he thought might allow for a personal face-to-face meeting on the streets of Moscow. The concept, which would come to be called identity transformation, was something that I had also been thinking about in my capacity as chief of disguise, but Jack was really the first person to put it into practice.

It happened during the winter of 1976, when a North Vietnam- ese walk-in had entered the embassy in Moscow and announced to the marine guard that he wanted to defect. Sent away, the defector was told that there would be another meeting at a site somewhere in Moscow. This was the CIA's standard protocol for when we were approached with a volunteer or a walk-in any- where in the world. Get the person out of the US embassy and back out on the street, and then plan to hook up with him or her at a more covert location.

As the deputy chief, Jack took it upon himself to be the one to meet with the individual, but he still had to find a way to slip past the embassy guardhouse and then shake any KGB tail he might pick up.

It was then that Jack had hit upon a novel idea. Out of despera- tion, he decided to disguise himself as Neal, one of our OTS tech- nical operations officers (TOPS) working at the embassy. Neal, who had administrative cover and was seldom on the street, had been considered "a person of no interest" by the KGB and there- fore had only light surveillance. Even better, he sported a unique yellow-fur shapka, or Russian hat; wore a distinctive handlebar moustache; and had possibly the only pair of cowboy boots in Moscow. Jack borrowed the hat, applied a mustache from some- body's disguise kit, and squeezed into Neal's boots in order to exit the embassy.

It worked. The militiaman at the gate took no notice of him, thinking he was Neal, and Jack was able to meet up with the defector without any problems. Afterward, he had the inkling that he'd stumbled upon a new operational tool that might allow case officers at the embassy to get free from their surveillance. However, even as he sat in his office feeling the adrenaline rush that comes from having conducted a successful operation, he began to wonder. Was it possible that he had just gotten lucky?

What he needed was a second opinion to evaluate the technique and see if it could work for an operation like TRIGON.

At the time, I was running the Disguise Branch, and Jack sent a tersely worded cable to headquarters asking for me to come out and do a survey of the station to examine the tactic and see if we could develop it further.

During the early 1970s, the Disguise Branch wasn't thought of very highly at the CIA. That had all changed by 1973, when I was able to disguise an African American case officer and his Laotian contact as two Caucasians so that they could link up for an important meeting. Effected with the help of a Hollywood special-effects expert and makeup genius named John Chambers, the disguises had been so realistic that they had allowed the two men to slip through a roadblock undetected, something that had never happened before. Afterward, in 1974, headquarters had promoted me to chief of disguise.

After the cable from Jack, I flew into Moscow's Sheremetyevo Airport on Air France, traveling with Jacob, a colleague and former mentor from one of our bases in Europe. We were traveling on official passports, one step below diplomatic and one step above tourist class. Thankfully, unlike when traveling in Africa on an official passport, the immigrations officers did *not* return the document while covering some of the letters with their outspread fingers, revealing only the "cia" in the word "official." We were trying our best to stay below the radar and not draw any attention to our visit by posing as lowly administrative types, bean counters, on a temporary duty assignment (TDY) to the embassy. We went first to the Peking Hotel up the Garden Ring from the embassy before reporting to the office. A CIA operative, usually a Type A personality, would go first to the office. A bean counter would not.

Jacob and I went way back, operationally speaking. Tall and elegantly lean, Jacob was straight out of North Dakota, although he presented himself at all times as an Anglophile, replete with navy blazers with pocket crests, club ties, and French cuffs. Ian Fleming could not have been prouder of his rendition of a James

Bond–type character, complete with the British tics and affectations that went along with his look—his "old boy" in every other sentence. But, to my and others' great amazement, Jacob, ever the aristocrat, was a solid intelligence officer. Steeped in the lore and techniques of espionage, with a penetrating mind and a penchant for inventiveness, he made for a highly entertaining travel companion and an insightful colleague when probing for solutions to operational problems.

Our initial mission was to inventory the city and its inhabitants. Jack wanted us to get a feel for what it was like to be under the constant pressure of surveillance as well as some of the other challenges that his case officers found themselves up against. Jacob and I spent hours walking the streets of Moscow, taking different forms of transport, observing the populace, and testing the rules currently in use by the station. We photographed tourist spots and gathered information on what city life was like.

My first impression was of a huge, drab, dirty town composed of medieval buildings surrounding the amazing architectural drama of Red Square. The Kremlin was a towering presence in the background. There were February snow squalls daily, reminding me that we were close to the latitude of northern Canada. There were a lot of pedestrians but not a lot of traffic, except for the ever-present KGB surveillance teams, which sped through the streets with reckless abandon. The aggressive Volga and Zhiguli autos the KGB used were so common that the Russians had a knack for swerving out of the way to let them pass and then continuing about their business as if nothing had just happened.

Jack, of course, was a gracious host and met with us inside the Bubble to brief us on his use of identity transformation. As he took us through how he had donned Neal's cowboy boots and slipped out of the embassy, essentially hiding in plain sight, I couldn't help but notice that Jack's technique used several elements that were traditionally associated with the world of magic.

I have always had a fascination with magic, even as a boy. I suppose that's natural; that was part of the world of deception and art. Of course, a lot of the dime-store magic I learned as a kid tended to deal with simple tricks, the wooden vases and cardboard boxes that you'd find in a basic magic set. I thought the success of the trick was in following the rules laid out in the manual. In that sense, the trick would either work, or it wouldn't, and then you could wow your friends by explaining what you'd done to fool them. However, the older I got, the more I learned that there was a lot more to really pulling off a good illusion than that.

My first introduction to the professional world of magic came when I went out to Hollywood to meet with the great Oscar winner and Hollywood makeup artist John Chambers in 1971. Originally acclaimed for his work on *The Planet of the Apes*, John took me under his wing and made me one of his protégés. This was before I had been made chief, and I'd been sent out there by my boss, who had seen an episode of the original *Mission Impossible* TV show, made famous for its use of overhead masks. At the time, our disguise capabilities were basic and underdeveloped, so much so that my boss thought we might be able to learn something from the visual effects people working out in Hollywood. Boy, was he right.

John had a stellar career under his belt, beginning with his work on *The List of Adrian Messenger* in the early 1960s, a film that was required viewing for our entry-level disguise officers. In that movie, Chambers disguised numerous movie stars with well-known faces to an unrecognizable degree, even turning Frank Sinatra into an old woman. I have always said that he was one of the only people I ever met whom I would call a genius. He would go on to become one of few makeup artists to have a star on the Hollywood Walk of Fame, on Hollywood Boulevard in Los Angeles, smack in front of the entrance to the Roosevelt Hotel.

I had no idea what to expect before I met him, but John turned out to be a warmhearted and generous man. He did not look like a makeup artist, or at least what I envisioned one should look like. Heavyset with a round face and nerd-like, black-rimmed eyeglasses, he had a large expressive face that would often split into a wide grin after he landed one of his many zingers. Chambers was a tough Irish guy with little tolerance for mistakes, and his politics were what I would call very conservative, but he was a great artist and became a good, loyal friend and a valuable ally in a fight. The actor John Goodman played him in the movie *Argo*, and it was actually a perfect choice.

Not long after John and I started working together, he told me that he had, in his studio, several life castings of women's chests. The life casts were from the base of the rib cage to the base of the neck, and their subjects were completely unidentifiable. He kept them covered. He told me that he used to play what he thought was a clever game when he had cocktail parties: Guess the Ingenue. He played it with Dudley Moore one night. Chambers unveiled the first cast, and when Dudley guessed wrong, Chambers corrected him, "No, that's Elizabeth Taylor." He had to make her an insert prosthetic for the movie *Cleopatra*. The next bust was then unveiled, and Dudley guessed, again wrong. John corrected him, "No, that is Tuesday Weld," and Dudley exclaimed in his droll British accent, "You're right!" John only then remembered that Dudley was once married to her.

John had a serious side to him as well. He was a true patriot through and through. He was a first-generation Irish American from Chicago who had served in the army during World War II. In fact, before he worked in the entertainment business, John created fake noses and glass eyes for wounded veterans in an early career in anaplastology. When he was first approached by the Agency about offering his services, John didn't hesitate. He invited me onto the sets of many of his projects and used to get a big kick out of introducing me as his "friend from the army."

I also found it amazing that none of his colleagues seemed to mind. If John said it was OK, then that was good enough for them. At one point, in the mid 1970s, I spent three weeks on the set of the science fiction movie *The Island of Dr. Moreau*, working side by side with John and a team of makeup artists. The movie was from an H. G. Wells novel about a scientist who attempts to convert animals into human beings. Chambers was making disguise appliances (i.e., overhead masks) for the movie, and I was shadowing his process, from sculpting the faces to pulling the molds and then adding the pigment and the hair goods.

Whenever I was in Los Angeles, I found myself connected to people involved in the fields of deception and illusion as well as people who were interested in magic or actually worked in the field as magicians or inventors of magic tricks. It turned out that there was an amazing community of magicians in Los Angeles, and of course, they all knew John. John took me to a place called the Magic Castle, a well-known magic club started by a family of magicians named Larsen. The Larsen boys had discovered an old Victorian mansion on a hill in Hollywood, renovated it, and formed an organization for magicians and others in the magic community to meet and exchange material. Even more important, they included small theaters so that guests could be invited to watch both traditional magic shows and what was called "close-up" magic.

John was a frequent guest and introduced me to the hallowed halls of professional magic. He was also the one who instructed me on the fine art of deception as it might apply to my line of work. "You have to realize, Tony," he said. "What you call an operation? We call it a performance. It is up to you, as the performer, to define both your stage and your audience. If you fail to do this, your performance will be a failure."

These were wise words to a young intelligence officer, and I took them to heart. John then proceeded to school me on the intricate connection between that audience and that stage. He showed me how the audience's point of view was a key component of designing a deception. Some tricks can be viewed in the round; they will work from any angle. Others, most others, require a fairly specific sight line. It may be that your performance would need to be done directly in front of your audience. Any deviation from either side would reveal the secret of the illusion.

When Jack recounted how he had come to utilize identity transformation to meet up with the North Vietnamese walk-in, I could see right away that the technique was very much like a performance. In a sense, Neal had set the stage for the illusion by deciding to wear cowboy boots and his Shapka hat. And then Jack had stepped in to pull off the deception after Neal had set everything up. They had worked as a team, much like a magician and his or her assistant work together to fool the crowd.

It was then that everything clicked. When Jim Steinmeyer, one of my favorite magicians, wrote his famous book, *Hiding the Elephant: How Magicians Invented the Impossible and Learned to Disappear*, his whole point was to get the reader to think like a magician. And this was exactly what I was going to have to do now. I was going to have to turn our case officers into amateur magicians.

The first order of business was to examine the current personnel at the Moscow Station and to identify potential donors and recipients—the magicians and their assistants—who could be paired together for a potential identity transfer, similar to what Jack had done with Neal. Jacob and I did facial impressions and gathered data and measurements for everyone at the station. We color matched their hair; took actual hair samples, clothing sizes, and shoe sizes; and characterized skin tones, tricks I had learned from John out in Los Angeles. By the time we were finished two weeks later, we had enough information on each station officer to fashion a custom-made suit, make a custom wig, or prepare a lifelike mask.

Back at headquarters, I tasked my disguise staff in our DC labs to use the details we had recorded for each officer in Moscow to create an all-points capability for identity transfer and identity transformation. The goal was to have maximum flexibility for any operational contingencies. This is a great example of how the Moscow Rules were constantly evolving. We tested the waters and found out what worked. Already Jack had scored a victory. Now it was time to take it to the next level. I recommended to SE Division that we institute a new disguise program, a proprietary scenario, just for Moscow Station. Every Pipeliner who was scheduled for Moscow would have an initial appointment in Disguise Branch. There we would escort the officer to our laboratories and do an initial light disguise, which would be used during IOC training. The purpose was to acclimate the officer in the proper use of disguise.

It should be pointed out here that entering a supermarket or a convenience store wearing a wig, a mustache, and a pair of plano glasses is a little more unsettling than you might think. Paranoia sets in, and you are pretty sure that everyone will recognize the fact that you have on a wig and then probably think you are going to shoot up the place or steal something. Our goal was to get our officers past this point, to where they realized that nobody noticed or cared as long as their demeanor was confident. We would send our officers to the CIA cafeteria, where their colleagues and, yes, even their bosses, would be having lunch.

We wanted them to understand how easy it was to blend in, to sit at a table next to their office crowd and not be recognized. A powerful lesson, it was better learned in a friendly environment than on the streets of Moscow. That was round one: entry-level disguise. For many of our officers, that would be the totality of their disguise experience. For officers going to Europe, or even to many African countries or the Far East, this would be the only disguise technique that would be necessary.

But for Moscow-bound CIA officers, light disguise was only the opening salvo. Over the duration of their training, they would come back to our laboratories for more elaborate preparations. That was when we would begin to assemble a file on each one of them that would enable us to replicate the officers, fully replicate them, in their absence. We would measure them in the same way that a fine tailor would measure—inseam, neck, sleeve length, waist, and chest. This applied, by the way, to women as well as men. Our officers photographed the Pipeliners from all angles, capturing 360-degree images. Full profile. Three-quarter profile. Back of head. We would note shoe size, hat size, and glove size. We would note clothing sizes in general. We would take their optical prescriptions if they had glasses or contacts. Height, weight, tattoos—nothing escaped our notice.

We would take clippings of each officer's hair to characterize its texture and color. We would note their skin color, using a unique, proprietary skin-tone system internal to our labs. We would note their natural eye color.

For each Moscow-bound officer, we would make a wig pattern. This was a relatively simple process, somewhat humble in its materials, but it produced a world-class product. The tools consisted of Scotch tape, Saran wrap, and a black Sharpie. With those three materials, we could make a wig pattern to our wig maker's specifications, with which she could construct just about anything we requested, from a toupee to a full head of hair. Male or female. Black or white.

At the end of the disguise preparation for a Moscow assignment came the face impression, the preliminary step in the fabrication of a unique mask for the officer. The face impression was uncomfortable for the officer, and we usually saved it until the end—just to ensure that the officer wouldn't hold it against us.

The rest of the work was all done in the laboratories, after the SE officer had departed. When we were finished, we had all the pieces and all the information necessary to re-create the officer from a distance, from halfway around the world if necessary.

And by the way, we often took this information on the spouses as well. We were looking for total flexibility, the ability to switch people around, to have one person pose as another, to have two copies of the same person available. That total flexibility included readiness for operations that we couldn't even yet envisage, but once they were conceived, we wanted to ensure that we had the information and the material necessary to execute them. Our goal was to give SE Division, both the case officers with boots on the ground and SE managers sitting in their offices at headquarters at Langley, the wherewithal to design any operation they required with the knowledge that we could support it in just about any way they could imagine.

★   ★   ★

A few months after my initial visit to Moscow, our hard work was to pay off, when I would get another cable from Jack saying that he was trying to set up a rare face-to-face meeting with TRIGON in Moscow. It seemed that Jack had some concerns about the

Russian's well-being and was worried that the agent might go to ground or, worse, panic and take his own life now that he had gotten his L-pill. Jack was convinced that by setting up a meeting, he could reassure the spy, let him know that he was making a huge difference, and thereby convince him to keep going.

It was a tricky operation, but Jack was in a favorable environment for taking risks: if he was caught and kicked out of the country, the station wouldn't be substantially affected, since his replacement had already been trained and was ready to step in. Of course, there would be no such kindness extended toward TRIGON. If Jack was unable to get away from the KGB and they followed him to the meeting site, then this incredibly valuable Russian spy would be arrested and almost certainly executed. The stakes could not have been higher.

Jack had originally hoped to use identity transfer in order to get free for the meeting, but there were a few problems. Since Jack was scheduled to leave at the end of the summer, we hadn't built a scenario for him. The other problem was that Neal, the officer he'd used for the original ID scenario, was not going to be in Moscow during the time of the operation.

We were in a bit of a conundrum until I discovered that another of our technical officers, Ron, was going to be heading out to Moscow for temporary duty. Ron was getting ready for his overseas posting, and as part of his training as a TOPS officer—a designation given to technical officers that have been cross-trained in a variety of disciplines—he had already taken the IOC course. In addition to that, he'd been required to go through nearly a year of training in various disciplines, such as audio devices, lock picking, documents, disguise, concealment fabrication, photography, and whatever else might be needed to help support an ongoing operation. A way to move beyond the cumbersome tradition of sending for a tech from headquarters whenever the need arose, this training meant that we could forward deploy our TOPS officers, which would give our stations much more flexibility to tackle any problem that might arise.

I'd actually met Ron during his disguise training, so I knew him well. A chemist by trade, Ron was a no-frills kind of guy, the type who tends to get things done without making too much noise. Upon the completion of his training, he had initially been assigned to another station, but Neal, of all people, had convinced him that Moscow was the better choice.

Ron readily agreed to help us out by posing as the donor for Jack's identity transfer scenario, but I am not sure that he knew what he was getting himself into. By that time, I had come to realize that the tactics' success relied on our donor officers standing out—the more distinctive, the better. What we needed was someone the Russians could see coming a mile away. I asked Ron to grow a handlebar mustache and to grow his hair long. Then I sent my first wife, Karen, and Ron's wife out to do a little shopping.

As the day of his departure approached, Jack flew to Washington, DC, so that we could run through the scenario. John Chambers was also in town from Hollywood, and he decided to join us as well. We set up the demonstration in one of our OTS disguise labs. I wanted Jack to get a sense for how Ron moved, to be able to mimic his walk, but I don't think Jack was prepared for what he saw when Ron entered through the door. Ron had on bright-orange pants, a pair of matching orange cowboy boots, a tan safari jacket, and a creamy white Stetson hat. When John had initially seen the outfit, he'd nicknamed Ron the Rhinestone Cowboy. Indeed, the only thing missing was the Glen Campbell song itself. For a moment, I thought we had overdone it, but the year was 1976, and by some standards, Ron's outfit could actually be considered tame.

We had Ron take a couple of turns up and down the hallway, and then we asked Jack to try to mimic Ron's walk. Perhaps it was the cowboy boots, but it was a testament to Chambers's professionalism that he didn't burst out laughing. However, despite the ridiculousness of the moment, we all knew that we held TRIGON's life in our hands. This operation had to go smoothly; there was absolutely no margin for error.

I headed back to Moscow toward the end of August. Officially, I was bringing with me the disguise kits my department had been working on, but I also knew that Jack's operation to meet with TRIGON was scheduled to launch at any moment. I wanted to be on hand to lend my support if it was needed.

Ron had already been at the embassy for over a month, in a job that would allow him access to just about every section of the embassy. For the most part, things had gone smoothly; however, there was one incident. Ron had moved in to an apartment on the fourth floor that was still filled with some of Neal's stuff. And in the process of wrapping these items up and putting them into boxes to ship back home, Ron accidently cut his upper lip when the fiber-tape dispenser smacked him in the face. The cut was pretty bad, but despite the fact that there was blood dripping down his face, he couldn't shave off his mustache or even put a bandage under his nose, because the mustache was an integral part of his ID donor disguise.[1]

When I arrived, Jack was happy to see me and filled me in on the status of the TRIGON operation. A message had been sent to the Russian spy using OWVL telling him about the meeting and asking if he would reply by laying down a drop at a prearranged site. The date for the drop was fast approaching, and Jack was clearly anxious. We had put so much effort into setting up this operation, but ultimately it was TRIGON's call. If he said no, there was really nothing Jack could do about it. But I think most of us assumed that Ogorodnik would be excited about seeing his friend one last time before Jack left Moscow for good.

On the night of the drop, we screened the movie *Jaws* and created around it a scenario intended to provide cover for the pickup. Movies were a popular way of breaking the tension during foreign postings, and they were also a great excuse for having a group of people clustered in one area. Of course, in 1976, the movie was shown on a sixteen-millimeter projector. When the film "broke" and repairs were being made, one member of the group announced that he would dash out to the local kiosk to pick up cigarettes. The cover was perfect, and within ten minutes, he was back with TRIGON's dead drop—a crushed can dripping with used engine oil.

It was fitting that the all-important job of developing the secret writing (SW) message fell to Ron. Ogorodnik's modus operandi was to include a note inside the package with a message in Russian that said, "If you find this, throw it in the river." The note's purpose was obviously to protect an unsuspecting citizen who might discover the package from becoming harmed; however, the note also served a double meaning, as TRIGON would use the reverse side to communicate with the CIA through secret writing.

In this case, TRIGON had used the equivalent of butcher-block paper for his message, with one side waxed and the other unwaxed. Unfortunately, he had written the secret text on the waxed surface. In order to confirm the presence of the SW message, Ron did a routine "comb-off," putting a blank piece of paper on top of the message and applying pressure, using a comb, to transfer some of the secret writing onto the blank sheet of paper. Then that was developed, and when a faint reverse image of the text revealed itself, it confirmed that there was a message being sent. The comb-off process is a form of insurance used in developing almost all secret writing messages.

Ron then proceeded to do a classic development of the secret message, putting it in a cardboard paper tray with alcohol and the secret-writing developer solution. He slid in TRIGON's message, and it started to come up, not unlike processing a photograph in a bath of film developer. It looked great. But when Ron started to slide the message out of the liquid, it all blurred. The alcohol in the developer had dissolved the wax coating on the paper; all the letters disintegrated. It was like drawing your hand through a freshly painted image while it was still wet. At that point, Ron's eyes went wide with horror. There was so much riding on this message, and it had been inadvertently destroyed. There was going to be hell to pay.

As Ron came out of the darkroom, I could see by his demeanor that something was wrong. It appeared that our operation might be canceled. Jack was particularly devastated, but we weren't quite ready to give up just yet. As a professional forger and artist, I had a hunch that we might be able to salvage something.

"Do you have copies of TRIGON's handwriting in Cyrillic?" I asked. While the original message was illegible, there was enough left for me to see that TRIGON had used his own Cyrillic alphabet instead of the block letters we had trained him in.

The truth was that TRIGON had made a poor choice by writing his secret message on waxed paper. Even worse, I saw that the paper was clay coated, which posed its own set of difficulties, since the microscopic clay particles tended to bleed into the invisible ink during the development process.

Ron took the original message back into the darkroom for more exposures. Using photo processing and colored filters, he over- and underexposed some of the prints to see if we could get the text of the message. Comparing the blotches on the paper to TRIGON's handwriting, I managed to produce a fair copy of the writing in Cyrillic, which was totally meaningless to me, of course. It was then that Jack, peering over my shoulder and literally breathing down my neck, announced in a hoarse whisper that he could read the message: "I accept your proposal for a meeting. If you feel it is safe to do this . . . Wish us good luck."

I turned to see Jack grinning ear to ear. This was the moment he'd been waiting for. TRIGON had agreed, and we had an operation. Now all Jack had to do was get free from surveillance in order to meet up with him.

Since Ron was staying in Neal's old apartment inside the embassy compound, we decided to use this to our advantage. As we assumed that the apartment was compromised with audio bugs, we made a series of calls from that phone during the week leading up to the meet, ostensibly to arrange for a dinner out for a small group: Ron, a communicator named John, and John's wife. Having heard the plans being made, the watchers would be expecting this trip, which would give us the cover we needed.

The night of the meeting, Jack and his wife, Suzie, went to happy hour at the Marine House. He and Suzie eventually eased out of that scene and worked their way around to a secured elevator not in common use that would go directly up to the CIA station. They walked from the station to Neal's apartment, almost right next door.

Once inside, Jack and Suzie were mute. Ron and I were waiting in the apartment, and I worked on Jack, getting him ready to wear not one disguise but two. The outer disguise would turn Jack into Ron in order to get him past the militiaman guard at the gate in John's car on the way to dinner. Underneath the Ron disguise, Jack was dressed in typical Russian clothing, glasses, and a facial prosthesis: a new nose, a forehead with heavy brows, and a dental facade to conceal his real features so that he could move on the street.

John called to have his car brought into the courtyard. Normally, he would drive, but this evening we wanted his wife, a more accomplished operator than her husband, at the wheel. To give him an excuse to ride shotgun, we had sent him to Helsinki by train a few days earlier, where he had an "accident" that forced him to use crutches. John waited, talking to the real Ron, who then "realized" he needed his keys and disappeared back into the embassy.

The moment of truth came as Jack, dressed as Ron, emerged from the building and piled into John's car, along with the others. If the militiaman in the guardhouse even suspected that something was not right, all he would need to do would be to pick up a radio, and nearby KGB agents would swarm down upon them. John tried to keep the mood light, cracking a joke as they pulled out through the archway. Jack was wearing a small receiver, an SRR-100, which could pick up the frequency of the KGB surveillance teams. If the guard had notified any of them, Jack was bound to hear the telltale squawk. As they drove out onto the street, Jack heard nothing; the disguise had worked.

When he arrived at the target site, Jack removed the Ron disguise to reveal his Russian clothes underneath. Then, in a rolling car escape—in which the vehicle only slowed down but did not stop—he bailed out of the car while John and his wife went on to dinner. Jack stood for a moment to make sure that no trailing surveillance car might come tearing around the corner. Satisfied that he was completely in the black, he turned and melted into the city. Amazingly, everything had gone according to plan. He was now free to meet with TRIGON.

Jack told me later that that evening was one of the highlights of his long and illustrious career. When the two men saw each other, they embraced, caught up in the moment. Jack had taken off his Russian disguise by then so that Ogorodnik could easily recognize him. The two spent nearly an hour walking and talking in the grounds of Fili Park, an unprecedented operational act that would have been unthinkable in the age of Penkovsky.

During the meeting, Jack was careful to reiterate how thankful we were for everything the spy had accomplished so far, even telling Ogorodnik that the director of the CIA personally passed on the information he had given us directly to the US president. The material was considered to be so sensitive that it was also hand carried to Secretary of State Henry Kissinger. Kissinger had said the material included "the most important piece of intelligence" he had read as secretary of state.[2]

Jack also reaffirmed our promise to do everything we could to keep Ogorodnik safe and reminded the spy that if anything happened to go wrong, we had a plan to exfiltrate him out of the country. The implications were clear: Jack wanted to make sure that Ogorodnik didn't get spooked and use his L-pill. When it was over, both men expressed how amazing it had been to be able to meet in the Soviet capital.

There were times during the Cold War when success was hard to gauge. Or the payoff came months down the line. However, Jack's face-to-face meeting with TRIGON was like a seismic shift. Face-to-face meetings were the coin of the realm in the espionage business. Looking into your agents' eyes and reassuring them, evaluating them, praising them, questioning and then observing them—all these assessment and reinforcement tools were wrapped up in personal meetings. The partnerships that formed in such dangerous circumstances became the fuel that propelled an operation forward.

Jack and TRIGON's meeting was also an immense morale booster, and it went a long way in scoring points with the more cautious individuals at headquarters, who tended to look down on human intelligence. It was a clear indication of just how much progress we had made since Penkovsky.

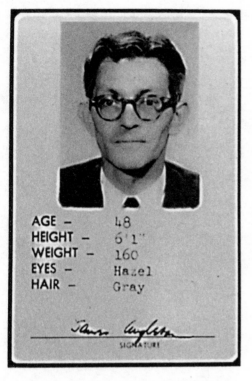

As the chief of the CIA's counterintelligence staff, James Jesus Angleton became suspicious that there may have been moles in the CIA. (Collection of H. Keith Melton at the International Spy Museum)

Aleksandr Dmitryevich Ogorodnik, a.k.a. TRIGON, was a crucial asset for the CIA during the Cold War. (Collection of H. Keith Melton at the International Spy Museum)

An illustration of TRIGON at his desk, with many of the gadgets the CIA used to communicate with him. (Collection of H. Keith Melton at the International Spy Museum)

Martha Peterson was the first female CIA case officer sent to Moscow. She was a liaison with TRIGON, among others. (Collection of H. Keith Melton at the International Spy Museum)

A railroad bridge over the Moscow River was the site of a dead drop left by TRIGON for Martha Peterson. (Collection of H. Keith Melton at the International Spy Museum)

An illustration of the Moscow bridge site given to TRIGON.
(Collection of H. Keith Melton at the International Spy Museum)

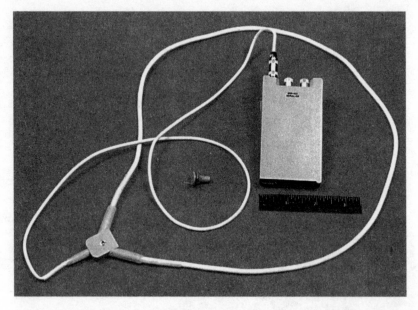

Martha Peterson used an SRR-100 listening device to monitor KGB frequencies during her time in Moscow. (Collection of H. Keith Melton at the International Spy Museum)

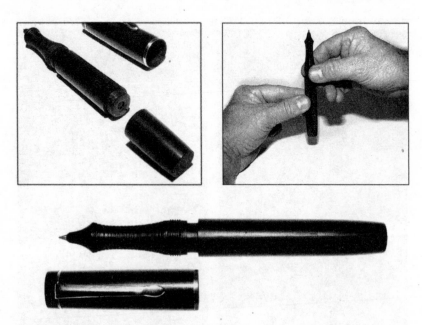

Peterson also carried a miniature TROPEL camera, small enough to hide inside of a pen. (Collection of H. Keith Melton at the International Spy Museum)

Tony Mendez with President Jimmy Carter and Stansfield Turner, the head of the CIA. (Collection of H. Keith Melton at the International Spy Museum)

Adolf G. Tolkachev, a KGB defector who provided crucial information to the CIA. (Collection of H. Keith Melton at the International Spy Museum)

Jonna Mendez meets President George H. W. Bush in a state-of-the-art mask. (Courtesy of the authors)

Jonna Mendez, in true face, at a magician's studio in Los Angeles. (Courtesy of the authors)

Tony Mendez in true face.
(Courtesy of the authors)

Tony Mendez in disguise.
(Courtesy of the authors)

This painting of Tony Mendez hangs in the CIA headquarters at Langley, Virginia, as a testament to his career and service. (Courtesy of the authors)

CHAPTER 5

"Only approach the site when you are sure it is clean."

In the early years, the CIA's technical capabilities were woefully behind those of our adversaries. The United States was late to the spy game. As one US general put it, US intelligence before World War II was "little more than what a military attaché could learn at a dinner, more or less, over the coffee cups."[1] Most of our allies and all of our enemies had long-established intelligence organizations with the equipment and trained personnel in place, whereas America didn't get around to setting up a permanent intelligence agency until after World War II. Initially this put our officers at a distinct disadvantage. Similar to how a Hollywood director from the 1960s was limited in what he or she could do creatively based on the quality of the visual effects of the era, so were our case officers limited in the kinds of operations they were able carry out due to the lack of technical support.

The Penkovsky operation during the early 1960s had been a low-technology affair. For example, since the CIA had yet to create a reliable subminiature camera, the GRU colonel used a commercially available Minox Model III camera in order to photograph documents, a use it was not really intended for. The Minox was a long, slender aluminum camera measuring about three inches by one inch, roughly the size of an index finger. While easily hidden on the body, the camera was anything but clandestine when in operation, as it required two hands to activate and made a lot of noise with each shutter actuation, limiting its usefulness. It could not be used in an office, for instance, or with others around. This meant that the only type of operation we could run involved Penkovsky taking the documents out of a secure area to photograph them. However, since the Soviets had strict restrictions on which types of documents could be brought out of the various ministries, this increased the danger that Penkovsky might be found out. The number one benchmark for an intelligence operation is, can we keep our source safe? If not, it wouldn't be considered a success.

In order to shoot photos, Penkovsky would center the target in the viewfinder and then press the tiny shutter button on the top of the camera for each exposure. Each film cassette contained fifty exposures. He had to close and then open the camera again for his next shot. Using a fine chain attached to the camera, the focus could be set with knots tied at eight, ten, twelve, and eighteen inches. It was a time-consuming procedure and could only be conducted in a secure area.

The Penkovsky operation was also forced to rely on a relatively low-technology communication plan. His primary electronic contact with the West was his one-way voice link, commonly known as OWVL. Penkovsky had a fixed schedule telling him the day, time, and frequency to listen on his Panasonic radio for our shortwave transmissions. The broadcasts, sent from a CIA transmitter in Europe, consisted of a robotic voice reading off groups of numbers that were meaningless to a normal listener. Most were done by a female robotic voice, and she would read long strings of numbers, generally in groups of five. German seemed to be the most commonly used language, as it was widely understood and would have raised fewer alerts than English. The message would sound something like this: *"ein, vier, sieben, neun, acht"* (one, four, seven, nine, eight). This would repeat before moving on to the next five-digit group. Penkovsky would be required to dutifully, and tediously, write down the five-number groups. The end of the message would be some version of zero or "null."

The messages were simple but effective, due to the fact that they were encrypted using a one-time pad, which Penkovsky would immediately destroy after decoding the messages. (That

pad was one of the incriminating pieces of spy equipment presented at his trial.) The downside was that Penkovsky was mute
in this exchange; this was a receive-only, one-way system. These
communications allowed us to task Penkovsky with new reporting requirements. But he could only respond with material that
he could drop to us. The greatest danger to him was not obtain-
ing the secret information but trying to communicate the intelligence to his case officer.

Despite these technological limitations, the operation was
actually a major success, due in large part to the fact that Penkovsky was allowed to travel abroad to London, where he was
able to hand over more than one hundred film cassettes as well as
collateral material, resulting in an estimated ten thousand pages
of reports.[2]

At first, the CIA imported an inexperienced young field officer from the Soviet Division at headquarters in Langley. The officer, thankfully known at this point in history only by his code
name, COMPASS, was ill equipped to handle this operation.
COMPASS's initial idea was for Penkovsky to throw his intelligence packages over the twelve-foot wall of America House, the
American bachelor living quarters, and hope to God that the Soviets didn't observe him doing it. That was it. That was the plan.[3]
Needless to say, Penkovsky wasn't impressed, and after several
months, COMPASS was unable to establish any kind of contact
with the Russian spy.

In the end, the job of running Penkovsky was handed over to
our British "cousins" in MI-6. However, even they seemed to be
overwhelmed by the challenge at hand; Janet Chisholm, the wife
of the MI6 station chief, quickly drew the attention of the KGB
when she met with Penkovsky on several occasions. As it turned
out, the KGB became suspicious when they saw Penkovsky hand
a box of chocolates to one of Chisholm's children. At that point,
the KGB didn't even know who Penkovsky was, but it wouldn't
take long for them to figure out what was going on. Penkovsky
was arrested, and his execution followed shortly thereafter on
May 16, 1963.

Contrast this with the TRIGON operation, and the differences could not be more obvious. New strategies—such as ID transfer, subminiature cameras, advanced disguise techniques, portable scanners to eavesdrop on KGB transmissions, new concealment devices, and better communications plans—had all been created by our techs at the Office of Technical Services to allow our case officers to carry out an operation that in the past would have been considered impossible.

★   ★   ★

The Office of Technical Services was hidden in plain sight in the heart of Washington, DC, directly across the street from State Department at 2430 E Street. When I reported for duty, the office that had begun in 1951 with a complement of about four dozen officers had changed rapidly, expanding and adding skill sets that we would never have imagined. During my tenure, roughly 1966 to 1991, we had grown to a total of one thousand officers. Physically removed from our Ivy League colleagues at CIA Headquarters in Langley by a distance of seven miles, we were also cut from rougher cloth than our case-officer brethren.

OTS was originally staffed with techs from the Midwest; I can mentally count the number of young officers who hailed from Texas, for instance. With a global responsibility and a world-wide presence (20 percent of us were assigned overseas in a military-style forward deployment), we existed with the sole purpose of supporting international CIA operations. Later, a focused recruitment effort was made to upgrade the credentials of our new hires, resulting in an influx of mechanical and electrical engineers with advanced degrees, scientists, artists, printers, psychologists, graphologists, and craftspeople of many types in order to better reflect current technical capabilities and needs. These officers represented the new possibilities in miniaturization and reliable electronics. The predigital, analog technology of the past would be set aside.

At our complex in DC, we occupied three buildings. Central Building housed both our Disguise Branch and its sister, Documents, upstairs. On the ground floor were enough printing presses to produce a daily newspaper in DC. We had a full staff of press operators and, at a separate facility, a papermaking site where we could duplicate any paper in the world, starting with the pulp—handy when making another country's identity documents.

East Building, with the former offices of our founders, General Wild Bill Donovan and Allan Dulles, also housed the Audio Branch, the group responsible for bugging devices. On the second floor of the building was Systems Branch, and at the other end of the hall were Special Devices Branch, electronics R&D, and paramilitary units.

South Building was the home of our Training Branch, our director, the chiefs of Operations and R&D, the Applied Physics Branch, and the Battery Lab. In the basement was Covert Communications, which was responsible for small cameras, video requirements, film technology, secret writing, and microdots. Just down the hall stood a small, locked refrigerator holding the remnants of the US government biological-warfare efforts in the form of cobra venom. Good thing we didn't know that at the time. When it was discovered years later, all hell broke loose, because the venom was supposed to have been destroyed with the rest of America's biological agents.

Following Penkovsky's arrest and execution, the CIA and OTS turned their attention to improving the tradecraft available for running clandestine operations in the Soviet Union. By the mid-1960s, technology was changing, and with the transistor replacing vacuum tubes, the miniaturization of our equipment became a reality. Our battery people were chasing low-power technologies, working to make our batteries smaller and longer lasting. And reliable electronics were the goal of our engineers.

The next agent might not be able to leave the Soviet Union or might have information that needed to be captured from a secure facility, and we couldn't risk losing out on it as a result of inferior technology. There were also instances when a scientist might have access to a blueprint relating to a new Soviet ballistic missile. In the predigital age, these schematics could be quite large, which meant that it was nearly impossible to sneak them out of a secure location. Under those circumstances, the only way for the spy to carry out his or her mission would be to photograph the documents while still inside the institute. As mentioned earlier, this was not something that the Minox was ideally suited to do.

Desperation is indeed the mother of invention, and this was one of our bedrocks for the CIA's development of new and ingenious technology. Our customer drove these developments, and in the case of our Moscow operations, SE Division defined the new requirements. When left to their own devices, the R&D side of our house—the engineers, chemists, physicists, and so on—would focus on the areas of interest to them, but perhaps not to our clients, resulting in black boxes that were typically too big, on the wrong frequencies, or impossible to use in a clandestine mode. But when challenged by real-world problems, clearly defined, they were able to create new technical breakthroughs to solve them.

★   ★   ★

The Tropel camera, or T-100, as it was called, was only one and a half inches long. Get out a ruler and look at that! Inside the camera was a tiny film cassette containing enough film, fifteen inches in fact, to hold one hundred exposures. The camera had an automatic advance system, so the spy did not have to bring his or her other hand up to advance the film. The small size of the device lent itself to a multitude of concealment devices—some of them active concealments, which meant the camera could be used while in its disguised mode. It could be concealed, and it was, in a fountain pen that would still write, a lipstick that could be applied, a key fob that carried keys, a perfume atomizer that sprayed perfume, or a cigarette lighter that would produce a flame when needed. It could fit into almost any small item commonly carried in a man's pocket or a woman's purse.

The only downside was that the camera was somewhat difficult to use. You couldn't just hand it over to an agent with a slap on the back. The agent would first have to be trained. The camera was so small that it didn't have a viewfinder, meaning that the operator would need to know the exact distance for an optimal photograph. The agent would also need to keep the tiny device absolutely still. The best way to pull this off was to have the agent use his or her own body to form a kind of tripod for the camera.

We trained agents to place both elbows on their desks, the page to be copied centered between their elbows. Then we would find the proper height for the camera relative to the agent's body; we were looking for eleven inches. In practice sessions, we would work to find a comfortable, easily repeated position. It was a lot like grooving a golf swing, where over time, the agent could simply feel it and know that he or she was eleven inches off the page. But the agent would have only one chance to get it right. Once he or she pushed that button, it was game over. Since the process of loading the film was so complicated, the agents would use the camera as a one-off and then return it to their case officer with the film cassette still inside. At that point, the cameras would be sent by diplomatic courier back to headquarters, where our techs would go through the process of developing the film.

Not surprisingly, the tiny cameras were incredibly difficult to handle in the laboratory and in the darkroom. Loading and unloading the film cassettes and developing the one hundred exposures per cassette were mind-numbingly tedious tasks. But the knowledge that an agent had risked his or her life to shoot the negatives in each cassette or was going to take the freshly loaded film into a denied area and take his or her chances in stealing more secrets imbued the usually mundane darkroom tasks with a highly charged sense of drama and pressure.

Jonna tells me how her heart would race when developing the film; each step of the process, from the tall glass beakers of developer and fixative to the infrared-sensitive night-vision goggles required to navigate the process, presented a new chance of something going wrong. And when loading new film into the cassettes, there was always the possibility of loading the film backward—because there was no way to determine the emulsion side of the film in the darkroom after it was cut from the supply reel. Of course, there was also no way to check except to expose a few frames and develop the film. And then you would have to start all over.

This all might sound cumbersome by modern standards, and it was. But it was widely understood during the Cold War that these tiny cameras were collecting more significant intelligence than any other tool the US intelligence community had in operation, including our new satellite systems. While the satellites could show us what was going on at the present time, the Tropel cameras were busy imaging the agendas and minutes of important meetings, where the future was being mapped out. Plans and intentions—those were our goals. What were our enemies going to do next? These cameras supplied some of the answers.

★   ★   ★

Technology took many forms. Sometimes it was a new advanced electronic device; other times it was more akin to an artistic creation. OTS didn't differentiate. Our officers presented a dazzling array of skills and aptitudes. For instance, while Marti was in Moscow, she worked closely with our TOPS officers, who helped to fabricate all her dead drops. Some of these were so realistic that, unless you knew what you were looking for, there was absolutely no way you could spot the fake. We actually had problems in the past with some agents going to the drop site and then not being able to find the concealment device, in one instance disguised as a brick among the detritus of a construction site. Thankfully, by the time the TRIGON operation rolled around, we had fixed this problem by including a careful description of the package in the communications plan. It was another way to add a level of security and ensure that only the agent would be able to identify the drop.

Another groundbreaking device came about not as a means to capture information but as a means to communicate it. From 1973 to 1976, the CIA began work on a short-range agent communication system (SRAC) that was years ahead of its time. It was undertaken at the direct request of SE Division for a "short-range, high-speed, two-way communications device that encrypted the transmitted information, was small in size to allow for concealment, was portable, and would function for years."[4]

Known as BUSTER, the device would eventually force OTS to team up with other offices in the Directorate of Science and Technology in order to shoulder the heavy development costs. In fact, at one point the budget got so out of control that the project nearly threatened to bankrupt our office. However, despite the cost overrun, BUSTER was truly revolutionary—a two-way burst transmitter that could send and receive fifteen hundred securely encrypted characters in less than five seconds at the touch of a button. And while it might seem primitive by today's standards, in the 1970s, it allowed two people to surreptitiously communicate at a distance without ever having to break cover. The only downside was that the officers still had to be in an approximate vicinity of each other, which meant that communications plans needed to be established first. And it was a time-consuming device that required a person to input the message one key, or letter, at a time.

As the requirements became more specialized, so did our staff. While the Office of Technical Service had originally been staffed with techs from a variety of backgrounds, our recruiting had become more focused over the years and our hiring more pinpointed. But as we became more specific in the skills we needed, we became less able to describe the nature of the work to our potential employees. We were looking for advanced degrees in esoteric specialties, and at the same time, we needed a cadre of officers with an adventurous spirit and a healthy amount of ingenuity.

"Genius is where you find it," we used to say, and genius was what we were looking for. Some of our officers would go on to fame within the intelligence community. Others would gain respect only within our OTS walls for their derring-do. Still others would hunker down at their workbenches in their laboratories and invent the technologies of the future.

We had a small group of technical officers whom we kept almost under house arrest. Young, arrogant, gifted, and oftentimes without social skills, they were not allowed to visit outside contractors. It seemed at times that the more brilliant the mind, the more outrageous the package it was wrapped in.

Jonna was working for Dave Brandwein, the director of OTS in the early 1970s. In the front office of South Building, every November the preparations for the office Christmas party would begin with a visit from the Price brothers. We had to start early, because at OTS the party was much more than decorating a tree with lights and tinsel. First, the electronics would gradually be installed. The Price brothers would stay late almost every night during the second half of November, just before Thanksgiving, wiring the hallways for their grand production. It would happen slowly, and you really wouldn't notice that it was going on unless you absentmindedly tripped on one of their connections that weren't taped down tightly. If you tried to engage the brothers in small talk, you would be disappointed; while polite, they didn't want to be distracted. They were on a mission.

The Price brothers, both engineers, were two of our youngest professional employees. They had not been working with us for that long, but they set out to make a mark on our population of scientific R&D types, and they achieved their goal early on. It wasn't until years later that I realized that this Christmas party was their way of announcing their arrival and then reminding our officers, yearly, of their technical wizardry. You could say that they were establishing their brand, before the idea of branding really took off. We all knew who they were soon enough, and we were always thankful that they were ours and were working on our side.

The brothers were both so focused on their engineering skills that it was difficult to engage them in a conversation about almost anything else. This close focus would last throughout their careers, and their initial demonstration of this ability was manifested in our Christmas party preparation and execution. What we witnessed at the office was not only the beginning of the arrangements for the event, six weeks in advance, but the end of their months of organization at home.

They didn't have special resources to work with, so they accumulated a good portion of their materials from dumpster diving. They would recycle anything electric or electronic. A discarded vacuum cleaner, an old TV set, a lamp, a toaster—all of these were retrieved from sidewalks and alleys and carted back home. There, while the rest of us were going about our evenings at home, the brothers would be disassembling their finds into their separate electronic components and then reworking them into futuristic devices.

My favorites each year were the assortment of robots that they created and controlled during our party. While you were chatting with a colleague over a drink, courtesy of our skilled chemists, one of their bots would roll up to you and speak to you, beginning with your name. Some only spoke through words on a screen, in a font that was difficult to read. Other parts that they had salvaged would be rewired into a lighting system that pulsated with the music on the walls and ceilings of our hallway, synchronized with the Christmas music that they controlled.

You would never actually see one of the Price brothers at the party. It was necessary for them to be out of sight, barricaded in a tiny room that they had adapted as their control center, the nervous nexus of their electronic wonderland. While we mere mortals drank a little more than we meant to and marveled at their skills, our chemists and physicists and mechanical and electrical engineers and graphic artists and forgers and press operators and forensic specialists would all be highly entertained by what our young brothers had most recently concocted for us.

And so their branding endeavor worked. We were reminded on an annual basis of their technical wizardry, and we called upon them during the year, over and over, for some of our most challenging tests.

Another of our most gifted engineers should be mentioned. Known for his flamboyant red-plaid pants mixed with a yellow-and-brown-striped shirt, long blond hair, and white socks with black sandals, George Methlie spent his early career in OTS working his magic with our battery program. Many years later, when he finally retired from the CIA, the Agency had one of our four CIA schools of excellence named for him: the DDS&T's George Methlie School. It was an incredible honor.

His battery work over a career impacted America's space program, and his advice to NASA extended the life of the Hubble Space Telescope. While he was working for OTS, his work touched on our Moscow problems, as he created smaller, longer-lived, more powerful batteries to run our devices. After all, once you had your third-story guys enter a denied building and install a bug underneath the conference table in the VIP conference room, the odds of getting back in a year later to change out the batteries were laughably small. Our intel lasted only as long as our batteries, so we needed especially good ones. If you wear a watch or a hearing aid today, you are likely another beneficiary of his remarkable work.

★   ★   ★

Since the KGB surveillance teams were such an ever-present backdrop to life in Moscow, our case officers spent an inordinate amount of time on the streets conducting surveillance-detection runs. Sometimes they could last for hours, and while tedious, they were the only way for case officers to ensure that they had gone black. But what if our officers could tell that they had surveillance because they could secretly listen in on the KGB's frequencies? This was a concept put forward by a communications technician who happened across the frequency used by the KGB surveillance teams.

At that point, our TOPS in the station tried to correlate the frequencies with our case officers' travel around the city. To test this theory, a series of "hounds and hares" exercises were choreographed with an in-house set of scanners to monitor the surveillance. Eventually the station was able to see KGB patterns and extrapolate some KGB double-talk. Just as our SST surveillance team did in training exercises in DC, so the KGB developed a verbal shorthand, a code of sorts, to position themselves and maintain the eye on the target. KGB surveillants would also use many of the other techniques that our team in DC used, to include changing clothing, bags, even cars.

And so, in a partnership with the Office of Communications but produced by OTS, we developed a body-worn receiver that was able to listen in to the radio frequencies that KGB surveillance teams were using. The channels might move around, and we had to pay close attention, but eventually we were able to anticipate who had surveillance by sitting in the station and spinning the dials on the surveillance radio channels until we found the ones the Soviets were using that day to monitor our case officers.

In the end, we built a body-worn version of the SRR-100 receiver with five channels. Small, it was worn with a special harness underneath normal clothing, but we still needed a way for the case officers to clandestinely listen to the receiver without the telltale wire going up to the earpiece. Our engineers then came up with an induction loop that could be worn around the neck, like a necklace. Worn under clothing, it connected to the body-worn receiver. The third piece of the technology was called a Phonak, a small receiver manufactured in Switzerland that resembled a hearing aid device. Tiny, not much larger than an eraser on the end of a pencil, it fit comfortably into the ear. But it was still visible.

That is where the disguise labs came into the picture, sculpting the silicone flaps that fit over and completely covered the Phonak device. This was actually the first job that Jonna performed when she transferred over to the Disguise Department, and it became something that we required all our disguise techs to master. Each was custom-made for a specific officer; sculpted in clay and made to fit into a dental-stone replica of that officer's ear, it was then painted to replicate the inner shadows and contours of the ear canal. When inserted into the ear, the Phonak was invisible. We gave them out in pairs, one for the receiver and the other to cancel out ambient street noise.

The SRR-100 became an invaluable tool for our officers in Moscow, who would often never take it off. It gave them one more piece of information about the tight net of surveillance that could be invisibly shadowing them at any time. The first indication of surveillance would come when exiting the embassy compound; a pop or a crackle on the frequencies would be your first indication that they were falling in behind you as you left, whether on foot or in a car. During your day, you could actually hear voices on the receiver and could try to correlate them with your movements. It was an excellent tool.

Over time, the TOPS and the case officers broke the numeric code that the surveillance teams were using, figuring out their terms for left and right and changing the "eye." The station also had a receiver set up and could track your surveillance along with you. While you could never be absolutely certain, the absence of any static or voices in your Phonak was a good indication that you were free of surveillance for the time being. Combined with extensive SDRs, it gave our case officers the necessary confidence to carry out their missions. At least that was the theory. But the KGB, it seemed, weren't quite ready to throw in the towel.

*　*　*

By the fall of 1976, something seemed to be going wrong with the TRIGON operation. At least, that was how Marti saw it. There wasn't one glaring problem or warning sign that she could point to, but a bunch of little details were beginning to add up. In September, Marti had spotted TRIGON with a woman she labeled Ponytail drive past the drop site, setting off her alarms.[5] He should not have been there in advance, and certainly not with a companion. After that, there were a series of empty packages or no packages left for the Moscow Station. The winter of 1977 gave Marti a knot in her stomach as TRIGON missed delivery dates. She had a gnawing unease that something bad had happened to him.

In April, he sent a note saying that he was having bad health, and the TOPS noted that the quality of his photography, always meticulous, was falling off. The photography continued to decline; TRIGON was becoming erratic. The unasked question was, was it still TRIGON? Or was he under KGB control? At the June dead drop, Marti spotted a small van on the street and encountered a man with a flashlight in the park where she was putting down her drop.[6] She was startled and horrified. She found herself incredibly sad, in deep distress over concern for her agent. *Always listen to your gut; it is your operational antennae. A Moscow Rule.*

The station had asked TRIGON to park at the site they called PARKPLATZ, in front of his mother's apartment building, or to make a signal at a designated site. On July 14, Marti drove by the signal site, and the signal was stenciled in red. She went into the office with this news and had a bad feeling about it. Signals were not *stenciled*. But they had a new chief of station, Gus Hathaway, and he said, "We have to make this meeting tonight." Marti understood the politics; this would be Gus's first operation as chief of station, and he wanted to prove that he was aggressive, in control. There was an operational meeting before she went out to do the drop, and she said later that "we all suspected" the KGB had put up that signal.[7] But she had to go and find out.

When Marti drove away from her apartment on the evening of July 15, 1977, she made a provocative turn—heading off on a route that did not suggest any logical destination—in the hopes of drawing out any surveillance, but her SRR-100 was silent. Even so, throughout her two-and-a-half-hour SDR, as she weaved her way through the city, Marti couldn't shake this bad feeling that something was wrong. There had been too many anomalies as of late, too many clues that something was amiss.

Similar to her previous outings, after completing her long meandering SDR, Marti parked her car and entered the subway.

While on the train, she focused on pants, shoes, and bags and did not make eye contact with anyone. Marti knew that surveillants changed hats or jackets but rarely changed shoes or bags when they wanted to alter their appearance.[8]

Switching trains, she traveled across the city until she reached the Lenin Stadium stop. As she emerged from the underground, Marti took a second to take in her surroundings. Her earpiece was still quiet, a good sign that she had no surveillance. If she was going to abort, it was going to be now. She waited a few extra seconds just to be sure, and then she set off on foot toward the drop site. She had made her decision.

When Marti arrived at the railroad bridge over the Moscow River, she walked up forty-seven stairs to the pedestrian walkway and put her package, a large piece of asphalt, down on a ledge inside a pillar. It was quiet. She could see, in Moscow's endless summer twilight, that there was nobody on the bridge. Her SRR-100 remained silent. But as she headed back down the stairs, suddenly three men emerged from the shadows and reached out to grab her.

"Fan out!" one of them yelled. "Don't let her run!"

Marti started yelling in Russian at the top of her voice, hoping to warn TRIGON away if he was in the area. She responded to being manhandled with red-hot anger. She remembers kicking a couple of them. Later, one showed her a bruise, while a segment on Russian TV later reported that another man had been hospitalized as a result of a severe kick to the groin. From under the bridge, a van appeared, and dozens of men emerged from the vehicle, reminding Marti of a clown car. She continued to protest loudly, repeatedly, trying to alert TRIGON even as they threw her in the van and drove her to Lubyanka Prison for interrogation.[9]

It was in Lubyanka that Marti became certain that TRIGON had been compromised. The CIA had given him three identical fountain pens. One was an actual pen. The second was a pen concealment device containing his subminiature Tropel camera. The third look-alike pen contained the L-pill. When the interrogation at Lubyanka got underway, Marti watched closely as the chief interrogator removed a pen from her asphalt concealment device. He handled it daintily with the tips of his fingers and set it to the side, away from the other materials in the device. He could not know yet that this pen contained a camera, but just by the way he had reacted to it, she realized that he knew that this pen might contain another poison capsule. The only explanation was that, somehow, they had discovered the L-pill in TRIGON's possession.[10]

As it turned out, there was to be no interrogation, only a drama acted out for the camera, as she recalled. Later, she learned that after the KGB had arrested TRIGON, he sat at his desk, stripped down to his briefs, and asked for a pen. It was well known that Soviet ballpoint pens didn't work well, and TRIGON said, "Give me my pen, and I will write out my confession." Remember that he said he would not work for us unless he had the ability to commit suicide if necessary. When he bit down on the hollowed-out housing of the pen and broke the glass capsule that contained the poison, his death was almost instantaneous.

So why did the SRR-100 not pick up the surveillance team that apprehended Marti Peterson? Simple. She did not have surveillance that July evening. She was not being followed. There was no need for the KGB to engage in chatter. They were simply waiting for someone to turn up at the Krasnoluzhskiy Most Bridge, spanning the Moscow River. They had arrested her agent, and he had committed suicide. They had found TRIGON's communication schedules, the site sketches, and the signals he would use to call out a meeting. They were the ones who had put up the stenciled signal. And then they drove to the bridge, receded into the shadows, lit a few cigarettes, and waited for someone to show up to load the drop.

At the time of Marti's arrest, the KGB could not have realized the degree to which the Americans were monitoring and exploiting their radio transmissions. Certainly, the small SRR-100 receiver, no larger than two packs of cigarettes, and the induction loop that she wore around her neck like a necklace confounded them. She carried the receiver in a small pocket that she had hand-sewn herself, and she used Velcro to attach it to her bra. Our office, in a casually misogynistic oversight, had neglected to provide her with a harness that would fit a feminine physique.

The KGB never noticed the Phonak device that Marti wore in her ear throughout her interrogation. While listening to the interrogators with one ear, she could also hear the KGB surveillance team that had arrested her whooping it up in the other.

Following protocol, Marti was turned over to an American embassy official, passing out of the prison and into the night air two and a half hours after her arrest. Entering the embassy, she spotted the TOPS officer talking to the marine guard and was shortly relieved to be back in the safety of the station's Yellow Submarine and the company of her fellow CIA officers. However, as per the stipulation of her release, her time in Moscow was finished.

Marti left a trail of glass from the shattered virtual glass ceiling over her head when she boarded the flight back to Washington, DC. Arrested by the KGB early Saturday morning, she left Moscow the following day for Dulles Airport, where Jack and Suzie Downing were waiting for her outside International Arrivals. Jack had been the deputy chief of station, Moscow, for almost the whole duration of the operation. When she walked through the arrival doors, two burly men at the back of the airport crowd faded into the distance; they were the last she would see of KGB surveillance for the rest of her long career.

Given that it was not surveillance that led the KGB to Ogorodnik, how was he identified? How did they find him? The answer goes back to the city of his recruitment: Bogota, Colombia. The CIA had a telephone tap on the Russian embassy in Bogota, which had led us to Ogorodnik. It was not until 1984, seven years after TRIGON's arrest and suicide, that it was discovered that a transcriber, under contract with the CIA, had been translating our telephone taps from the Bogota embassy.

He had been working for the Czech intelligence service simultaneously, and they passed the data to the KGB.[11] The translator, a Czech named Karl Koecher, surmised that we were looking at someone from the Soviet embassy in Bogota, perhaps for recruitment. When the taps stopped, Koecher figured out that the person of interest had left. The KGB had three candidates for possible spies. It took them three years to figure it out. And it led them to TRIGON's doorstep.

The intelligence that TRIGON gave to us changed the face of the Cold War. He provided us with a window inside the Soviet Union and their intellectual and policy processes that we would not have had without him. When Marti briefed the head of the CIA, Stansfield Turner, he asked few questions. It was well known, at that time, that Turner preferred the less risky techniques of collecting intelligence rather than human intelligence, and TRIGON was a prime example of HUMINT. This briefing with Turner seemed to be Marti's audition for an Oval Office visit. Her five minutes with President Carter went long, engrossing the president and stretching to more than twenty minutes, but it was Zbigniew Brzezinski, Carter's national security advisor, with a long and deep understanding of international politics, who seemed most knowledgeable and truly realized what Marti had done, what the CIA in Moscow had done, and how important this work was to American foreign policy at that time.

CHAPTER 6

"Float like a butterfly; sting like a bee."

It was early evening in Moscow in 1977, but it was also early in May, and so the twilight had begun to stretch out late; the sun would not set until around 9:30 p.m. It was a fine evening; however, a strange Russian man was furiously banging on the car window of the Moscow chief of station, Bob Fulton. Trying to get his attention, the Russian made a clumsy attempt to run alongside of Fulton's vehicle as it pulled out of the gas station. Bob had seen him before, and while he wanted to talk to him, he had been advised by CIA Headquarters in Langley to ignore the man and under no circumstances to respond to his repeated attempts to make contact. On another occasion, the man had dropped a note into Bob's car, declaring that he had information for the Americans. The CIA was afraid that the whole thing was a trap. And so nothing happened. After all, what were the chances that a random walk-in would just happen to contact the chief of station? But what if he wasn't a dangle? It was the age-old argument that had been making the rounds since the days of Angleton during the 1960s. How could you trust that a person who claimed to have secret information, who was volunteering to spy on his own government, was not a double agent? Burton Gerber had proven with his rules that the CIA couldn't turn everybody away. So then how was it possible to tell that a potential spy could be trusted?

Why do people spy? What causes a person to betray his or her country and make the decision to engage in espionage?

What draws a particular individual to the field of intelligence? Why would someone choose to spend a life hiding in the shadows? Why harm his or her country? Who will risk their careers, freedom, and, in the case of the Soviet Union, their very life, in order to provide America with the closely guarded secrets of their homeland? Who are these people, and what motivates them?

A former KGB officer, Major Stanislav Levchenko, who defected to the United States in 1979, suggested the use of the acronym MICE as a mnemonic for categorizing the four basic motives for espionage: money, ideology, compromise, and ego. Ergo, MICE.

The categories are, of necessity, loose. It is difficult to distill human behaviors into four simple categories, harder still to choose one and only one of these attributes as the motivator of traitorous behavior, but they serve as a starting point in exploring the causes of betrayal. Taking a look at some of the most well-known American spies, we can find examples of each.

Money

Money is the most commonly cited motive among Americans who are willing to betray their country. Since the end of World War II, Americans have most consistently cited money as the dominant motive for espionage. In the 1980s, it was cited as the predominant motivator in more than half of all espionage cases prosecuted in the United States. While before 1945 most Americans convicted of espionage were motivated by ideology, the tables have turned as the years rolled by. In recent decades, as in the well-known case of CIA officer Aldrich Ames, a need or desire for money was the primary rationale for his betraying his country and his own agents. It was a case of dollars for pounds of flesh.

Ideology

One of America's premier cryptologists, Meredith Gardner, decrypted messages passed between the United States and Moscow during the 1940s. What those messages revealed was staggering: more than two hundred Americans had become Soviet agents during the war. Moscow had spies in the Treasury Department, the State Department, and the OSS. The decrypted messages were eventually known as the Venona Papers and are most famous for exposing Ethel and Julius Rosenberg in their involvement with a Soviet spy ring, the purpose of which was to gain information on the US atomic-bomb research and the Manhattan Project.[1]

The KGB, it turned out, had cultivated an extensive network of informants in American institutions. What caused these two hundred US citizens to work for the Soviet government? The American spies often acted from idealistic calculations about a world order so changed today that it is difficult to recapture. The world depression of the 1930s shook the complacency of many about capitalism's merits and led progressive-minded Americans to take a friendly interest in the Soviet experiment. In fact, membership in the American Communist Party grew sevenfold during the Great Depression.[2]

Compromise

Compromise, or coercion, is a negative form of motivation. It is sometimes conflated with blackmail and can even be compared to torture. The idea of compromise is to gain leverage against the proposed spy and to force him or her to act through fear of punishment. As has been argued about waterboarding, the validity of a subject's cooperation is considered unreliable because the target's main purpose is to make the torture or coercion stop. The use of a swallow, or seductress, to compromise a target would be considered a common example of this type of coercion. In a classic example of the threat of compromise in an intelligence operation, Clayton Lonetree, a US marine guard at the American embassy in Moscow, was undone by a KGB swallow named Violetta Seina. In all forms of compromise, an individual does not cooperate freely. It is the least common of the four motivators found in the MICE acronym.

Ego

Called by several other names, including revenge and disgruntle-ment, ego can be broadly applied as a prime motivator of those who betray their country or government. Among volunteer spies, disgruntlement with the workplace was significant; one-fifth of prosecuted spies with a single motive have cited revenge or dis-gruntlement as their primary motive. Disappointment, anger, frustration, or alienation can arise from interactions among coworkers or between employees and supervisors.

People's egos are wrapped up in every aspect of their profes-sional and personal life, and it is hard to differentiate its effects when trying to assign cause and result. In the case of Robert Hanssen, who spied for the Russians in arguably the worst intel-ligence disaster in US history, the betrayal was closely bound to his sense of being undervalued and underrewarded by the FBI for his years of work and his contributions to the bureau's suc-cess. He was, at the heart of the matter, determined to demon-strate his competence, and he successfully maintained a secret life parallel to his FBI career in order to make clear that his skill surpassed that of his colleagues.

When looking at the Russians who worked for the American intelligence community—whether for the CIA, DIA, FBI, or other elements of the intelligence community (IC)—it is interesting to note that the scale works almost in reverse. For the Russians, the primary motivation was ideology, not money. Over time, they had become disillusioned with the Soviet system, in which the average citizen couldn't even buy vegetables, and decided that by betraying their own country, they were really saving its people.

During my tenure at the CIA, the best of the spies who worked for us were what we called "volunteers." While considerable time and effort was spent on targeting, assessing, developing, and recruiting likely candidates to work for us, the spies who brought us the best intelligence were invariably the ones who self-recruited, who stepped out of the shadows and insisted that they would work for us.

Penkovsky was a great example of this. He had to persist, despite being turned away by CIA officers multiple times. In addition to his political beliefs, he harbored a simmering resentment for what the Soviet Union had done to his career. His advancement was always limited because of his father's involvement with the White Russians at the time of the Bolshevik Revolution. Once on board, these volunteers were willing to take incredible risks and, indeed, provided the CIA with some of the most valuable intelligence of the Cold War.

So then, what to make of this new individual who kept making approaches? Was he the real thing, or was he a dangle?

The man had first approached Bob Fulton on a brutally cold evening in January of 1977. Identifying himself only as Adolf, the man had a folded note in his pocket that he intended to pass to the first American he saw at the Fili gas station, which was popular among foreigners.[3] The temperature was a brutal minus-thirty degrees Fahrenheit. Looking for an American license plate, the Russian observed one in particular who seemed a likely subject to approach, as he told Bob Fulton later. *He has to be an American*, the Russian had thought at the time, *and not a Russian chauffeur. Look at his trousers, which have never seen an iron. No Russian chauffeur of a diplomatic vehicle would ever dress like that.* When Fulton told me this story years later, it was relayed with a broad grin.

Who would guess he had stumbled on the CIA's chief of station, a rumpled bachelor named Bob Fulton who wasn't keen on ironing his casual clothing? What passed as Saturday-afternoon casual in Georgetown presented as slovenly by old-fashioned Russian standards. It didn't matter that while Bob had well-pressed sets of business clothing for his official and social functions, he liked to relax on his time off and not worry about his grooming. Bob took the note, and the bureaucrats in DC advised him not to respond.

A month later, Adolf made overtures to Bob again, this time in front of the US embassy, where Bob had parked his car, out of sight of the militiaman at the gate. Like before, Adolf slowly approached the car and dropped another note in through the window.

Two weeks later, the volunteer attempted to engage Bob for the third time and dropped a four-page note into his car. This time he included more data about himself, and he suggested making further contact. Again headquarters vetoed Bob's request to respond. CIA headquarters was concerned that the approach was a KGB trap, a dangle; no real spy would ever be that brazen, and the station was told once again to ignore the man.

And so when Adolf approached Bob Fulton again, for the fourth time, actually beating on the station chief's car to get his attention, Bob had to ignore him—as he had been instructed—and drove away.

Several months later, on a typically dreary winter evening, a determined Adolf made one more attempt to engage with the Americans, this time passing a letter to a different American on the street, who passed it to the newly arrived chief of station, Gus Hathaway. This was when the CIA, not knowing the Russian's true identity, gave him the CIA code name CKSPHERE. But even though the operation had progressed enough for the man to be assigned a code name, that still didn't mean that the Moscow Station was given a green light to speak to him.[4]

One of the main reasons for this extreme level of caution had to do with a new director back at headquarters. Back in March 1977, Admiral Stansfield Turner was appointed by President Jimmy Carter to be the new head of the CIA, replacing George H. W. Bush. Bush wanted to remain in office, but Carter wanted to have his own man take over the job. Turner emerged from a distinguished military career that included a term as president of the US Navy War College, commander of the US Second Fleet, and the commander in chief of Allied Forces for Southern Europe, with a headquarters in Naples. Turner harbored an ambition to become chief of naval operations; however, the president called on him to lead the CIA instead. At that time, in January 1977, the CIA had turned over three directors in four years. Nothing in his formidable military past could have prepared

Admiral Turner for his new position at the top of America's intelligence structure.

Settling in as the new director of central intelligence, Turner emphasized satellite imagery, signals intelligence, and eavesdropping devices—technologies that are still widely used today. The CIA was still reeling from the wave of congressional hearings into clandestine operations, such as experimental drug tests on humans and plots to assassinate foreign officials—all of which my office was involved with. He decided to support intelligence collection through technology rather than relying on spies with feet on the ground—that is, HUMINT. The career officers in the clandestine service did not concur. Turner's ramrod-straight military bearing and strict adherence to the rules did not go over well in their CIA operational environment.

By September, Turner was firmly in place, and he and his new Public Relations Office, headed by Herb Hetu, were determined to get this new policy out to the American public in order to counter what they considered to be the demonization of the CIA after the Watergate scandals. Together they concocted a daring and novel event in the eyes of CIA careerists: an overt celebration of the thirtieth anniversary of the founding of the CIA.

Within the intelligence community, celebrating so publicly was unprecedented. Herb Hetu, however, sank his teeth into the project, choosing to go with a live TV program discussing "What the CIA Does and How It Operates." The proposal was to produce a one-hour show, with four eight-minute recorded segments followed by a live interview with the new DCI. Possible subjects included a tour of the spy library at Langley, security issues like the CIA's management of classified trash, the use of safes and vaults for protecting classified materials, and the preparation of various analytical reports.[5]

Herb Hetu's optimism was not misplaced. ABC, in the form of David Hartman, the host of *Good Morning America*, agreed to his plan. At the last minute, the network also decided to move the location of DCI Turner's live interview to Foggy Bottom at 2430 E Street, a white limestone building that housed first the OSS

and then the CIA from 1947 to 1961. There was a nice sym-
metry in Turner proselytizing the CIA from the very same location where both Bill Donovan and Allen Dulles, the two great
salesmen of US intelligence, had worked.[6]

At the time, Jonna was working for Dave Brandwein, the OTS
director, in our own offices at 2430 E Street, and she remembers being recruited to refresh Wild Bill Donovan's original office
in South Building with a gigantic dieffenbachia from her own
office, a couple flags, and a silver tea service on a sideboard.
Leather chairs were brought in, as was an oriental rug, to give the
otherwise-dreary room some historic character, a little elegance.
This was to be an interview on live TV, after all, and there were
expectations from the producers and their production assistants
(and the American public) to be met.

In fact, this was just the beginning of a public-relations effort
to rebrand the CIA. In 1979 the CIA would boast that the DCI
and the DD/CIA had carried the CIA's message to some thirty
major audiences, while other officers had addressed some thirty
individual groups locally and outside of the DC metropolitan
area.[7] I can say with some confidence that SE Division was not
amused.

★   ★   ★

Gus Hathaway arrived in Moscow as the new CIA chief of station in June 1977, and two months afterward, the US embassy
there erupted in flames. On August 26, 1977, *ABC Evening News*
reported that there was a major fire at the American embassy
in Moscow. Beginning on the eighth floor, it spread rapidly.
Embassy officers quickly scrambled to save what they could, but
a significant amount of material would be lost. Despite the sever-
ity of the fire, all personnel were evacuated safely.

Old and crowded, the embassy was a firetrap. While the US
government had been, and would continue to be, in negotiations
for a new office building, or NOB, too many people continued
to work in the cramped space. This was especially true of the

CIA station, located on the floor just below the blaze in a small, oppressively confined space affectionately known as the Yellow Submarine.

Deputy chief of mission Jack Matlock initially raised the alarm. At about 10:30 p.m., he located the American ambassador, Malcolm Toon, who was dining at the Romanian ambassador's residence, to alert him, and the ambassador left for his embassy almost immediately, still in black tie.

By the time he arrived, most of the eighth floor of the embassy was in flames, and the fire was racing down the south side of the building. The US Marines had been fighting the fire from the start, but it was rapidly getting away from them. The General Services Office had called the Moscow Fire Department, but they were slow to respond. About two hundred people, those living in apartments on the lower floors of the building, were milling around beside Ring Road.

According to a State Department report, "The fire broke out in the upper stories of the building . . . and rapidly got out of control. Soviet fire trucks were pulling into the area, ladders were going up against the building, and . . . a first wave of so-called firemen, wearing worn uniforms and carrying leaking hoses were racing up these ladders. They were followed a short time later with a more professional looking crew in brand new, firefighting uniforms and with much more sophisticated equipment."[8] The suspicious second crew of "firefighters" was, as it turned out, from the KGB.

Ambassador Toon, who had only been in the country for eight months, was standing out on the curb in full diplomatic regalia, fresh from that formal dinner with several other ambassadors. He directed that the "firemen" not be allowed on the tenth and other floors where the most sensitive equipment and materials were stored. The fire marshal, equally impressive in the military finery of a Soviet general, eventually told Toon that the building would be a total loss if the firefighters did not have complete access. The somewhat-curmudgeonly American ambassador reluctantly gave ground, granting permission. He ordered all Americans out of the building, including the marine guards.

When the fire spread to the seventh, ninth, and tenth floors, it gradually became obvious that the attic, which contained a lot of sensitive equipment under the eaves, was in danger. Toon, a notorious hard-liner when it came to the Soviets, did an about-face. He turned on his heel and famously said, "Let it burn," knowing full well by then that KGB officers were mixed in with genuine firefighters.[9]

As the flames moved up the building, it turned out that at least two of the American embassy employees had disobeyed Toon's orders to get out. They were the new CIA chief of station, Gus Hathaway, and a senior sergeant in the Defense attaché office, carrying out the destruction of classified and sensitive materials as best they could. Gus was guarding his station dressed in a London Fog raincoat and armed with a .38-caliber revolver. On hearing the ambassador's order, Gus gave a rather undiplomatic response, the gist of which was that he wasn't going to leave under any circumstances, even if the building was burning down around him.[10]

Ambassador Toon, not the most congenial of diplomats even under normal circumstances, was not happy, but there was nothing he could do, and Gus stayed behind. Gus, like Toon, was a World War II veteran and knew his duty. This became a celebrated incident in Gus's career—when he barred arriving firefighters from entering the CIA station, *his* station, located the floor below the blaze. Like Toon, Gus correctly suspected that some of the firefighters were KGB agents. Knowing that the KGB would be hoping to collect sensitive information or enter restricted areas, he refused to evacuate until the fire was contained. Gus was later awarded the Intelligence Star by the CIA for his actions, with a citation noting that he had protected sensitive areas from penetration "at great personal risk."[11]

For several days after the fire, Soviet helicopters flew low over the embassy to try to get a closer look into the attic, an area that had always been off-limits to uncleared personnel. They were too late, however, to see anything of consequence. This fire made the front pages of most papers in the United States, with morning-after pictures of the embassy prominently featured. It would take almost five months to repair the damage, a massive headache for our personnel, who found themselves spending the majority of their tours doing nothing but rebuilding the station.[12]

Days later, when Gus asked embassy security whether the second wave of firefighters, in their brand-new uniforms, took a lot of material from the embassy, the answer, following a quick survey, was an emphatic yes. It was patently clear to senior embassy officials afterward that the "firefighters" had gone through the embassy, opened safes and cipher-protected areas, and leveraged the situation. As a result, the United States had to deal with serious theft of classified materials.[13] It would seem, however, that the CIA's stash, guarded by its chief of station, had fared better, according to meetings with Gus back at headquarters after the fire.

A few months later, a KGB shed located on a nearby rooftop went up in flames. When the US Marines, who had heroically fought the blaze at their embassy, saw that conflagration, they opened their bar on the second floor and played "Disco Inferno" by the Tramps ("Burn, baby, burn") at top volume out the windows of the embassy. The ambassador got a protest note from the Ministry of Foreign Affairs.[14]

Coincidently, shortly after the embassy fire, station officer Vince Crockett and his wife, Becky, were arrested, declared persona non grata, and sent home from Moscow. This followed the identification and arrest of a GRU colonel, Anatoli Filatov. The CIA had recruited Filatov when he was stationed in Algiers, and when he returned to Moscow, he was caught loading a classic dead drop. He was known at the CIA as GTBLIP. When Vince and his wife went out to do a car toss to the agent, our TOPS officer prepared a CD package for them containing a Tropel camera. The Crocketts rounded a corner after executing the car toss, and the KGB stopped and arrested them. GTBLIP had already been exposed elsewhere, without their knowledge.

All these losses hit the CIA station hard. With the unexpected loss of TRIGON and the subsequent arrest and expelling of

Marti Peterson, followed by the fire and the arrest of GTBLIP as well as the arrest and expulsion of Crockett, it appeared that perhaps a tradecraft flaw was gnawing away at the station's ability to collect intelligence.

As a result of these setbacks, during September 1977, Stansfield Turner, the relatively new director of the CIA, announced that he was going to turn the Agency's ship around. An austere man who had always abided by a strict code of honor and discipline, Turner had a natural mistrust for the Moscow Rules, or "techniques," as he called them. How could anyone trust a person who was willing to betray his or her country? In the end, Turner ordered a total stand-down on all CIA operations in Moscow. There was even concern that he might go so far as to close the station permanently.

Only six months into his job, Turner believed that the CIA was incapable of operating against the KGB, and he wanted no more public, humiliating embarrassments. At Langley, the Soviet and East Europe Division was in an uproar. Critical intelligence streams were truncated, and all espionage activities ceased. In effect, the Agency's Moscow Station was closed for business. One of our long-term cases, the Polyakov operation, which was using the brilliantly engineered BUSTER shortwave communications link to enable secure, encrypted two-way communications with the agent, was shut down. In the middle of the Cold War, the CIA's eyes and ears were being closed.

Just as the brakes squealed to a halt in Moscow, however, an important agent code-named FEDORA sent a signal to the station. Alexei Kulak was a science and technology officer who had been awarded the prestigious Hero of the Soviet Union medal. The agent had originally met with the FBI in New York in the early 1960s, and he had been working for them off and on until he was transferred to the Soviet capital in 1976. Before leaving the United States, he'd been recruited by the CIA to work for us in Moscow. Reluctantly, Kulak had agreed, and as part of the arrangement, he was given a communications plan and information for a potential drop site.

Then, in the summer of 1977, he had filled the drop, providing the CIA with a list of Soviet officials in the United States who were trying to steal technical and scientific secrets. Further, in a letter accompanying the list, Kulak promised to divulge even more sensitive information about the USSR's worldwide operation for stealing American technical secrets. The Moscow station chief was thrilled, but by the time Kulak signaled a second time that the drop was ready, Turner's operations ban had taken effect.

As a result, the CIA now sat mute. Kulak signaled again; the drop was loaded. But again, the Moscow Station remained silent, unable to respond. And then there was the mysterious and persistent Adolf, who had hinted in his letter that he worked at one of the premiere Soviet technical institutes. However, despite this potential goldmine for intelligence, the CIA was forced to turn him away.

Then, on October 31, 1977, Admiral Turner took a long look at the old boys' club that had run CIA operations for years, perhaps too many years in his estimation, and decided, in concert with President Carter, to remove some deadwood from the Agency's ranks. Still considered to be an outsider by the career Clandestine Services officers and with no professional or personal ties to that community, Turner, with one stroke of a pen, terminated 820 positions in the Directorate of Operations. The media called it the Halloween Massacre, in which 649 jobs were dissolved, 154 officers were asked to retire involuntarily, and 17 were fired.[15]

CIA insiders called it a bloodbath, and the furor in SE Division could be heard up and down the halls of Langley. Some of the officers who left had been with CIA since its inception, including Jonna's father-in-law at the time. They were dismissed with an impersonal and abrupt, two-paragraph letter perfunctorily thanking them for their service. Turner's demands were quite simple: risk-free operations and guarantees of no more "incidents" on his watch. Of course, there was no way that his demands could be met. There was no such thing as a risk-free operation.

"Ethical espionage" is a contradiction in terms. Espionage is, by definition, illegal. It is the theft of secrets from a foreign state. It involves bribing, blackmailing, or otherwise persuading a foreign national, in defiance of the laws of his or her country, to supply another government with secret material. In addition, it is almost invariably necessary to use false identities, lies, and other deceptions to execute and ensure the theft itself. As such, espionage can hardly be elevated to an ethical plane. It was as if Turner did not trust the CIA, the very agency he'd been tasked to lead, and it didn't take long for the feeling to become mutual. He was never forgiven for this reduction in force.[16]

To those of us who had dedicated our lives to serving our country, it felt like the CIA was dying. However, after a year and a half of being on lockdown, Gus Hathaway decided to push back. Gus was a legendary hands-on CIA operations guy, one of the exalted "barons" of SE Division, and he was not used to being told no. Adolf, the Russian, had now made four desperate but unsuccessful attempts to contact the CIA before Turner had slammed Moscow Station's door closed. Now, in this last encounter, Adolf included detailed instructions for a meeting and two pages of data on a Soviet aircraft. Gus had recently been the chief of the Soviet and East European Division at CIA Headquarters overseeing Moscow operations. He had been the one saying no to Bob Fulton's requests to meet with this potential asset. Now Hathaway, the last and final CIA officer approached on the street in Moscow by this mysterious man, argued that meeting him was worth the risk.

Taciturn but courtly, Gus Hathaway was already well known at the CIA. He was well respected but not particularly well liked. He was admired for his mastery of espionage tradecraft and aggressive efforts to best the Soviet KGB. "Gus was a risk taker," said Jack Downing. "We needed good intelligence and we needed to be aggressive to get it. He was canny and smart about how to do it."[17]

After a decent interval, Gus Hathaway again asked headquarters for permission to contact the volunteer, and to his very real surprise, headquarters, which had had a chance to digest the two pages of data on a Soviet aircraft that Adolf had provided, finally agreed. What nobody knew at the time was that this shadowy figure known only as Adolf would go on to become one of the most productive agents in the history of the Cold War. His full name was Adolf G. Tolkachev.

At this early stage in the operation, however, Gus still had very little to go on, apart from the loose theory that this individual might have something to do with Soviet aircraft development. When assessing the potential value of a volunteer, it is vital that the case officer first gauge his or her state of mind. At this point, Gus had been allowed to open the door, but he still couldn't let Tolkachev come walking in until he learned a little bit more about him. Turner had been right about one thing: 1977 had been a terrible year for operations in Moscow, and Gus couldn't afford to do anything that might damage the station further.

There were various steps for vetting potential volunteers. The first step was to examine their background and current work history. The next step would be to actually meet with the individual if possible and assess his or her motivation. However, one of the first things that the CIA did for Tolkachev was to examine a handwriting sample. The art of graphology, or handwriting analysis, has fallen out of favor, but during the 1970s, we used it to discern a person's state of mind.

So a sample of Tolkachev's handwriting was sent to a team of OTS graphologists, who weighed in with their conclusions. "The writer is intelligent, purposeful, and generally self-confident. He is self-disciplined but not overly rigid. He has well above average intelligence and has a good organizing ability. He is observant and conscientious and pays meticulous attention to details. He is quite self-assured and may plow ahead at times in a way, which is not discreet or subtle. All in all, he is a reasonable, well-adjusted individual and appears intellectually and psychologically equipped to become a useful, versatile asset."[18]

In February, Gus and his wife had a brief encounter with Tolkachev, and another note was passed. At this point, the Moscow

Station decided to test him out for real and asked Tolkachev to mail three letters in secret writing to the CIA. One side, written by the CIA, would look like a simple letter from an American tourist being sent to a friend back home. But on the other side, Tolkachev was told to fill out a questionnaire about himself and add a piece of intelligence that might be valuable. It was an overt act, one that would put the engineer's life in danger if the letters were found out. Gus arranged for the three letters to be given to Tolkachev through a dead drop.

Then the station waited. Soon they would know whether Tolkachev was a dangle. Dangles would never include real actionable intelligence. But as it turned out, three weeks later, the letters arrived at their destinations, and we had them in hand. As expected, the Soviet censors had opened them to examine their contents but decided that they were innocuous. Gus and everybody at the Moscow Station was thrilled. Tolkachev had just performed his first operational act. On June 1, 1978, seventeen months after Adolf's first approach to Bob Fulton at the Fili gas station, Gus Hathaway's operational plan for the agent they had code-named CKSPHERE was approved. They had an operation, at least in theory.

Across the pond, despite the promise that Tolkachev represented, Turner was having second thoughts. However, just when it looked like he might pull the plug on the budding operation, an emergency involving FEDORA changed everything.

FEDORA, recently retired from KGB service, was about to be identified in a book called *Legend: The Secret World of Lee Harvey Oswald*, written by Jay Epstein, and if this happened, he would be arrested and executed, the normal sentence for a Soviet found guilty of espionage. Gus had actually been the one to re-recruit FEDORA, Alexei Isidorovich Kulak, when he heard the Russian was heading back to Moscow, and he was determined to protect the Russian's life.

When the warning came from headquarters that FEDORA was in danger, Gus decided to push back against Turner's skittish policy of no contact with the enemy, a year and a half after the stand-down order was imposed. He concluded that he needed to go black and warn the source face-to-face that he should flee the Soviet Union before he was exposed. OTS already had an exfiltration plan in preparation if Kulak decided to escape; in fact, one of our officers was on a ferry in Sweden doing a probe, looking for potential exfiltration routes in case Kulak signaled his willingness to flee. To Gus's amazement, headquarters' SE Division agreed that FEDORA should be contacted and warned of the potential of exposure, and Turner approved warning him as well.

Although very active on the streets of Moscow, at least for a chief of station, Gus had not tried to use disguise to escape his watchers in Moscow. On two different nights, he attempted to reach Kulak by driving out through the embassy gate in true face, without a disguise; however, on each occasion the KGB surveillance teams quickly fell in behind him, and he had to abort. So while he had previously discounted the proprietary disguise techniques we had fielded earlier with two former Moscow chiefs of station to give them the options to go black (i.e., our identity-transfer silver bullets), Gus's hand was forced. The third time he went out, he used a contingency package I had left on the station's shelf. It was an overhead mask and accessories called the Carol disguise, and it would make an officer, any officer, look like Carol, one of the embassy wives. Gus put on the mask, a dress, and a coat. He got in a car with Carol's husband, holding a pair of her ice skates in his lap (Carol was an ardent ice-skater), and they drove out of the gate, past the militiaman, without a problem.

Once free and out of the embassy, Gus removed the mask and the dress and stowed them on the floorboard, along with the skates. But when he contacted FEDORA after hours of walking, doing the same SDR he expected of his officers, the agent's response to the warning, loosely translated, was the Russian equivalent of "Screw them. I'm too old and too tired to leave Russia at this late date. To hell with the bastards. They can't do anything worse than has already been done. I will die here as I have tried to live, with dignity."

The success of the operation, at least the part involving the ease with which Gus was able to escape surveillance, was another benchmark for the Moscow Rules. It proved that while a few operations had gone bad, the rules were still sound. It was also a source of amusement for longtime operatives who knew Gus, as they got a kick out of the idea of him challenging the Second Chief Directorate and its hordes of surveillants while wearing a skirt. It was so out of character and preposterous that it had to work, and it did. Gus was pleased and astounded at the power of the disguise technique. Disguise had a new fan.

Gus declared the extraordinary disguise technique his most valuable, fail-safe tradecraft option. Stansfield Turner, the nay-saying DCI, declared it to be a fine piece of work. Back at headquarters, Jack and Gus had a meeting about disguise, which ended with Gus sending a cable from Langley to Moscow saying that disguise would be the be-all and end-all extreme fallback on any operation run in Moscow. *Hold it in a precious place. Protect it.* Gus sent it.

The new Moscow Rules were coming into focus now, and Adolf Tolkachev was at hand to help improve them. The aggression of the KGB and Turner's threat to close Moscow Station created extraordinary circumstances that propelled the evolution of the Moscow Rules forward. The CIA's notoriously conservative SE Division was forced to consider techniques they deemed risky, and OTS used this new energy to turbocharge its technology.

Kulak died in 1983 of natural causes. Evidently, he was protected by his history as a war hero of the USSR. He was never arrested.

As for Adolph Tolkachev, it was only after the Moscow Station carried out an actual face-to-face meeting, one of many, that they began to realize just how incredibly important he was.

CHAPTER 7

"There is no limit to a human being's
ability to rationalize the truth."

On the evening of December 7, 1982, a car pulled onto the
streets of Moscow. The chief of station (COS) was sitting behind
the wheel, while a young case officer named Bill Plunkert sat
next to him in the passenger seat. The rest of the group consisted
of the men's wives, who sat in the back seat. The four of them
were dressed for a party; in fact, the wife of the COS had a birthday cake on her lap. The whole thing had been arranged several
days earlier, when a diplomat at the embassy had called to organize the party at one of the apartments in the city. It was known
that the KGB would be listening in and wouldn't necessarily pay
the party group any attention. Or at least that's what was hoped.

Plunkert had arrived at the Moscow Station earlier that summer. A former naval aviator who thrived in difficult situations
and a Soviet specialist, he was excited about getting a chance to
prove himself.

His sole mission was to take care of Adolf Tolkachev, who
had become one of the most valuable agents the Agency had ever
run inside the Soviet capital. Over the course of the previous two
years, the Russian spy had been able to meet face-to-face with
CIA case officers roughly a dozen times, handing over several
hundred rolls of film, thousands of sensitive documents, and even
electronic components, including circuit boards. Tolkachev did
not want to use dead drops. He thought personal meetings would
be no riskier than drops, because in each case, a CIA officer had

to be free of surveillance. He also noted that he preferred personal meetings. Over the total course of the operation, more than twenty face-to-face meetings took place.

Headquarters considered the operation to be nothing short of a miracle. Tolkachev's product compelled the US Air Force to completely reverse its direction on a multimillion-dollar electronics package for one of its latest fighter aircraft. He also provided intelligence on the newest Soviet surface-to-air missile systems. A Department of Defense memo to the DCI reported that "we never before obtained such detail . . . of such systems until years after they were actually deployed."[1]

However, by the autumn of 1982, it appeared as if something had gone wrong. The Soviet spy had missed five meetings in a row, which had never happened before. Tolkachev was a meticulous engineer, but he had absolutely no training when it came to clandestine operations. Had he made a mistake that had tipped off the KGB?

It was vital that the station reestablish contact, but for some reason, there had been an uptick in KGB surveillance, making it nearly impossible to get free.

With the next meeting set for December 7, Plunkert hatched a daring plan. The station had recently been provided with a new piece of OTS technology that was so secret that it was considered proprietary to Moscow. Engineered with the help of a well-known but unnamed magician out in Los Angeles, it was specifically designed to help our officers get black and avoid surveillance. Known as the Jack-in-the-Box, the device was intended to fool the trailing surveillance vehicle into thinking that our case officer was still in the car when, in fact, he or she had actually bailed out. And believe it or not, it was hiding in the birthday cake.

The premise of the JIB revolved around the idea of creating a twin, something very common in the world of magic. Early on, it was discovered that the KGB's vehicular surveillance teams would usually stay back at a distance. This meant that when they were following their target they tended to count heads or look at silhouettes. A good illusionist always knows that a person's mind wants to tell itself a story; it tries to rationalize what it sees. In this case, the goal was to get the KGB to believe that the silhouette they were watching belonged to the target they were following, when in fact it didn't.

The trick was in the timing. If the case officer bailed out too soon or the device didn't deploy fast enough, the illusion wouldn't work. It was a complex ballet, and Plunkert and his companions had been rehearsing and working on it for several days.

The first stage of the operation involved trying to create a gap in the surveillance. The COS had spent the past month planning a careful route that would allow him to make two right-hand turns in quick succession, which would open up a natural break. It might only be for a few seconds, but it would be enough to shield the car from the trailing surveillance team and give Plunkert a chance to leap from the car. All of it had to look natural, though, which meant that there could be no unexpected or aggressive turns or any sudden bursts of acceleration. No brake lights. If the COS altered his pace in any way, the KGB would instantly race in and bumper-lock him, and the operation would have to be aborted.

In the car, Plunkert had on a second set of Russian-style clothes underneath his own, which allowed him to alter his appearance to look like a typical Russian old man. In this way, the operation was like an onion, composed of translucent layers of deception that, when combined, served to obscure the heart of the matter. Our disguise offices had also fitted him with a face mask, heavy black-rimmed Russian spectacles with plano lenses, and a dental facade, all of which he put on while the COS approached the drop-off site.

Time tended to stand still in these moments. Plunkert knew that the JIB had never been used operationally before. He was taking a huge risk, but he tried not to think about that. Instead, he focused on the mission, checking and rechecking that he had everything ready.

A few minutes later, they made the crucial turn, and Plunkert had his hand on the door, ready to go. He waited until the COS used the emergency brake to slow the car down just enough and then flung open the door and leaped out onto the sidewalk.

At the same moment, the COS's wife reached forward and placed the birthday cake on the passenger seat. All it took was a touch of a button, and the JIB leaped into position. The JIB dummy had been dressed with clothing from Plunkert's closet; formed from Plunkert's facial impression, the head was realistic, and the dummy even had a small trigger that allowed the COS to swivel the head for lifelike effect.

The whole exchange took only a few seconds, but now came the moment of truth as the KGB surveillance team rounded the corner. The car's headlights washed over Plunkert, who did his best to stoop, playing the part of an aging pensioner. The COS, meanwhile, had made it to the end of the block and was just about to make another turn. From the rear, the silhouette of four individuals was clearly visible in the car. Plunkert held his breath, his skin pulled tight by the features of the mask. He was the only one on the street, but the KGB paid him no notice as they raced past to keep pace with the COS. A moment later, both cars turned onto a side street, leaving Plunkert alone. The ruse had worked. He was in the black and free now to meet up with Tolkachev.

When Plunkert finally made it to the site of the meeting, he was relieved to see Tolkachev waiting for him in the park. Plunkert had read up on the Soviet spy and so knew what to expect. Tolkachev looked like a little gray man, someone who could disappear into a crowd. He had a diminutive stature, standing only around five feet six inches, and wore the dreary clothes of a midlevel engineer: a nondescript coat, leather gloves, and a brown fedora. By this time, Plunkert had removed his mask and exchanged it for a lighter disguise. The two exchanged verbal paroles and then went for a walk.

Plunkert was exhilarated. After so much buildup, it felt surreal to finally be meeting the Russian face-to-face. Tolkachev, however, looked tired. He explained that he was suffering from a variety of ailments and hadn't been well. This was the main reason he'd missed the previous meetings. Even so, it hadn't stopped him from photographing documents, and he handed Plunkert a package containing approximately sixteen rolls of film.[2]

After returning to the embassy, Plunkert relayed the details of the meeting to the chief of station and to Langley. Headquarters was relieved to hear that Tolkachev was still operational, though it seemed that he'd been pushing himself too hard. His preferred method was to check out documents from his workplace and bring them home on his lunch break, where he could then photograph them in the relative safety of his apartment. In order to check out the documents, Tolkachev was required to leave his building pass with the clerk; under normal circumstances, this would have prohibited him from leaving work, since he was required to have his building pass to enter and leave the premises. The CIA had gotten around this by fabricating a second building pass so that he could leave one with the clerk.

However, as Tolkachev explained to Plunkert, his institute had just issued new passes, meaning that he was back to the old problem of having to leave his ID with the clerk. Unwilling to curb his production, Tolkachev had resorted to lying on several occasions, taking his pass back while telling the clerk that his boss was still reviewing the documents. This allowed him to take the documents home, but it was a risky strategy, and one that he couldn't continue to use. The Moscow Station needed to come up with a solution.

Plunkert told the Russian to lie low for a while until they could figure things out. In the back of his mind, the CIA case officer couldn't help but wonder why the institute had suddenly decided to change the passes. Was it just a coincidence? Or did the authorities know something? Either way it was not a good sign.[3]

* * *

As the Cold War progressed, the Moscow Rules became increasingly dependent on innovation and creativity. An operational need would arise for a particular requirement, which would then force our techs go out and find the solution, either by repurposing something or building it from scratch. The JIB was a perfect example of this.

The origin of the JIB came about in 1973, when I received a message from a chief of base in the subcontinent, looking for help with their surveillance problems. Our officers who were stationed in one of the countries in that region were under massive surveillance by the local Internal Branch, part of their intelligence service that at that time was in bed with the Russians. We needed a tool that could give a case officer the opportunity to exit a vehicle being driven by a partner while under vehicular surveillance.

In those days, I was a traveling technical officer assigned to Southeast Asia, representing both the CIA's documents and disguise capabilities. As part of the routine duties of traveling technical officers, I would probe border controls and also characterize hostile surveillance. For this trip, Dan, a photo-operations officer, was with me, also traveling from our regional base. I had worked with Dan in a previous assignment and would continue to work with him throughout my career. A droll cynic with a wicked sense of humor, he never failed to lighten the mood. He was a great traveling partner.

On a hot and humid early evening in early July, we sat down together at a local version of a coffee shop and ordered a couple of cold Kingfisher beers and a plate of samosas after making some dry runs on the street. Classic paper napkin spread out on the rusty tin table, we conjured up an idea to have a "Johnny Jump Up," an inflatable silhouette, replace the figure of a passenger in a car escape scenario. We wrote up this requirement to get it into development back at headquarters and fired it off, like a rocket, to our colleagues in Langley. While this request came from the subcontinent, we recognized that our network of colleagues had similar problems in other parts of the world, and the tool could be used worldwide.

After we returned to our base, we went shopping. The city robustly lived up to its reputation as the sex capital of Southeast Asia, and we had no problem finding just the right solution to our high-tech problem. Anatomically correct plastic sex dolls were readily available, although I found that confounding, given the plentitude of the real thing in the local bars. Nevertheless, for a few coins, we headed back to our office with an assortment of these devices stuffed into shopping bags. Experimenting in our labs, we found old gas canisters to use in inflating the dolls. However, we initially found that the gas came out so fast that it would freeze the plastic dolls, and they would become brittle and shatter, showering the lab with plastic shards. Adding a flash tube to the gas canisters allowed the gas to slow down long enough to warm up. All of this was put into a briefcase, James Bond style. Because we didn't need the whole torso, initially we taped the doll tight at the waist so that only the top half would inflate.

I returned to headquarters in 1974, becoming chief of disguise before arriving, and hit the ground running. Because of our Johnny Jump Up cable, there was already a program in place to develop our idea of an inflatable, pop-up device. Disguise Branch was running the program, and the device, somewhere along the line, had acquired the Jack-in-the-Box, or JIB, moniker. Dan also returned home in 1974 and was fortuitously assigned as the OTS representative in the CIA's Soviet and East European Division—the division that housed Moscow Station, among others. This was a partnership that would bear significant fruit in the future.

At headquarters, the JIB was built out of a Judy doll—a sexy, life-size party doll, blonde, nude, and made of cheap plastic. The CIA bought the Judy dolls from Al's Magic Shop at Twelfth Street and Pennsylvania Avenue near the White House, within walking distance of our 2430 E Street offices. We needed multiple dolls over multiple weeks, and over time, our officers became embarrassed about going back and acquiring more.

The doll inflated well enough, but it deflated too slowly, wilting like one of those undulating wind socks that you see outside of car dealerships today. Because we did not have an actual sponsor for the device yet, I went into collusion with an old friend, Pete, now a chief of station on the subcontinent. A serious friend of OTS and our spy gadgets, Pete was always an early adopter of spy technology, and when he saw the JIB, he wanted one.

The JIB prototype was sent to Pete in 1974 and tested there. They used it for their surveillance problem, and it worked well. In the meantime, we sent another test model for a dry run in Eastern Europe, but the device exploded when it was inflated in the car. The female driver, the wife of a case officer who had already bailed out of the car, was so stunned that she almost crashed.

When I was promoted to chief of the Disguise Branch in 1974, I set about convincing the R&D side of OTS to develop the technology required for this pop-up silhouette. The JIB was in an early "breadboard" mode, the initial development phase of the device in our laboratories at this time, and the project was given to George, who had been trained by our Hollywood makeup specialist in mold making and who became our in-house JIB guy. I had brought George out with me to visit John Chambers when he was working on *The Island of Dr. Moreau,* and the two of us had worked on our sculpting right alongside Chambers's team of makeup artists. In a spirited bit of life imitating art, H. G. Wells's novel is about a doctor who creates humanlike hybrid beings from animals via vivisection. *Close enough,* I thought.

"You guys make spies; our guys make monsters," Chambers had said. The makeup guys thought they had the better deal. Time would tell.

When Jack Downing asked me to do the disguise survey for Moscow Station in 1976, I took the prototype with me. At the time, the JIB was still based on the Judy doll and used a pressurized tank. We had added an overhead mask with a bunch of tape to hold it on, all in an attaché case. I showed the rudimentary device to Jack and the rest of Moscow Station and got an official request, otherwise known as a requirement, to make one.

The official request from Jack was really what kicked the program into high gear. The compartmentalized nature of the CIA can be a nightmare to navigate sometimes, but Jack was the kind of person who could cut through all of that. Before I knew it, I had the funding I needed to make it all a reality.

The project was given to Clint, one of several engineers from Texas, who explained right away, with his slow Texas drawl, that our fixation on an inflatable device was creating unnecessary problems. His solution was to reengineer the equipment by turning it into a complex scissor mechanism that would lift and retract, collapsing when not in use. This meant that we no longer needed the gas canisters, and it would also allow us to create a more realistic three-dimensional torso, doing away with the Judy doll. When he was finished, the device was small enough to fit into a large briefcase, but it still had problems. It was incredibly heavy, and there were just too many moving parts.

I sent it to our magic consultant, Josh, out in Los Angeles and asked him to take a look. Originally from Kansas, Josh had begun working for the CIA after John Chambers contacted him during the mid-1970s. The two were working on a film that involved a magic trick at the time, and Chambers saw right away that the man had a talent for building devices. By this time, Chambers knew all about the JIB, and he thought that Josh might be the guy to help. And so at one point, Chambers approached him on set when they were finished for the day and asked, "You ever do any side work or anything? I got some people who would love to see what you do." It was then that Chambers gave him the speech about serving his country, something that Josh felt strongly about as well.

After I sent the JIB out to Los Angeles, I got a call from Josh a few days later telling me that he was confused. "I know you wanted to know how I could improve on this, but I'm not so sure," he said. "This thing is built like a Swiss clock." Then we got to talking about its practicality, and Josh had to admit that the prototype could never be used in the real world.

"I want you to think of it this way," I said to him. "You know what we need the device to do, so just build it the way you would have done it."

Josh stripped the thing down and simplified it, getting rid of the gears and replacing them with a hinge-like mechanism very similar to an umbrella. This decreased the weight and size dramatically, which allowed the JIB to be carried in a large purse or even a backpack. He also added a handheld trigger for the driver of the car to use to animate the head, giving the doll an ability to turn its head toward the driver or toward the passenger window, which reinforced the illusion of a live passenger. The last time I saw it, the JIB was an elegant, sophisticated piece of equipment. Foolproof. And guaranteed not to explode.

The JIB wasn't the only innovation employed by the CIA when it came to the Tolkachev operation. A new wireless communications device known as DISCUS, secret and anonymous case officers, improved ID scenarios, and simultaneous drops would all have a part to play in helping the CIA carry out one of the most productive espionage operations in the history of the Moscow Station.

Perhaps the most impressive thing to say about the operation is that the CIA was able to meet with the Russian engineer nearly twenty times over the course of a five-year period. Such a thing would have been considered impossible during the Penkovsky era, but it showed just how much had changed since the early days of the Moscow Rules.

*   *   *

The first meeting with our Russian engineer took place on New Year's Day in 1979. By this time, Tolkachev had mailed us the three letters containing secret writing, proving that he wasn't a KGB dangle. However, before the operation could really kick off, we first needed to know a little bit more about him and his motivations for spying.

A man by the name of John Guilsher was initially assigned to be his case officer. Despite being only forty-seven years old, Guilsher sported a full head of gray hair, which he wore slicked back. He also had a penchant for wearing suits, even though they weren't required, which caused some of his colleagues to joke that he looked more like a politician than a clandestine officer.

Guilsher had a unique history that positioned him well for the job at hand. Most people who joined the CIA strongly disliked the Soviet Union, but for Guilsher, it was personal. The CIA officer's father had fought against the Bolsheviks as a member of the White Army, like Penkovsky's father. He had an uncle who was killed in the revolution as well. Guilsher grew up in New York. At one point, it seems, he had thought about becoming a park ranger; however, the Korean War intervened, and he joined the army. As a talented linguist who spoke fluent Russian, he was assigned to work for the National Security Agency. Guilsher enjoyed what he did and saw that he could make a difference, and after he left the army in 1955, he decided to join the CIA.

The early portion of Guilsher's career was spent in London and Berlin, working on some of the Agency's most sensitive operations. He even spent some time on the Penkovsky case. He was a natural fit for the SE Division. In addition to his language skills and family history, he had also married a woman named Kissa, who was the scion of a wealthy Russian family. Like Guilsher, Kissa's family had been forced to flee their homeland as a result of the Bolshevik Revolution, and when she found out that her husband had a chance to be stationed in Moscow, she pushed him to go.[4]

Guilsher's first few months at the station were difficult. He arrived on the same day that Marti Peterson was arrested, and then a few short weeks after that, the whole embassy nearly burned to the ground. Turner's suspension of all operations came as another blow. Here Guilsher was, finally on the front lines and able to strike back against the regime that had caused his family so much heartache, and yet he was told not to do anything. It would take more than a year before he would finally be given permission to meet with Tolkachev.

Guilsher had drawn heavy surveillance ever since he'd arrived in the Soviet capital, which is why he'd chosen to launch on New Year's Eve. It was a bitter and cold night, but with the help of a light disguise, he was able to get free and meet up with Tolkachev. The plan called for Guilsher to call the Soviet spy from a phone booth and introduce himself as Nikolai. Afterward, the two of them met in a nearby park. Tolkachev seemed well prepared and handed over almost one hundred pages of handwritten data, along with a letter.

In it, Tolkachev described himself as a designer at the Scientific Research Institute of Radio Building (NIIR), one of the most important research institutes for Soviet military radars, the kind that were used in advanced fighter jets. He claimed to be a "leading systems designer" and that he worked in a large office that he shared with twenty-four other people. Later, when Guilsher got back to the station and examined the pages, he found out that Tolkachev had taken copious notes on a variety of sensitive issues, even going so far as to include complex formulas and diagrams on oversized graph paper.[5]

Throughout the meeting, Guilsher was impressed by Tolkachev's calm demeanor. And when asked about his motivations for spying, the Russian responded by saying that he was "a dissident at heart."[6] Over the course of the operation, the CIA would come to learn a little bit more about the spy. In a letter sent to Guilsher in April, he wrote of how he loathed the Soviet system, which he claimed wasted massive amounts of money. He and his wife, Natalia, also felt resentment about the way in which her parents had been treated. Natalia's mother had been executed by Stalin's regime in 1938, when Natalia was only two years old, and her father had spent nearly ten years in a Soviet labor camp. This was all during the purges, but it was clear that Tolkachev and his wife had never absolved the government of responsibility for its brutal actions.[7]

Initially the CIA attempted to run Tolkachev by using dead drops, the first of which was left behind a phone booth near the Russian's apartment and disguised to look like a dirty construction glove. Since Tolkachev had no clandestine training, the drop included a communications note explaining how he would be required to signal when he was ready to load a drop and how he should put up a recovery signal once he had picked up the package. Tolkachev was told to wait by the phone on certain days and at certain times, at which point the CIA would perform a "wrong-number call." Depending on the name the caller asked for, Tolkachev would then know which site had been selected for the drop.

The arrangement lasted only a few months, though, before the Russian asked if he could go back to face-to-face meetings. His reasons were varied, but it basically came down to the fact that he was worried about leaving the material out unattended, since the information could be traced back to him. He also preferred the psychological benefit of meeting with a case officer in person. This put more pressure on the Moscow Station, but in the end, Hathaway supported his decision, noting that Tolkachev's relative inexperience would be less of an issue if he wasn't forced to load and recover packages. The Russian was also impatient and suggested that even if there were a greater chance that he might be caught, he was willing to take that chance and wrote in an operations note, "I have chosen a course which does not permit one to move backward, and I have no intention of veering from this course."[8]

This made the operation slightly more complicated, but luckily Tolkachev's apartment was only four hundred meters from the US embassy, which gave natural cover for both the Russian engineer and his CIA officers to be moving around in the area. The result was that communications were that much easier, as the geographical proximity provided a natural cover for putting down signals.

During one of the early dead drops, Guilsher supplied Tolkachev with a miniature camera so that he could take photos in his office. The camera was small enough to be disguised as a box of matches and was good for seventy to eighty exposures. It wasn't as advanced as the Tropel, but at this point, the CIA wasn't willing to risk such an important piece of technology on an untested agent. It was also thought that the matchbox camera would be easier to use, but as it turned out, Tolkachev had a lot of trouble with it. It was hard to hold and required more light than was available in his office. On two occasions during the spring of 1979, he gave Guilsher several canisters of film, but when headquarters went to develop them, almost all the shots were out of focus.

As it happened, Tolkachev was permitted to check out unlimited amounts of sensitive documents from the institute library, as long as he brought them back before the end of the day. As such, he was able to sneak them out on his lunch break and bring them back to his apartment, where he could photograph them in relative safety, negating the need for a miniature camera. At that point, the Agency decided on a low-tech approach, supplying Tolkachev with a thirty-five-millimeter Pentax camera and a clamp that would allow him to hold the camera steady by attaching it to the back of a chair.

The difference in the quality as well as quantity of his output was dramatic. In the previous two meetings with Guilsher before being given the Pentax, Tolkachev had only been able to hand over around a dozen rolls of film, most of which were useless. But in the two meetings held in October and December 1979, Tolkachev handed Guilsher more than 150 rolls of exposed film. In fact, he had taken so many images that the shutter had jammed and wouldn't advance. In addition to the film, Tolkachev also included hundreds of pages of hand-copied documents as well as notes and diagrams that helped to explain the photographs.[9]

Headquarters was ecstatic. Not only had the material provided information on the capabilities of Soviet radar and avionics, but also Tolkachev had included schematics on a host of other technologies, such as surface-to-air missiles and even Soviet fighter aircraft still in the developmental stage. It gave American military planners a much clearer picture of the threats they would have to counter at that point and in the future, information that could never have been provided by a spy satellite or other technological means.

At a three-day seminar in May 1979, representatives from the civilian and military intelligence agencies concurred that the information that Tolkachev had included was "devastating" to the Soviet Union. Military representatives at the symposium even went so far as to say that it had saved them "up to five years of R&D time."[10]

There is always a concern in any clandestine operation that as information is disseminated to a wider audience, word of it might leak back to the enemy. For this reason, SE Division instituted a sign-out sheet to keep track of the people who had read the reports and even broke the Tolkachev material up and included it with other intelligence so as to make it seem as if it came from a variety of sources. SE Division also began drawing up contingency plans in the eventuality that Tolkachev might come under suspicion. Guilsher was asked to broach the topic of exfiltration with the Soviet spy to see if he might be amenable to relocating outside the Soviet Union. But even in the event that Tolkachev agreed, headquarters hoped to delay any departure as long as possible in order to keep the operation up and running.[11]

Tolkachev's response was rather ambiguous, though. Instead of giving the CIA the green light to begin laying the groundwork for an eventual exfiltration, the spy asked Guilsher if he could have an L-pill. "I would not like to carry out a conversation with the organs of the KGB," he explained when pressed.[12] At first, Guilsher tried to put him off, knowing that the subject of an L-pill would be a sensitive one, especially in the wake of Ogorodnik. Headquarters also gave him a list of talking points to use to discourage the Soviet spy. However, Tolkachev would not let the matter drop, even writing a personal letter to the DCI in order to press his case. Turner refused.[13]

Another major point of contention between Tolkachev and headquarters was the question of money. In an early letter, Tolkachev laid out his plans to pass information over a twelve-year period that he said would be broken up into seven stages. And at the completion of each stage, he expected to be paid a set amount. During their first face-to-face meeting, Tolkachev asked to be paid for the work that he had already turned over, including his ninety-one-page notebook.

Guilsher had brought with him 1,000 rubles, but Tolkachev seemed offended by the amount (roughly $300 in the day's exchange). When asked to give a figure that he thought might be fair, Tolkachev referenced Soviet pilot Victor Belenko, who had recently defected to the West by flying his MiG-25 jet interceptor to Japan. According to Tolkachev, the Russian pilot had been paid an amount in the six-figure range, and he expected to get something similar.

Headquarters was initially worried about handing over so much money. If Tolkachev were to use the money to purchase something extravagant, then the whole operation could be jeopardized. Besides, there weren't many goods in the Soviet Union, meaning that a new radio or even a fancy coat might draw undue attention. Guilsher cautioned Tolkachev about the dangers of receiving so much money, but the Russian insisted, saying that it was the one way that he would know for sure that the CIA valued his services.[14]

Headquarters countered that they would set up a foreign interest-bearing account in the West. But Tolkachev wanted to be paid in rubles. It was also apparent that he wanted to be able to see the money. Even so, headquarters continued to drag its feet.

The quibbling over money annoyed Guilsher and everybody else at the Moscow Station. The intelligence that Tolkachev was providing was saving the US government hundreds of millions, if not billions, of dollars, so it seemed ridiculous to be nickel-and-diming the man. Hathaway outlined their thinking in a cable to headquarters in May 1979, stating that he thought Tolkachev should be offered $300,000. Eventually the DCI approved the ruble equivalent of $100,000. When Guilsher relayed the news, however, the Russian responded that when he said he wanted to be paid in the six-figure range, he meant a number followed by six zeroes, meaning he wanted to be paid millions.

Guilsher was at a loss for words, but it seemed that even Tolkachev realized that his request was unrealistic, as he changed his mind during the next meeting in December 1979. By the spring of the following year, thirteen months after the discussion began, a salary would finally be agreed upon, and Tolkachev was told that he would be paid an annual amount greater than "the salary of the president of the United States." The majority of the funds were to be held in escrow, to be available if and when the Russian ever decided to relocate to the United States.

While not exactly thrilled by this arrangement, Tolkachev seemed delighted when Guilsher handed over a block of 100,000 rubles ($92,000) as compensation for the work that the Russian had already done. Keep in mind that Tolkachev's monthly income was around 250 rubles, which was considered a good salary. However, even as Tolkachev asked for the money, Guilsher got the sense that it was more about respect. Tolkachev was a midlevel engineer who had absolutely no opportunity to advance thanks to his family history and lack of connections. The money was his way to prove that he was worth something.[15]

In addition to the money, Tolkachev also asked for things for his family. He was incredibly dedicated to his son, Oleg, who was fourteen years old in 1979. Oleg was studying art, and Tolkachev asked for ink and drawing materials as well as a set of headphones and rock albums, including Alice Cooper and Led Zeppelin.[16] At first, the Moscow Station was reticent to give him too many Western items, for fear that one of his son's friends or even a relative might comment on them to somebody and then draw the attention of the KGB. But since the items were available on the black market, Hathaway didn't see any problem in including them in the packages along with the rubles and new cameras.

Apart from the squabbles over the monetary compensation, things seemed to run smoothly until December 1979, when Tolkachev's institute began requiring that all employees leave their building pass ID in order to check out classified materials. This meant that Tolkachev wouldn't be able to take the documents home, as he would be without his building pass and so unable to leave or reenter the premises. In order to get around the problem, OTS was asked if they could duplicate the building pass. Tolkachev took photos of his pass and even removed a small section of card so that our fabricators in the documents section could make an identical copy.

Another issue was brought to light when Tolkachev mentioned that in order to check out documents unrelated to his department, he first had to sign a permission sheet. This wasn't much of an issue early on, but as the operation progressed, he became concerned about the amount of material he had signed out.

If word was ever to get out that somebody in his institute was stealing information, he reasoned that the first thing the KGB would do would be to check out the list. Over time, the permission sheet became a huge security risk that the Moscow Station realized it had to address. At first it asked Tolkachev to simply concoct a cover story, and then much later, headquarters asked OTS to fabricate the sign-out sheet to make it look like Tolkachev had only signed out a few documents.[17]

In response to the crisis involving the building pass, the Moscow Station also began including several Tropel cameras in the packages that it was sending. However, Tolkachev rarely used the cameras, and only at home. Hathaway, who remained COS until the winter of 1980, also tried to get Tolkachev to use the SRAC system known as DISCUS. DISCUS was an improved version of BUSTER and allowed the agent to encrypt a message containing several thousand characters and then send it at the push of a button. The text could be read by scrolling down the screen, very much like a BlackBerry.

The technology wouldn't play much of a role until 1982, when Tolkachev would use it to communicate with his case officer in order to ask for an unscheduled meeting. This was during the period when OTS was attempting to fabricate Tolkachev's building pass, and the spy was anxious to move up a meeting so that he could hand over a sliver of the card to speed up the process.

In the fall of 1980, the operation overcame a major hurdle when Guilsher finished his tour and David Rolph was assigned as Tolkachev's new case officer. Up until that point, the Russian spy had only really known Guilsher. The handoff of an agent from one case officer to another can prove to be difficult. However, Rolph had been in Moscow for nearly a year at that point and so proved to be a steady hand when taking over the case.

The partnership between Tolkachev and Guilsher produced uncommonly valuable intelligence during the Cold War, intelligence that enabled the CIA to anticipate the Soviet Union's next military technologies and begin to counter them before they were even produced. The effects of this foreknowledge extended many years into the future, enabling the United States to exploit his information for another five years.

David Rolph was another former US Army officer who had worked in intelligence before joining the CIA. Rolph had served in West Berlin, where his job was to interview potential recruits from the refugees fleeing Eastern Europe, but the work was frustrating. Most of the refugees just wanted to get on with their life, and if he did come across an interesting case, it would be immediately transferred over to the CIA.

After his time in the army, Rolph went back to school and became a lawyer; however, his heart wasn't in it. He missed the excitement of running cases in denied areas and decided to join the CIA in 1977.

By the time Rolph had taken over the Tolkachev case in the fall of 1980, tensions were beginning to mount between America and the Soviet Union. The USSR had just invaded Afghanistan, and the Moscow Station found itself under increased scrutiny, making it harder for our officers to get black. In order to get free for his first meeting with Tolkachev, Rolph decided to use an ID scenario involving Mike, another one of our TOPS officers. Much like we had with Ron, we'd asked Mike to cultivate a unique appearance, and the tech had shown up for his TDY assignment sporting shaggy, shoulder-length hair and a thick beard.

Over the course of his assignment, Mike had built in a routine of heading out into the city with the station's senior technical officer in order to search for equipment and other supplies. At first, these outings drew the attention of our friends in the KGB's Seventh Directorate. The senior tech had purchased an old mint-green Volkswagen van, perhaps the only one in Moscow, to use for his excursions, so they were easy to spot. But after a while, the minders lost interest and stopped caring.

For this reason, on the day of the meeting, the militiaman at the gate took no notice of Rolph, now disguised in a shaggy wig and thick beard, and the senior tech as the two of them drove out through the gate in the old Volkswagen van.[18]

Once free of the embassy, the senior tech took a circuitous route through the streets of Moscow, the two of them keeping their eyes open for surveillance. Rolph was also wearing an SRR-100 to listen in on KGB transmissions. The tech knew the city well, and he drove the van at a slow and steady pace, trying to draw the surveillance out. The point wasn't to try to outrun them but to discover if they were there. If there was surveillance, you aborted—simple as that. It was a lesson that Rolph had learned time and time again at the IOC.

The SDR stretched out for several hours until finally both men were convinced they had indeed gotten free and were in the black. By that time, night had fallen, and the tech found a quiet spot and slowed the van so that Rolph could get out.

The case officer had taken off his shaggy wig and put on a light Russian disguise so that he would blend in more on the streets. The meeting with Tolkachev was still three hours off, and Rolph planned to use that time to flush out any potential surveillance that might still be out there. He had to be absolutely certain, or else Tolkachev's life would be in danger.

By the time Rolph made it to the meeting site, the Soviet spy was waiting for him. The two exchanged code words, and then Tolkachev motioned for him to follow. Rolph wasn't sure what he meant, so the Russian explained that he had recently purchased a new Zhiguli and thought it might be better for them to talk inside the car rather than out on the street.

Rolph's main mission was to explain that the CIA had finally approved an L-pill, which Tolkachev was happy to hear. Rolph also gave the Russian a list of questions that could help him in the event that they might need to exfiltrate Tolkachev and his family.[19] Tolkachev handed over twenty-five rolls of film, along with nine pages of notes.

A few weeks later, the L-pill would arrive in Moscow. Once again, our techs in OTS had hidden the capsule in a fountain pen, similar to Ogorodnik. Rolph was finally able to give the pen to Tolkachev in December. The two of them met in a park adjacent to the Moscow Zoo, and later, Rolph would report that the Russian had looked pleased after receiving the pen.

Rolph would meet with Tolkachev several times over the course of the following year, as the operation settled into a kind of pattern. The case officer would always be disguised as an ordinary Russian. The majority of meetings dealt with OTS attempts to fabricate Tolkachev's building pass as well as the sign-in sheet. Tolkachev's production had been severely hampered by the new restrictions at the institute, and so he was forced to take the documents into the bathroom at work, where he would photograph them with Tropel cameras.

The toilet stall had a ledge upon which he could rest the documents, but the light wasn't ideal, and if he didn't hold the cameras perfectly steady, the images would be out of focus. It was stressful work, and Rolph reported after one of their meetings that the Soviet spy was looking worn down. At the same time, the intelligence that Tolkachev was providing was so valuable that the military planners back in the States were constantly asking for more. At one meeting with Rolph, the Russian spy was given a wish list of items, including actual circuit boards and other parts, which the Pentagon was hoping he would be able to obtain.[20]

By this time in the operation, Burton Gerber had taken over as chief of the Moscow Station, while Hathaway had returned to headquarters to run the SE Division. Gerber was a good COS; he was very hands-on and went over every operation as if it were his own. He was also very demanding and expected his case officers to plan for every contingency. Naturally, with two alpha lions like Gerber and Hathaway working in the SE Division, there were bound to be disagreements, but the two found a way to make it work.

During the fall of 1981, there was talk that the Soviets might invade Poland. Gerber, for one, didn't believe it, but he was told by headquarters to prepare to shut down the station if tensions moved past the boiling point. While the invasion never happened, Gerber decided on a new strategy in order to confound the KGB.

Rather than rely on the traditional model of a single case officer, he began using a host of deep cover officers, not unlike Marti Peterson in the TRIGON case, sending two or even three out at a time on simultaneous surveillance-detection runs in order to increase the chance that at least one of them could get free and meet up with the Russian.[21]

This new system seemed to work well until the fall of 1982, when Tolkachev appeared to fall off the map. It was at that point that Plunkert decided to use the JIB in order to reestablish contact.

After meeting with Tolkachev, Plunkert reported back to headquarters about the situation with the new building pass. The CIA had worked so long to fabricate Tolkachev's old pass that just when they had gotten it right, the institute had changed policies. It was a heavy blow to the operation, and it wasn't the only one. In addition to the new pass, the institute had begun requiring that all personnel have a signed permission slip from their boss in order to leave the institute during working hours.

Why the new level of security? It appeared as if somebody must have leaked something, which, if true, meant that Tolkachev's life was in danger. Despite the risks, the Soviet spy seemed determined to press on. At a meeting during the winter of 1983, he provided a sample from his new building pass for OTS to duplicate. He also handed over several rolls of film that he'd been able to produce by sneaking documents into the bathroom. On another occasion, he had even asked a colleague to check out documents on his behalf so that he could take them home and use the Pentax.

After he heard about that, the case officer said that it was an incredibly dangerous thing to do.

Tolkachev responded, "Everything is dangerous."[22]

★ ★ ★

In the autumn of 1983, Moscow Station failed to meet up with Tolkachev on five separate occasions, either because the Russian spy had signaled and failed to show or because the CIA had been unable to shake surveillance and get free. Fearing the worst, the station was finally able to meet up with him in mid-November. Overall things went well. Tolkachev appeared to be in good spirits, and the case officer resupplied him with new spy cameras along with a light meter. The Russian, meanwhile, handed over sixteen pages of written notes but claimed that he hadn't been able to successfully photograph any documents due to the increased security measures.

For the most part, the night's mission was seen as a success. Moscow Station had reestablished contact with Tolkachev, and the spy seemed to be happy and healthy. Opinions changed, however, when Tolkachev's operations note was finally translated, indicating that the Russian had been through a trying ordeal the previous spring.

As it turned out, the security office for Tolkachev's institute had launched a major investigation in April. Tolkachev had been standing in his boss's office at the time when the call came in, so he was one of the first people to hear about it. The security office wanted a list of all the people who might have had access to a project related to a target-recognition system for a brand-new fighter that was just going into service. The request sent the Russian spy into a panic, as he had actually included information on the target-recognition system in a package only the month before. It was clear to Tolkachev now that somebody had indeed leaked the information, which meant that he was in huge trouble.

Fearing for his life, he took the following day off and drove out to his country house outside of Moscow. He had loaded up everything the CIA had given him into a box and spent the better part of the morning burning everything inside the dacha's fireplace, including several hundred thousand dollars' worth of rubles.

On his way back into town, Tolkachev expected to be jumped at any moment, and his sense of anxiety only grew once the workweek started. He was certain that his boss was going to call him into his office, where a team of security agents would be waiting to take him into custody. As the paranoia spread, he began bringing the L-pill into work, even taking the cyanide capsule out of the pen and placing it under his tongue whenever his boss asked for him. However, after several days of living in a state of near-total panic, the arrest never came, and Tolkachev began to relax.

A sense of shock and dismay settled over the Moscow Station. It was clear that the KGB had gotten some information from somebody, or else why zero in on that particular program? An internal review of the material quickly showed that it hadn't been disseminated until June, so a mole within the military establishment didn't seem logical. But somehow word had gotten out, which meant that even if the KGB didn't yet know Tolkachev's identity, it would only be a matter of time before all roads would lead to the Russian engineer.

After the November meeting, plans were immediately put into the works for a possible exfiltration to get Tolkachev and his family out of the country. The most logical solution would be to have them take a train to Leningrad and then smuggle them across the border into Finland by car. The CIA had modified several vehicles with hidden compartments for just such a scenario. Another option would be for the family to be picked up on the outskirts of Moscow and then smuggled to a safe house until an airplane could pick them up.

In the following meeting with the Soviet spy, a CIA officer laid out the options. Tolkachev turned them all down. He explained that he would never be able to convince his wife and son to leave Moscow. And as for trying to settle somewhere in the West, Tolkachev said that he and his wife knew a couple who had immigrated to the United States and that they complained about how homesick they were for Russia. He also noted when discussing the light-aircraft option that such an aircraft, designed to evade Soviet aircraft-detection systems, might have trouble accommodating his wife, due to her weight! In the end, Tolkachev reported that he would never be able to leave his family, which meant that he was staying put.[23]

The case officer tried to convince the Russian engineer to rethink his position, but much like FEDORA—Alexei Kulak, who had turned down the exfiltration option—it was clear that he had made up his mind. At that point, the Moscow Station had little else to do but to watch and wait.

a clear line of sight onto the area. In order to accomplish their mission, the Moscow Station relied on clandestine photography and patience, and over the course of several months, field officers were able to take enough photographs of the manholes and even test the difficulty of removing the cover, in order to create an accurate enough picture of what they were up against.[2] The next step would be to send an officer down into one of the manholes.

Jim Olson, that officer, fit well into the US embassy diplomatic milieu. Quiet and thoughtful, he always manifested a powerful personality, which would lead him to senior management positions in his long and successful career.

Olson had grown up in the small town of Le Mars in Iowa. He loved the state and was a midwesterner through and through. However, while he was attending the University of Iowa, he had decided to join the US Navy Reserve and was accepted. After graduation, Olson served as an ensign on a guided-missile destroyer.[3] He saw the world and appreciated the adventure that came with the job but couldn't see himself making a career out of it. Instead, he decided to return to Iowa to get his law degree. Olson was planning on practicing law in a small town and maybe one day running for office. Then he got a phone call out of the blue from a mysterious recruiter who asked Olson if he would be interested in a job that would allow him to serve his country.

Olson was convinced that the caller was from the US Navy and figured he would go and hear what the man had to say. As it turned out, the caller was a CIA recruiter from Kansas City.

When Olson got into the Career Trainee program, he felt lucky to be there. He was a part of the Cold War generation who believed that communism was contradictory to the freedoms and values that America represented. Olson was one of three individuals selected for the CKTAW program. By this time, the Moscow Station had conducted their initial surveillance, and before he began his training, Olson was read in on the mission. The CIA's DDS&T, the science and technology directorate, was anxious to get somebody down into the manhole, but it was thought that the covers might be locked or fitted with an alarm. They were also

CHAPTER 8

"Don't look back; you are never completely alone.
Use your gut."

At the same time that the Tolkachev operation was heating up, the Moscow Station was in the midst of another equally import-ant but very different sort of activity: setting up and running CKTAW, a wiretap on a communication line that ran under-ground through Moscow from a nuclear-weapons institute south-west of the city to the Ministry of Defense. The CIA already had a long history of tapping into seemingly secure communication links, the Berlin tunnel being Exhibit A, but CKTAW would top them all.

During the early 1970s, a new digital-imaging satellite known as the KH-11 revealed that the Soviets were digging a communi-cations trench along a major highway that ran from the Ministry of Defense in the capital to a nuclear-weapons-research institute, located in Troitsk.[1] Upon closer inspection, the CIA was able to confirm that the workers were installing a series of manholes along the tunnel at fifty-yard intervals, which would allow main-tenance workers to have access to the cable.

The Moscow Station was then ordered to conduct a casing operation to see which of the manholes might be accessible. It was a tricky job, since the road was not typically heavily traf-ficked by Americans during their normal activities and the CIA didn't want to draw any undue attention to the fact that they were interested in the cable. And if that wasn't bad enough, there also just happened to be a KGB monitoring station with out in the open, near a wide avenue frequented by KGB surveillance teams. When Olson heard about the mission, he thought it might be a joke. How did they expect him to pull off something like that?

A contractor had built a mock-up of the manhole complex at a CIA training facility known as the Farm, and day after day, Olson and his colleagues practiced lifting the lid and slipping inside undetected. OTS had made a special grappling tool that would allow them to quickly remove the lid; however, the instructors were fond of putting obstacles in their way in order to see how they would respond. Olson was intimidated, but he persevered. His fellow cadets had shown up on the first day sporting combat pants and military-style gear, while Olson had on a pair of jeans and sneakers, knowing full well that a paramilitary demeanor was not going to work. During one exercise, they asked them to try to open the lid blindfolded, and then, just to make it harder, they decided to add some screws around the rim.[4] Olson cut himself badly when he tried to use his pocketknife to remove the screws, but he showed grit by not giving up. Eventually he was able to complete the assignment, which impressed the instructors, although he was still marked down for leaving blood all over the operational site. In the end, apparently it didn't matter, as he was chosen to be the first one to enter the CKTAW manhole.

Apart from the actual physical challenge of getting into the target, perhaps the most worrisome aspect of the entire mission was the approach. In order to reach the manhole, Olson would first have to figure out a way to elude surveillance and cross a wide-open avenue that was pretty much devoid of any cover. Was there a way to ensure that he could get black even while out in the open?

It just so happened that I had been working on a new disguise scenario that I thought might be able to help. The concept was called Disguise-on-the-Run, or DOTR for short. The idea had occurred to me after I traveled to Moscow and did the disguise survey of the station. After I was out on the streets and observed the KGB surveillance teams, I wondered if there might be a way for officers to exploit a medium-size gap, say thirty to forty seconds, by having them disguise their appearance while on the move. It was an audacious concept, and one that I immediately ran by John Chambers once I got back from my trip.

This was in the late 1970s, around the time of the birth of our original semianimated mask, known as a SAM, a capability that would become one of our workhorse disguise appliances. Initially it was a half-face mask that began with the lower jaw and mouth area obscured by a beard. The wearer was able to animate his or her mouth, talk, drink, smoke, and, if the moment required it, laugh. The fit around the eyes was critical, as it was what gave the mask its lifelike appearance. The result was extraordinary, and it owed a lot of its technology to the *Planet of the Apes* work that Chambers had done.

Chambers was intrigued by my idea for DOTR, but he had too much on his plate and told me, half seriously and half in jest, that he was thinking about quitting. "I need to retire, Tony," he said, shaking his head. But he left the door open. By this time in my career, Chambers and I had become close friends, and I knew that he would be there for me whenever I needed him.

In the meantime, Chambers let me raid his supplies, and I returned to Washington to get started on the scenario. Jack Downing was now back from Moscow and working as the chief of the USSR branch, but I knew that before I was ever going to be able to show the DOTR technique to him, I would first have to iron out the kinks. I would also need to get the go-ahead of my boss, Dave Brandwein. It would take several months of fine-tuning, including using the technique on the Washington, DC, streets during practice runs, before I thought we were finally ready to show it off.

David Brandwein was the director of the Office of Technical Service. A chemist by training, he was many other things. He was a national authority on rocketry and arms negotiations and had written the *Britannica* entry on rockets and missiles. Additionally, he headed an interagency committee on foreign strategic-missiles arms control. He was also a diagnosed narcoleptic and a stereotypical absentminded professor. His staff worried that if they went on vacation for more than a week, he would forget their names. Dark haired with horn-rimmed glasses, he stood over six feet tall, and while heavyset, he was light on his feet. Taciturn and lethargic, he could give the wrong first impression, but his natural curiosity and droll sense of humor quickly set things right.

He drove a battered black VW Beatle so old that you could actually look through the floorboard and watch the pavement stream by. His Agency badge on its lanyard chain would sail out his side window as he sped from our DC compound to the Headquarters Building at Langley. A lawn mower cord attached to the gas pedal returned the pedal to its neutral position. Not everybody would ride with Brandwein on his visits to headquarters.

Amazingly, this rocket scientist fully embraced our advancement of the use of magic, illusion, and deception for work on the streets of Moscow. He had an open mind, outside of and removed from the paranoid paradigm of CIA's SE Division, and he was eager to help us help them.

The OTS office at 2430 E Street is still an infamous address in the intelligence community. The cluster of buildings perched on the hill behind the Bureau of Naval Medicine and across Twenty-Third Street from the State Department, where Wild Bill Donovan began America's fledgling intelligence capability, the Office of Strategic Services, it is also where Bob Gates lived in a row of generals' quarters while he was President Obama's secretary of defense, just three blocks from the White House.

The compound consists of three buildings embracing an oval lawn—Central, South, and East Buildings. Donovan and eventually Allen Dulles had their offices in East Building. Today, with North Building demolished to build the E Street Expressway, the view is of the Kennedy Center, the Potomac River flowing down from Georgetown in the background. It was and is a historic view.

The top floor of South Building was a long, dark hall. We used this fourth-floor space as a photography test bed and a pretty clean field for path-loss measurements on our newest radio communications equipment, but today it was going to be used as a gap, a forty-five-second interlude in a surveillance scenario in

Moscow, when I would be out of sight of my KGB surveillance team. I had forty-five seconds and forty-five steps to completely change my appearance. This was my chance to demonstrate to my office director what DOTR was all about.

Dressed in a dark raincoat, dark pants, and black shoes, I was carrying an attaché case and nothing else. I looked into the dim light and could just barely make out Brandwein at the other end of the hall. He was seated or, more precisely, slumped in a chair about 120 feet from me. Next to him was his assistant, Jonna Goeser, who was taking notes of this exercise. Her secondary job was to ensure that Brandwein did not drift off during the demonstration, overwhelmed by his narcolepsy. I had arranged with Jonna that it would not overwhelm him this morning.

I looked at my watch, the second hand just sweeping past twelve, and began to move. One step a second, forty-five seconds to accomplish a complete transformation. While I had rehearsed this disguise numerous times on the streets of Washington, DC, with our SST, it didn't mean that my adrenaline wasn't going crazy. That my breath wasn't coming too fast. That my heart wasn't about to jump out of my chest.

I stopped and positioned my attaché case on the floor. *Slow down*, I told myself. *Take it slow. Maintain a natural pace.* I touched a button on the case, and it popped open, transforming into a grocery cart on wheels. The attaché handle became the top of the handle for the cart. At the same time, a brown paper bag inflated, and the contents, a loaf of bread and some vegetables, expanded to fill the newly available space.

I moved forward a few steps, and then I steadied the cart and began to remove my raincoat. I had to hold the tip of the sleeves tightly in order to reverse the coat; in effect, I was peeling it off, turning it inside out as my arms came out. The transformation was dramatic, as a man's black raincoat became a dark-pink woman's coat with a shawl attached around the shoulders. I slipped my arms back into the sleeves and pulled it together in front.

Pulling the cart, I moved toward Brandwein. Leaning forward, I pulled my pant legs up, first the left and then the right.

A Velcro-like material caught the pant legs and held them up, revealing black stockings. A few more steps, and I reached down and removed the slip-on rubber men's shoes, one at a time, stashing each inside of my dress, each shoe becoming a female breast. Black size-eleven Mary Janes were now revealed, adding more detail to the look.

Checking my watch, I saw that I was twenty seconds into the change. Good. Right on schedule. Brandwein, far from disappearing further into his sleeping disorder, was now sitting upright and appeared to be leaning forward, drawn into this performance.

As I continued down the dimly lit tunnel toward him, I reached into the pocket of the pink coat and extracted a mask that I had spent weekends creating, slipping it over my face and ever-present mustache with one hand. I reached back to the shawl attached to the coat with my free hand and pulled it up over my own hair. A gray-haired female wig attached to the shawl spilled forward, protruding from the shawl and falling slightly over my face.

Now, as I approached Brandwein, walking slowly and pushing my grocery cart almost like a walker, I saw a flash of appreciation on his face as he turned to Jonna and nodded. He knew that I had been working with unique contractors. A very special tailor in Pennsylvania who also worked for the magic industry had assembled the reversible coat, while one of our magic consultants, Will, out in Los Angeles, had developed the pop-up grocery cart.

Forty-five seconds, and we were done. Dave Brandwein's introduction to our Disguise-on-the-Run Program had been a success. The businessman in a raincoat with the attaché case had disappeared, transformed into a little old lady in a dirty pink coat wearing a shawl and pulling a fully loaded grocery cart. Would you be suspicious of a little old lady?

★   ★   ★

After Brandwein gave his stamp of approval, I took the technique over to headquarters to show it to Jack, who was equally impressed. Then when Olson was chosen for his assignment, we brought him over to our disguise labs and began running through some scenarios.

I commissioned a quick-change, three-piece suit for Olson from our New England tailor, and he made a totally reversible suit of clothes, head to toe. It included a vest with multiple pockets and a pair of pants that would drop down from the vest with a flip of a Velcro tab. Olson could basically walk into this second set of pants. He also carried a large book made of compressed foam, actually a concealment device for some of the materials he would need to take down into the hole.

All the above would enable Olson to transform from an elegant American diplomat in a three-piece suit to a bearded Russian professor in baggy pants and jacket, carrying a book, in less than forty-five seconds, even with trailing surveillance. It happened so quickly that even a casual passerby would not notice. The mask came out of his pants pocket and went on as easily as putting on a knit winter cap. All this was done while he was walking, on the move, strolling through a Moscow park and down the street along which the manholes were positioned.

Later, I would get confirmation that the disguise had worked and that Olson had been able to slip into the manhole undetected. As the first man in, it was his job to photograph the site and glean as much information as he could. Olson brought back images and diagrams of a small chamber intersected by a dozen or so lead-sheathed cables, which had been filled with gas in order to prevent tampering. The gas would pressurize the cables, which if penetrated, would then be able to trip a sensor due to the drop in pressure.[5]

Jim Olson was a colleague at the beginning of this disguise R&D, but by the time we had completed the work and he had rehearsed it again and again in Washington, DC, Olson had become a friend. He is a friend to this day. Thoughtful and introspective, he brought an intellect to the deconstruction of operational problems that proved to be very helpful.

With this information in hand, the CIA was then able to move on to the next stage of the operation. During this phase, one of our techs returned to the same manhole to run tests on the wires in order to see which of the cables led to the nuclear test facility. It was a painstaking job that involved wrapping a device containing two sensors around each of the cables to sample the signals.[6] The third and final phase involved placing the actual tap. OTS had built a kind of collar that could be placed around the outside of the cable so as to not trip up the pressurized sensors. Once installed, the wiretap worked to perfection, transmitting the intercepted signals to a recording device hidden nearby.

The operation was a massive achievement; technology and tactics came together to accomplish one of the most audacious missions ever conceived in Moscow. Here was the proof, if anyone still doubted, that the CIA had completely rewritten the rules when it came to conducting operations in the Soviet capital. There are some who have looked back on the Tolkachev operation and the CKTAW wiretap and referred to this period as a kind of golden age for the CIA. Not only were both operations massive success stories, but they had also been carried out in the most hostile environment ever conceived for an intelligence operation. It certainly appeared as if the KGB was powerless to stop us. Unfortunately, the feeling wouldn't last.

★   ★   ★

It was a little more than twenty years after the Penkovsky case, and the CIA, most specifically OTS, had conspired to provide Adolf Tolkachev and his billion-dollar spy operation with a carte du jour to draw upon that staggers the imagination. In the area of secure communications, the Tolkachev operation was using short-range agent communication systems, commercial shortwave-radio broadcasts, and a demodulator unit for those broadcasts. One-time pads were provided to decrypt the messages. Tropel subminiature cameras and special low-light film replaced the clunky Minox cameras and the special clamps for holding the cameras.

Our graphics people—forgers and counterfeiters par excellence—put together duplicates of security passes and library sign-out cards for Tolkachev to use at his work. Concealment devices were made by our officers at an off-site location to accommodate the many dead drop requirements in this operation. Even an exfiltration container was constructed in case Tolkachev needed an emergency rescue. And of course, the L-pill was a condition of his cooperation with us.

Clearly the secure communications portion of the problem had been taken in hand. With the addition of the short-range agent communication system, Tolkachev had an opportunity to contact his CIA handler instantly. He was no longer mute electronically. He could now pass his intelligence using a variety of techniques.

Of course, none of these technological advances would have amounted to much if our officers had been unable to get free from the embassy without being followed by the ever-present KGB surveillance teams. And to this effect, the Tolkachev operation owes a great debt of gratitude to the handful of legendary special effects wizards and magicians out in Hollywood who agreed to share their expertise with us. Not only did their knowledge allow our disguise program to accomplish the impossible, but it also allowed our officers to be more creative in their tradecraft.

In the spirit of the great Hollywood magicians, we captured some of their techniques to use on our stage: the streets of Moscow. If Hollywood could make a person disappear in broad daylight, so could we. If magicians used twins to fool their audience, so could we. In fact, we could not only make twins; we could make quadruplets—or as many of you as were needed.

The idea of identity transfer, first used by Jack Downing, was a good example. We used it again with Tolkachev when his case officer left the embassy compound using an ID transfer disguise. Then, while still in his car, he changed out of Western clothes and adopted the look of a working-class Russian, putting on a fur hat, eating a piece of raw garlic, and splashing some vodka on his jacket. He met with Tolkachev that evening.

The latest countersurveillance disguise tool was the Jack-in-the-Box. The pop-up dummy, inaugurated when Bill Plunkert used it to meet with Tolkachev, was yet another example of the bag of tricks we had on the shelf for our operations officers' use.

But despite all our best efforts, there was one aspect of operations that we couldn't account for. And it was about to rear its ugly head.

★   ★   ★

Approaching the meeting site code-named TRUBKA, Paul Stombaugh was ambushed, and to say that he was blindsided would not do justice to what happened. When the three thugs from the Seventh Directorate came crashing out of the underbrush and grabbed his arms from behind, he held on to his packages for dear life. Instantly, more men rushed forward, and blazing headlight beams shot out of the darkness, revealing multiple KGB vehicles encircling the scene.

Stombaugh knew it was over. The date was June 13, 1985, and Stombaugh had been carrying two trash bags of material to pass on to Adolf Tolkachev. Now it was clear that something had gone wrong. The KGB had been crouched around the site, patiently waiting for him. His blood was pumping, and as the packages were wrestled out of his hands, Stombaugh suddenly went limp. There was no point to resisting now.

One man, silver haired and unmoving, was sitting quietly in a Volga sedan. Rem Krassilnikov was not about to miss this arrest.

Stombaugh wasn't even supposed to be there. That afternoon, Tolkachev's primary case officer had been pulling so much surveillance that he had opted out of the meeting. Stombaugh was the first alternate on standby. Because he didn't normally receive a lot of surveillance, he was sent out on very short notice. Stombaugh was a former FBI agent on his first tour, and he decided not to wear a disguise. Instead, he put on a dress shirt and a

sports coat, making him look like exactly who and what he was—
an American diplomat.

As was standard practice at the time, he began his SDR inside
a car, which would give him a better chance to draw out the
surveillance and to control events. Thanks to past experience,
it had been discovered that the KGB teams were always at their
most vulnerable at the start of an SDR, and so Stombaugh kept
his eyes open while his wife sat behind the wheel and steered
their car through the streets of Moscow. After this first portion,
Stombaugh got out of the vehicle and then proceeded on foot,
walking a long SDR with the two heavy bags that he hoped to
pass to Tolkachev. He was looking for repeats, seeing the same
faces twice, over time and distance. There was an old mantra:
"Once is an accident, twice a coincidence, three times an act of
war!" Corny but true.

Stombaugh had arrived early at the meeting site and then
moved past it, just scoping the place out, checking the entrances
and exits. Everything looked normal, and he found a quiet place
to sit and wait on a park bench. When it was time, he approached
the meeting site again and noticed the agent's car, a ginger-colored
Zhiguli, parked a short distance away, just as it should have been.
But before he could turn his gaze back to the phone booths at
his destination, Stombaugh was rushed and apprehended. A van
pulled up, and he was muscled into the back seat and driven to
the KGB's headquarters at Lubyanka Prison.

As it turned out, it wouldn't have made a difference if he were
wearing a disguise or not, as the surveillance hadn't actually
been following him but instead had been in front of him. They
knew he was coming, or that somebody was coming, and it was
Stombaugh's bad luck that he happened to be the person they
were waiting for. The meeting had been set up after Tolkachev
responded by putting up the correct signal, opening the middle
transom window in his apartment. But if the Russian had put up
the correct signal, then why had Stombaugh walked into a trap?
And then it occurred to him: the only way they could have known
that he was coming was to have gotten that information from the

agent. It wasn't Tolkachev who had put up that signal but the KGB. It was a hard fact to swallow, but it seemed to be the only explanation. Somehow the KGB had discovered Tolkachev and arrested him.

Stombaugh's Russian-language skills weren't the reason he was picked for Moscow, but there was no mistaking the pumped-up Seventh Directorate watchers' glee at having apprehended an American spy. When they arrived at Lubyanka, he was guided into a conference room and motioned to a chair. His pockets were emptied, and the contents were displayed on a table in the middle of the room. The two packages that he had been planning on giving to Tolkachev were also on the table, still intact. Stombaugh sat there, arms crossed, mute.[7]

While waiting for interrogation, Stombaugh had time to go over the situation in his head. Again. Before coming to Moscow, he'd been read in on the operation and so knew how things stood.

After the meeting with Tolkachev during the fall of 1983, in which the Soviet agent had recounted his harrowing experience of nearly being discovered by an internal investigation at his institute, things had seemed to settle down. The CIA had broached the subject of exfiltration with him, but Tolkachev had declined, responding that he preferred to stay in the *Rodina*, Mother Russia, no matter what the result.

At that point, the CIA decided to slow down and meet with the Russian engineer only twice a year. The next meeting had taken place in April 1984.[8] Tolkachev seemed to be in good spirits at the time and reported that conditions had returned to normal at work. In his operations note, he even apologized for having destroyed all his spy gear after the brief security scare at his institute during the spring of 1983. It also seemed that he had been busy, handing over two Tropel cameras containing ninety-six frames of photos, along with thirty-nine pages of handwritten notes. In return, he was given two new Tropel cameras and nearly 100,000 rubles. As the meeting came to a close, Tolkachev thanked the case officer for the cameras but asked if he might be given another Pentax thirty-five-millimeter camera, claiming that he was anxious to return to his old habit of sneaking documents out of his institute at lunch.[9]

Going through the notes on the operation, headquarters had admired Tolkachev's dedication but decided that it would be too dangerous to give him a Pentax. For the time being, he was told not to take any unnecessary risks and to continue to make do with the Tropel subminiature cameras.

At the next meeting in October, it had appeared as if the operation might have turned a corner and was back on track. Tolkachev reported that everything was still calm at work, and he returned the two Tropels with ninety frames of clear images, along with nearly twenty-two pages of notes. By this time, Tolkachev was using the T-50, a Tropel with a capacity of only fifty frames per cassette. This was to correct a problem with the T-100, which began to jam with the higher-capacity film load of one hundred.

Then in January 1985, another routine meeting was held. Tolkachev returned the miniature cameras, along with sixteen pages of notes. Everything seemed to be fine. However, when headquarters went to develop the photos, every single one of them turned out to be blank. Tolkachev had explained in the operations note that he had taken the photos in the bathroom of the institute on a cloudy day and that he was afraid that the light might not have been adequate. He then gave a tantalizing clue as to what it was he had tried to photograph: new frontline fighters that would be coming out in the 1990s.[10]

Headquarters immediately asked the Moscow Station to set up an unscheduled meeting. OTS had recently created a new film that was faster, meaning that it worked better in low light, and headquarters was hoping that the Russian engineer could go back and photograph the new frontline fighters. In early March, one of our officers put up a signal for an unscheduled meeting, and Tolkachev failed to respond.

Then in mid-March, the Russian appeared to acknowledge his readiness by opening a window in his apartment just after noon. This was the signal that Tolkachev had been told to make; however, had the CIA been paying closer attention, they would have realized that he used a different window from usual. Was he trying to send a signal that something was not right? In hindsight, it's definitely possible; however, Moscow Station was so anxious to meet with him that they dismissed this as a minor detail. In any case, Tolkachev failed to show at the meeting site.

The station tried a third time in March, but once again, the Russian failed to respond by putting up the proper countersignal. At that point, headquarters decided that rather than continuing to try to signal, it would be safer just to wait until the normally scheduled June meeting, the very meeting that Stombaugh was on his way to when he was jumped.

When the door to the conference room in Lubyanka opened, a short, gray-haired, distinguished-looking Russian walked in. Rem Krassilnikov, the major general who was responsible for the KGB's First Department within their Second Chief Directorate, the organization that dealt with American spies, was clearly in charge of the formalities on this case. Stombaugh recognized him from a small black-and-white photograph tacked to a wall in the tiny, claustrophobic CIA station. By this time a legendary figure within the KGB, Krassilnikov was charged with investigating and disrupting CIA operations in Moscow. His presence in the room signaled to the American, if he had any doubts, the level of attention that this case was generating.

All manner of incriminating material from Stombaugh's pockets was spread out on the table: medicine for Tolkachev, the meeting agenda, a Tropel camera, and cryptic notes Stombaugh had made before the meeting about material he meant to go over with Tolkachev while they walked and talked.

Krassilnikov declared, "You have been arrested for committing espionage. Who are you?"[11]

Stombaugh spoke abruptly. "I am an American diplomat. I want to call the embassy. Now."

Krassilnikov continued to insist that Stombaugh was an American spy and then proceeded to open the two packages. A video camera was rolling as Krassilnikov opened the first package, which contained 100,000 rubles compressed into a brick of

50-ruble notes. Everyone in the room froze in silence, riveted by the sheer bulk of the banknotes. Surely they had never seen that much money at one time in their lives. Krassilnikov took out a Tropel camera and held it up, but Stombaugh simply shrugged as if it were the first time he had ever seen it. Then the Russian began to read the CIA's note to Tolkachev out loud, for the record, but he paused after a few lines and read the rest of the letter in silence as he learned the extent of Tolkachev's recent production of secret materials and the praise being heaped on him by the American government.[12]

As protocol demanded, the Soviet Foreign Ministry called the American embassy to say that they were holding an embassy employee, and the embassy duty officer came to represent Stombaugh. It was then that another heated confrontation erupted. Krassilnikov kept insisting that Stombaugh was a spy, and the embassy duty officer demanded that they be allowed to leave. Krassilnikov was normally patient, adept at blunting America's attacks on the motherland, the *Rodina*. But as he was the one who had arranged the ambush, he felt that he finally had Moscow Station over a barrel and was preparing to be even more aggressive. In the end, however, he had to relent, and Stombaugh and the duty officer were released.

Totally missed in the confusion of Stombaugh's arrest and the glaring lights that lit up the dark street and sent men running from all sides was the fact that the KGB had put an imposter resembling Tolkachev on the site. The imposter was to be used to lure Stombaugh into the meeting site, to convince Stombaugh that the clandestine meeting was going to proceed. He was even carrying their agreed-upon recognition signal, a white book.

Stombaugh never even saw the guy. While the KGB called the man an imposter, Stombaugh knew his role in this drama by another name. It seemed that the KGB was using our ID transfer technique against us, disguising one of their officers as our agent. They had also thoughtfully parked Tolkachev's car a few hundred meters away, another agreed-upon signal that all was well and the operation should go forward. The only thing missing that night was Tolkachev himself.

It's unknown exactly when Tolkachev was compromised. Most experts point to the period after the meeting in January 1985, but there is no way to know for sure. This supposition would seem logical, since Tolkachev appeared to be no different at that meeting than during his previous meetings. He had also given the case officer a long list of items that he wanted, including drafting pens for his son, more rock music, and medicine for a bad bout of gastritis. He even mentioned that the CIA should use the money they had put in an escrow account to hire somebody full time to find all the items on the list. It seems unlikely that he would have gone to all that trouble if he had already been compromised.[13]

Either way, one thing is for sure: by the time that the CIA had seen Tolkachev's signal in June indicating that he was ready to meet, the Russian engineer was already in custody. He had been arrested months before this faux meeting was set up by the KGB.

In the aftermath of his arrest, Stombaugh would be declared persona non grata and expelled; however, there would be no such hope for Tolkachev. He had always said that he would rather take his own life than let the KGB have their way with him in the interrogation rooms. Instead, he was firmly in the viselike grip of the KGB, his worst nightmare. He had left the L-pill in its hiding place in his apartment, beyond his reach. Now he was at the mercy of the KGB.

The CIA would get official confirmation of this fact in September, when it was publicly announced that the Soviet spy had been arrested in June for his involvement in an intelligence operation. Tolkachev would eventually undergo a brief trial before being executed on October 22, 1986.

Tolkachev had passed so much material to the CIA that in 1980 they estimated that it would take eight clerks and three Russian-language translators working full time for seven to eight weeks to process the data. On reviewing Tolkachev's product, a senior CIA analyst noted that Tolkachev's information was so voluminous and so valuable that, even though the agent was arrested in 1985, the task force continued to exploit his information until approximately 1990. From 1979 to 1980, the information could have meant the difference between victory and defeat should a military confrontation with the USSR have occurred.[14]

In the aftermath of Stombaugh's arrest, there was a lot of finger-pointing. The logical assumption was that the material had somehow gotten out to someone who had leaked it and compromised the agent. Certainly, with an operation like this one, in which Tolkachev had handed over thousands of pages of documents and photos over the course of five years, it would be hard to maintain absolute control of access to the material. Still, the Agency had put in safeguards to protect the operation from such a breach, and there were those who adamantly denied that such a thing had happened. Another possibility was that the Russian had made a mistake at work. He'd been known to take risks, and it didn't seem out of the realm of possibility that he might have slipped up and been discovered by one of his coworkers. In the end, nobody could really say what went wrong.

Perhaps the most troubling aspect of Tolkachev's arrest was that it wasn't the only setback the CIA faced during 1985. During the spring, the CKTAW wiretap mysteriously went off-line, and when a case officer went to investigate, he found that the device had been tampered with. Then in May, a Soviet agent, Sergei Bokhan, who was a colonel in the GRU, received a call from his headquarters telling him to return to Moscow immediately. A member of the military intelligence in the Soviet embassy in Athens, Bokhan instantly suspected that something was wrong. His supervisor had said that Bokhan's eighteen-year-old son was having problems, but Bokhan had just been speaking with his son and knew this to be a lie.[15] When he reported what had happened to his CIA handlers, they quickly organized an exfiltration and secreted him out of the country.

Losing each one of these operations on their own would have been a heavy blow. Three in succession was beyond a coincidence. It was clear that there was something seriously wrong, but what?

Then on August 1, 1985, a KGB defector named Vitaly Yurchenko would walk into the Rome embassy with a story to tell. According to Yurchenko, the KGB had a source, a mole in the CIA, code-named ROBERT. The Russian didn't know the man's real name, just that he was a former Pipeliner who had been kicked out of the CIA.

CHAPTER 9

"Betrayal may come from within."

Santa Fe, New Mexico, September 21, 1985. It had been over two years since the CIA had fired Edward Lee Howard, and in that time, he had demonstrated an emotional reaction that went beyond mere rage to a burning desire for retribution. There was evidence, at this point, that he was providing classified intelligence to the Soviets. The FBI was in Santa Fe to surveil the situation, and Howard had surmised that he would be watched. He was right, of course, and was impressed with their stealth. He could not see them. Dinner with his wife, Mary, had been tense, and Howard was becoming agitated at his inability to identify the surveillants. He had been trained to spot them but could not pick them out of this crowd. This bothered him, because he had run numerous exercises against FBI teams and prided himself on his ability to tease them out. But he and his wife could not hurry tonight. They had to sit and wait until after dark, and so he ordered another Dos Equis.

Finally, around 7:00 p.m., when the light was fading quickly as it does in the desert and the temperature began to drop, the two of them paid the check and went out to the car, a red Oldsmobile. Everything had been prepared in advance; the deception was primed and ready to go. The brake lights had been disconnected, as had the overhead dome light. The homemade JIB device was lying on the floorboard, just in front of the passenger seat, covered with a raincoat. It had been fabricated from a Styrofoam wig stand, on which was pinned a somewhat embarrassing brown wig Howard had used at the Farm during his disguise training.

On top of that was a baseball hat, and draped over a coat hanger, wired to a plumber's plunger, was a favorite safari-style jacket from Howard's closet that he wore frequently. The two of them got into the car, making final adjustments. Mary fastened her seat belt; Howard disregarded his. Mary was driving when they pulled out of the restaurant, and now they were on Garcia Street, driving away from the adobe-bedecked center of town, the tourist-heavy area, where, on this early fall evening, hundreds of out-of-town visitors would be sitting down at taquerias to enjoy fajitas, flautas, and enchiladas.

Howard spoke first, telling her that everything was ready, as they turned into the spot they had reconnoitered earlier in the day, the perfect place for a car bailout when under FBI surveillance. They passed the Indian Arts Research Center before taking a sharp curve to the right, where Garcia Street curved into Camino Corrales. Even though Howard had yet to spot the surveillance, he had to assume they were there. His training had taught him to expect this, which is why they had gone to such lengths to set up this elaborate deception. Assuming that the trailing surveillance was maintaining a discreet distance behind them, they would be out of the bureau's line of sight for perhaps ten seconds, in the gap, black. Ten seconds was enough.

Mary braked and tapped his arm without looking at him, her eyes glued to her rearview mirror, and Ed opened the car door while the car slowed. He was out the door, and the dummy deployed in two smooth motions. Mary reached over and adjusted the makeshift JIB, ensuring that it was securely wedged into the crack between the cushion and the backrest of the passenger seat. When the car behind them came sweeping around the curve, it would appear as if there were still two passengers in the car. Mary slowly picked up speed and headed toward the Old Santa Fe Trail.[1]

They had practiced this JIB escape many times down at the Farm, and we had exercised them in Washington, DC, just next to the Kennedy Center on an isolated configuration of grass and shrubs with our Special Surveillance Team standing in for KGB (or now FBI) surveillance. Howard had always performed it flawlessly, but this time he hit the ground hard, almost too hard. Wondering if he had perhaps broken his arm, Howard rolled into the bushes beside a house encircled by shrubbery and a fence. After sitting up for a moment, stunned, letting the pain calm down, Howard realized that they had done it. He was free. He got up and began half running, half walking to his office in the capital. He had a few loose ends to tidy up before heading to the airport.

When Mary pulled into their well-lit garage on Verano Loop, the illusion was complete. In training, they had called it "closing the loop." Mary nosed the car into the garage and powered the door closed with the remote before getting out. To the FBI surveillance team watching the house from a van parked just down the street, it would appear as if both Howard and his wife were now inside. Mary then dialed Howard's doctor from the house, knowing that she would get an answering machine, and played a prerecorded message from Howard asking for an appointment.

This twist would further confirm to the FBI, through their wiretap, that Howard had returned home with her, buying him even more time. Both assumptions were based on the techniques used by the FBI's surveillance teams. After the fact, it became clear that the FBI officers in the van had missed their departure from their home entirely and so had not been trailing them back from the restaurant. Howard had gotten away, and a few days later, he walked into the Russian embassy in Helsinki and asked for asylum.

When Howard first approached the CIA in 1980, he seemed like the perfect choice. He was incredibly bright and had had a colorful life that had taken him all over the world. His father had been in the air force, and Howard had moved around a lot, even spending time in West Germany and England as a kid. For the most part, though, he had spent his youth in and around Texas and the Southwest. He had a curious and intellectual mind, but he also loved the outdoors. On vacations, he would visit his grandparents in New Mexico to hunt rabbits and fish.[2]

After briefly flirting with joining the army's ROTC program as an engineer in 1969, Howard decided to go to university instead, where he studied international business and economics, graduating in the top 10 percent of his class. While at school, he had applied to join the CIA but was told he was too young. His next choice was graduate school, but before that could happen, a recruiter for the Peace Corps approached him. In the end, the prospect of being sent off to some far-flung part of the world appealed to his sense of adventure, and Howard decided to give it a try.[3]

He spent the majority of his tour in Colombia, working on a variety of agricultural projects. Howard enjoyed his time in South America. He met a young woman, Mary Cedarleaf, who was also in the Peace Corps, and a romance blossomed. Unfortunately, it seems, he also picked up a drug habit. This was during the 1970s, and drugs like cocaine and marijuana were readily available and cheap in Colombia. Even so, Howard was able to complete his tour in 1974 with a satisfactory rating.

After his time in the Peace Corps, Howard moved to Washington, DC, to get an MBA from American University. He and Mary stayed in touch and eventually decided to get married.

The next phase of Howard's life involved a stint in the Agency for International Development, helping small farmers and rural industries in Peru get loans from banks. After that, he returned to the States to work for a year in a consulting firm in Chicago, before being hired to work in an environmental firm called E&E. On the outside, it appeared that Howard had a pretty good life. E&E had recently been awarded a contract by the US government to identify hazardous toxic waste sites, and Howard was put in charge of the Kansas City office. He was just twenty-eight years old, owned his own house, and was moving up in the corporate world. However, Howard was restless and looking for more out of life, and in 1980, he applied to the CIA.

During the initial interview, Howard readily admitted to his past alcohol and drug use. As this was in the 1970s, it wasn't seen as being that big of an issue, especially since Howard claimed that it was no longer a problem. Our Agency recruiters often had to deal with applicants who had dabbled in recreational drugs.[4]

Initially, Howard thought that he might be assigned to Europe, perhaps gathering intelligence on economic matters. However, a position opened up in Moscow, and he was placed into the queue. The chief of the SE Division, David Forden, was told by the security and medical staff that Howard had admitted to using drugs in the past, but they said it shouldn't preclude him from being given a sensitive post. Forden had no way of knowing whether this was true, since internal rules in place at the time prevented the division chief from looking at an employee's medical records, but it is clear that he took the recommendation of the staff.[5]

From 1982 until April 1983, Howard was put on the Soviet desk, which gave him access to all cable traffic to and from Moscow. He and his wife, Mary, also attended the six-week Internal Operations Course and were trained in the Moscow Rules, which included access to the proprietary equipment and techniques that were only used in the Soviet Union.

As his assignment date approached, Howard was allowed deeper into the inner sanctum, where the most secret files containing the true identities of the Agency's most sensitive cases became his required reading. It should be noted that this information was so carefully guarded that the true identities of CIA agents were not even available at the Moscow Station. Finally, he was trained in how to service the übersensitive CKTAW wiretap and was told that he would be running a valuable agent named Adolf Tolkachev, first encrypted CKSPHERE and later GTVANQUISH.

Shortly before his assignment was to commence in April 1983, Howard was given a routine polygraph that indicated that he'd been less than forthcoming about the extent of his drinking and drug use. The examiners became suspicious that he might have lied about other things, and he was asked to take another test a short time later, in which he admitted to an episode of petty theft and to cheating on a training exercise involving the CKTAW mock-up. When he failed a third and fourth test, his case was put before the CIA's Office of Security. They didn't like what they saw, and within a matter of days, Howard was pulled off the Soviet desk and abruptly fired.

The firing was a massive humiliation for Howard, who had left a well-paying corporate job for what he thought would be a life of adventure and international intrigue. To make matters worse, Mary had recently given birth to a child, and her overbearing parents were breathing down their son-in-law's neck about his decision to return to government work. When Howard handed in his badge and was escorted out of CIA headquarters, he was a bitter and resentful man, and it didn't take long before his drinking problem escalated.[6]

Howard quickly left Washington and returned to New Mexico, where he got a job on the finance committee for the state legislature. He bought a house, and it appeared that he was trying to get his life back on track. However, it wouldn't be long before his anger and resentment toward the CIA would cause him to lash out.

After a few months, he began making mysterious late-night phone calls to Moscow, using a line that was designed for diplomats to make direct calls back and forth from the US embassy. Howard had been told about the line during his training, and he started dialing it repeatedly. During one call, he read off a list of numbers before hanging up. On another, he told the marine guard to pass a message on to the chief of station, Carl Gephardt, that he would not be able to make it for his physical. Since it was known that the line was not secure, this last message was a serious breach of his nondisclosure agreement. Essentially Howard had just let the KGB know that he was a CIA officer scheduled to be sent to Moscow.[7] Eventually, the calls were reported back to the CIA, but Forden was told that the CIA didn't have any power to monitor Howard's calls and that the matter would have to be turned over to the FBI. Forden brought the matter up with his superiors, but they told him that the issue wasn't worth pursuing.

Meanwhile, back in Santa Fe, Howard seemed ready to move on to the next level of his betrayal—reaching out directly to the Soviets. He'd actually tried to do it once before. In the immediate aftermath of his firing, he'd walked into the Soviet consulate in Washington, DC, and left a note, also containing a photocopy of his CIA badge. In it, he proposed to sell information for $60,000 and then left instructions on when and how to meet him.[8] In the end, Howard decided to back out of the meeting, telling his wife that he just couldn't go through with it. As it turned out, the KGB also stayed away from the meeting, thinking that the whole thing was a trap set by the FBI.

Now back in New Mexico, Howard decided to write a letter to the Soviet consulate in San Francisco. The note was innocuous, but he signed it with his real name, a clear provocation that he hoped would get the CIA's attention.

His drinking seemed to be getting worse, and in the winter of 1984, he was arrested for firing a gun during a fight outside a local bar. Things seemed to go downhill from there.

Thanks to a bureaucratic mix-up, Howard had received his passports even after he'd been kicked out of the CIA. During the summer of 1984, he decided to use this to his advantage and took a trip to Europe with Mary. The two of them ended up visiting several countries, including Italy. Howard later boasted to a friend that when he was in Milan, he'd been able to meet up with the Soviets and even fill a dead drop.

A few months after that, Howard received a mysterious phone call from a KGB agent in Washington, DC, offering to pay him for any information he might have. In reply, Howard sent a postcard to the consulate in San Francisco. The postcard, which was signed "Alex," was apparently an agreed-upon signal that indicated he was prepared to meet with the KGB in Vienna. The date for that meeting was January 1985, and before he left, Howard apparently told his wife that he was finally going to get revenge on the CIA.[9]

When Howard arrived in Vienna, he was picked up outside a movie theater and clandestinely transported to the Soviet embassy, where he talked with two Soviet KGB officers. The men had been told to find out whether Howard was the real deal, after which they would agree to pay him for his services. Howard obviously had a lot to tell them. Not only had he been trained in the Moscow Rules, including all the technology and tactics that had been developed, but also, since he had been so close to his assignment, he'd been able to read in on all the active cases going on in the Soviet capital. This meant that he knew names, or at least descriptions, of the Russians who were working for the CIA, information that the KGB would pay handsomely to obtain.

The officers were good at reading people, and they knew right away how to treat the disaffected ex-CIA trainee: pamper him with praise and make him feel special. The men seemed unable to verify everything that Howard told them, because another meeting was set up for the spring.

Howard returned to Vienna for the second time in August. And this time, it seems, the KGB took him more seriously. It is not known whether it was during this second meeting or the first that he betrayed Tolkachev, but either way, Howard definitely sold out the Russian engineer. Howard would later even brag to a friend that he had sold information to the Soviets.

It was also around this time that Howard reportedly started displaying a new collection of Swiss gold coins, a Rolex watch, and Russian-style hats that he and his son wore. And even if Howard didn't know or remember Tolkachev's real name, he could certainly provide enough details from his reading-in of the operation to give the KGB data to go on. It's also believed that Howard identified the CKTAW wiretap as well, since he had been trained extensively on it and could tell the Soviets exactly where to find it.[10]

Then, during the summer of 1985, the CIA received Vitaly Yurchenko's warning that the KGB had a valuable inside source code-named ROBERT. And even though Yurchenko hadn't named Howard, his description of the agent was plain enough: a former CIA trainee who had been in line to be stationed in Moscow but was subsequently fired.

Upon reading the initial cables, Burton Gerber, who became chief of SE Division in 1984, had a visceral and instant reaction. Knowing full well the significance of Yurchenko's words, Gerber suddenly felt overcome with emotion. Edward Lee Howard had betrayed Adolf Tolkachev. After everything that had been done to protect the Russian agent—the concealments, ID transfers, SDRs, electronic communications gear, Tropel cameras, and messages urging Tolkachev to be careful—the Russian agent had been destroyed by one of our own, an insider, a failed trainee!

At that point, the FBI was notified, and they sent a team to watch Howard's house in Santa Fe, New Mexico. They also received permission to tap his phone. But Howard was able to use the techniques he'd learned at the IOC to evade surveillance and then escape to Helsinki and eventually the Soviet Union.

Once in Moscow, Howard gave the Russians every bit of the CIA's classified information on technology, tradecraft, and the Moscow Rules that he had learned. Because he had been trained to take over the Tolkachev case upon arrival in the Soviet capitol, Tolkachev's identity was probably the first piece of information Howard gave them. This operation was so important that he would use it to solidify his standing with the KGB. The tradecraft that OTS had dedicated to this operation contained elements from almost every section of OTS: graphics work on security passes and duplicates or counterfeits for library sign-out cards; commercial and proprietary cameras for document copy, including multiple subminiature cameras; the JIB; the L-pill; concealments; disguises of several types, from light to the more advanced masks; secret writing materials; one-time pads; and more, too much to even mention. Howard was a human wrecking ball, demolishing years of effort in one convulsion of pissed-off rage at the organization that had fired him and taking down as many of our agents as he could remember.

The defection of Edward Lee Howard to the Soviet Union in 1985 marked the first time that a CIA staff officer had physically fled from America's shores and set up house in the USSR. Sure, a host of British and other foreign spies had led the way, including the infamous Kim Philby, followed by other members of the so-called Cambridge Five, who had fled London for Moscow, but the CIA had never experienced such a betrayal.

The loss of Tolkachev was a serious blow to operations in Moscow, but in truth, worse was yet to come. Around the same time that Howard had been setting up his meetings in Vienna, another rogue CIA officer stepped forward in April 1985 and agreed to spy on behalf of the KGB. His name was Aldrich Ames.

Ames was a counterintelligence officer working in SE Division at CIA Headquarters in Langley. He was a second-generation CIA officer; his father had worked for fifteen years in the Operations Directorate at the CIA, in a somewhat lackluster career, perhaps due to a serious alcohol dependency.

Ames began his CIA career in 1957 working as a summer employee and then obtained full-time work as a clerk typist. He slowly made his way up the career ladder, eventually becoming an operations officer, a case officer in spy lexicon. A close look at his early career would show several incidents with law enforcement involving speeding and reckless driving, as well as alcohol-related incidents, perhaps in a nod to his father. As a matter of fact, alcohol surfaced often as a problem during his performance evaluations and his career progression.[11]

Also noted repeatedly were his inattention to detail, tendency to procrastinate, and mediocre, unenthusiastic job performance. A performance review done while he was assigned to Ankara, Turkey, had made that point: "He lacked the necessary, fundamental personality skills. . . . He was in the wrong business or, at least, the wrong side of the intelligence trade. . . . He was introverted and devoid of interpersonal skills. He was never going to bring them along toward recruitment."[12] Nevertheless, Ames continued to rise in the hierarchy of the CIA and eventually was assigned to the Soviet-East European Division of the Directorate of Operations.

Sandy Grimes and Jeanne Vertefeuille, fellow colleagues of CIA's SE Division and part of the Agency's Mole Hunt Team, remember their early contacts with Ames. Jeanne remembers him as being mildly unkempt, with hair that badly needed styling, teeth stained from his cigarette habit, and outmoded frames for his glasses. Sandy noted that he was like an absentminded professor, unpretentious in dress and manner with messy hair, socks that often did not match, and shirts rarely pressed, and he was always late. They both agreed that he was a gentle soul whose company his fellow officers enjoyed and an interesting conversationalist, full of ideas. Neither could envision him as a traitor at the time they worked with him.[13]

In 1982, Ames accepted an unaccompanied tour to Mexico City, where his problems seemed to multiply. His first wife, Nancy, stayed behind in New York, and toward the end of the year, he was developing a mushrooming pattern of heavy drinking. Additionally, he established a romantic relationship with Rosario Casas Dupuy, a low-level Colombian-born paid CIA source whom he met while in Mexico. This relationship went against CIA policy regarding fraternizing with paid sources.[14] Ames would repeatedly ignore established norms. But despite his poor work performance and alcohol problems, it seems that the good-old-boy network kicked in, and his next assignment back at headquarters, in SE Division, was approved with no objections.

In 1983, he was made chief of the Counterintelligence Branch for Soviet operations, which meant that he had essentially taken over James Angleton's old job of ferreting out moles. It was a highly sensitive assignment that, in the wrong hands, could also prove to be very lucrative.

Ames's financial troubles began in 1984, when he divorced his first wife and married Rosario, the object of his affections in Mexico City. The stress of having to take care of a new family while paying alimony soon left him struggling under a mountain of credit card debts. Desperate and running out of options, it was then that he decided to turn to the KGB.[15]

All this led to arguably the most extensive and damaging compromise of Soviet agents in CIA history. While Ames's treachery began in 1985, it continued unabated for nine years. During that time, he identified over ten Soviet agents working for the CIA, leading to a virtual collapse of the CIA's Soviet operations and gutting Moscow Station's stable of resources and technical operations. He was responsible for over ten arrests and the executions of those US sources. In addition, he compromised more than a hundred Western intelligence operations. He gave the Soviets everything: anybody and everybody working for the CIA, the FBI, and other countries' intelligence services.

On April 15, 1985, Ames made his first delivery of intelligence to the Soviets. He stated later that he thought of it as a scam, an easy way to make money. He walked into the Russian embassy in Washington, DC, and left an envelope for the KGB *rezident*, the highest-ranking Soviet spy in the country. Inside were the names of two KGB officers working at the Soviet embassy, who, unbeknownst to their fellow countrymen, were both also working for the FBI. That was Ames's first approach, and the Russians paid him in US dollars for their pounds of flesh: $25,000 for each traitor, $50,000 total.[16]

Ames later claimed at his sentencing statement that he intended to stop there; he had the money he would need to clear up his finances and would just walk away from what he had done. But, of course, you cannot walk away from espionage. The money was so easy. Ames had so much more that he could provide, and he now knew that it would be worth millions. He decided that for that price, he could give them everything, and in the end, that is pretty much what he did. On June 13, 1985, when Ames scooped up a six-pound stack of documents from his desk and his files, stuffed them into a plastic bag, and walked through the turnstiles of the headquarters building and to his car, there was no going back.[17]

When Ames's betrayal began in 1985, there was initial confusion, as agents were swept up in Moscow, arrests were made, and executions reported. It was thought that some of this tumult was the result of Howard's earlier defection, but that proved not to be the case, as operations were compromised that Howard could not have known about. At that point, it was clear that there must be another traitor. However, it would take years for the CIA and the FBI to eventually finger Ames. During that time, in hindsight, there was a trail of breadcrumbs that might have given the IC a clue, had they been looking.

Initially, when Tolkachev was arrested, the CIA thought it must have been Howard who exposed him, and it was. But it was also Aldrich Ames, who confirmed to the Soviets that Tolkachev was indeed giving secrets to the US government. Howard also disclosed two other Russian agents: Boris Yuzhin, CKTWINE, sentenced to six years in the Gulag; and Vladimir Mikhailovich Vasilyev, GTACCORD, arrested and executed.

Immediately after learning the identities of Ames's list of traitors, the Soviets quickly began rounding them up, arresting them, and executing them. The list is long, containing KGB, GRU, and FBI assets. Ames subsequently sent a message to his masters in Moscow, begging them to slow down. He did not ask them to stop the killing; he asked them not to kill them all *so fast*, concerned that it would lead back to him. Ames also tried to divert the attention of the CIA's mole hunters by placing blame onto Jeanne Vertefeuille, who was a longtime acquaintance and member of the counterintelligence team.[18]

Additionally, FBI officers monitoring the tapes of Ames's residence before his arrest noted that he was encouraged, if not actually aided, by Rosario. His Mexican wife demanded a lifestyle and an income that he could not possibly realize on his government salary. She berated and belittled Ames, admonishing and correcting him if she thought his tradecraft was sloppy. The FBI agents who monitored the tapes came to dislike this woman intensely.

Ames and Rosario were routinely charging $18,000 to $30,000 per month on their credit cards. In one year, Ames was charged an extra $18,000 in finance charges because he neglected to pay his monthly statements on time. His salary at the time was $69,843 a year, and obviously he could not afford to pay $200,000 per year in credit card bills. In Rosario's closet were sixty purses, some still wrapped in the packages from the store; five hundred pairs of shoes; 150 unopened boxes of pantyhose; and dozens of dresses with the price tags still attached.[19]

Ames was sentenced to life in prison without the possibility of parole. He is currently serving out his sentence at a federal prison in Allenwood, Pennsylvania, and is allowed one hour a day outside of his cell. Rosario was sentenced to five years and three months.

While Howard and Ames went a long way to damage operations connected to the CIA, the FBI fell victim as well. Robert Hanssen's betrayal began in 1979, just three years after he had joined the FBI. Prior to that, the Chicago native had received an MBA from Northwestern and had been a lead investigator for the Chicago Police Department. His early FBI career was rather unremarkable. He served in the field office in Indiana before being transferred to New York, where he was assigned to the counterintelligence unit.

In 1979, Hanssen approached the GRU in New York and volunteered his services. As a relatively new agent, at that point he didn't have much to offer, but he did give them the name of one of American intelligence's most important spies, known by his code name as TOP HAT. The code name belonged to a GRU general named Dmitri Polyakov, who decided to switch sides in 1961.[20] Polyakov had become disillusioned during his second tour in New York, when his youngest son became ill. The KGB denied his request to allow his son to enter a hospital in New York City for a lifesaving operation. The boy died.

Soon after, Polyakov offered his services to an American at a diplomatic event. Over the years, Polyakov had come to be seen as one of our most important assets within the military intelligence community, so much so that former CIA director James Woolsey once called him "the jewel in the crown."[21] Polyakov was serving in India around the time that Hanssen identified him, but the Soviets seemed to take a cautious wait-and-see approach toward the GRU general. In fact, it wouldn't be until 1986, when Aldrich Ames also mentioned Polyakov, that the spy would finally be arrested.

After providing the GRU with information on Polyakov, it appears that Hanssen took a hiatus of sorts during the early

1980s. As it turned out, his wife happened to come upon him while he was putting together a package for the Soviets. He tried to cover it up by telling her it was actually fake information designed to mislead the GRU, but she became fearful that he might lose his job if the FBI ever found out. A devout Catholic, his wife convinced him to speak to the family priest, who told him that in order make things right, he needed to give the money he'd been paid to charity and agree to never spy again.[22]

It seems that Hanssen kept his promise until 1985, when he again decided to pass along information, this time to the KGB. He had just been promoted to supervisor of a foreign counterintelligence squad in New York, and the position gave him access to a wealth of information, including material related to technical projects the FBI had launched to combat Soviet penetrations. His new position also put him into direct communication with the CIA, allowing him to pass along secrets that might normally be beyond the purview of the FBI.[23]

Hanssen has always said that he was motivated purely by money, but a closer look at his career indicates that there was a clear case of revenge against a system that did not recognize or appreciate his professional skills. It was thought that he resented his FBI colleagues, who were steadily rising higher in the ranks while he languished in relative obscurity. Did they think they were better than him? He decided that he would show them how much he was worth.

Hanssen proved to be incredibly good at covering his tracks. Indeed, one of the reasons he was able to last as long as he did was his paranoia about being caught. Throughout the twenty-two years that he was spying on behalf of the Russians, he never once provided his real name, instead alternately signing his communications "Ramon" or "Ramon Garcia." He also refused to meet with his KGB handlers face-to-face, and he exchanged material for cash by using dead drops. He was apparently so cautious that he even refused to use the sites chosen by his Soviet case officer, Victor Cherkashin, instead preferring to choose his own.[24]

The information Hanssen passed along to the KGB was incredibly damaging to America's national security interests. Not only did he give up the names of people, both in the FBI and the CIA, but he told the Russians about operations, programs, and technology as well. In October 1985, he sent a letter to the KGB demanding $100,000 and offering up the names of three Soviets working for the FBI. He was not aware of the fact that all three of these men had already been betrayed by Aldrich Ames. Two of them would subsequently be executed.[25]

After recommitting himself in 1985, Hanssen embarked on what can only be described as a long and uninterrupted career as a Russian spy. In 1989, he compromised the FBI investigation of Felix Bloch, a high-ranking US State Department employee who was working for the Soviets. Tipped off by Hanssen, the KGB warned Bloch that he was under suspicion. He supplied the Soviets with thousands of pages of intelligence documents, helping to negate many of the NSA's newest and most technologically advanced electronic-surveillance plans.[26] He provided a wide range of information on American Measurement and Signature Intelligence, or MASINT, a technical branch of intelligence gathering that tracks, detects, identifies, or describes the signatures left by electronic devices such as radar, spy satellites, and signal intercepts.

He also compromised the secret tunnel that had been dug underneath Russia's new embassy building on Wisconsin Avenue in Washington, DC, code-named MONOPOLY, and betrayed the CKTAW operation on the outskirts of Moscow. Hanssen's goal, which he seemed to accomplish, was to betray everything—not just American operations but those of all our allies around the world—almost as if he were a gambling addict who couldn't pull himself away from the craps table.

Hanssen went on spying until February 18, 2001, when he was arrested at a park in Virginia while making a dead drop. The FBI had finally been able to identify him, thanks to an ex-KGB paid informer. When he was caught, it is reported that Hanssen asked his captors, "What took you so long?"[27]

Time magazine dubbed 1985 the "Year of the Spy," and for good reason. The betrayal of Howard, Ames, and Hanssen would cause untold damage to clandestine operations around the world.

These are the agents disclosed by Howard:

Boris Yuzhin, CKTWINE, sentenced to six years in the
   Gulag
Adolf Tolkachev, CKSPHERE, civilian, executed
Vladimir Mikhailovich Vasilyev, GTACCORD, executed

These were the ten agents executed after Aldrich Ames gave them up to the KGB:

Dmitriy Fedorovich Polyakov, GTBEEP, TOP HAT, GRU
   general
Valery F. Martynov, GTGENTILE, FBI PIMENTA, KGB
   lieutenant colonel
Sergei Motorin, GTGAUZE, FBI MEGAS, KGB major
Vladimir M. Piguzov, GTJOGGER, KGB lieutenant colonel
Vladimiir Mikhallovich Vasilyev, GRU colonel
Sergei Vorontsov, GTCOWL, KGB
Gennady Smetanin, GTMILLION, GRU lieutenant colonel
Gennady Grigorievich Varanik, GTFITNESS, KGB
Leonid Polyshuk, GTWEIGH, KGB
Adolf Tolkachev, GTSPHERE, civilian, also betrayed by
   Howard

Some of the agents identified by Aldrich Ames escaped execution:

Vladimir V. Potashov
Oleg Gordievsky
Sergei Fedorenko
Sergei Bokhan

Robert G. Hanssen identified these agents:

Dmitriy Fedorovich Polyakov (later betrayed by Ames)
Boris Yuzhin (also betrayed by Howard)
Valery Martynov (also betrayed by Ames)
Sergei Motorin (also betrayed by Ames)

For many reasons, the year 1985 marked a turning point for the Moscow Station. It wasn't just the loss of our valuable agents that affected operations in Moscow but also the fact that so many of our new methods and technologies had been passed along to the KGB. This was a serious blow. From now on, it was going to be that much harder for the CIA to conduct clandestine operations in the Soviet capital.

CHAPTER 10

"Murphy is right."

On the night of March 10, 1986, Michael Sellers set out from his apartment in Moscow with the hopes of meeting up with a Russian agent known as GTCOWL. The agent had first made contact in 1984, when he had slipped an envelope through the open window of an American diplomat's car. The man refused to identify himself, but due to the material he'd included in the letter, it was thought that he must be connected to the KGB's counterintelligence unit in Moscow.

At that point, the man was given the code name GTCOWL, and the Moscow Station attempted to establish contact. The first meeting didn't go that well. GTCOWL was a tough streetwise individual who spoke a colloquial Russian that made him hard to understand.[1] As Sellers had tested near the top end of Russian fluency, it was up to him to go and see what the man wanted. As it turned out, GTCOWL was looking to exchange information for cash.

He told Sellers about an operation involving a KGB informant named Father Roman Potemkin who had somehow been able to disrupt a sensitive operation with the unwitting help of an American journalist. Journalist Nicholas Daniloff had taken an envelope he had received from a mysterious source to the US embassy in Moscow. Daniloff assumed that the envelope was from Father Roman, who had recently approached him, and he told the CIA as much. GTCOWL told Sellers that the letter had been from a legitimate source but that when the CIA had approached Father

Roman, they'd basically burned the source and killed the whole operation.

GTCOWL also confirmed a rumor that the KGB was using a substance called Spy Dust that allowed them to keep tabs on anyone they deemed suspicious. The chemical powder was mixed with water and sprayed on car-door handles, doormats— anything and everything that might come in contact with the target. The Russian agent even produced a bottle of the liquid and sprayed it into a plastic sack so that Sellers could take it back to the embassy and have it analyzed.

After this meeting, GTCOWL gave Sellers a phone number that he could call at various agreed-upon times, which basically ensured that the Russian agent, and only the Russian agent, would be the one to pick up the phone. Sellers followed through a few months later, but GTCOWL never picked up. Then the KGB double agent seemed to disappear for the better part of a year until March of 1986, when he finally responded and signaled that he was ready to meet. By this time, Tolkachev had been rolled up, and the Moscow Station was eager to reestablish contact with the KGB counterintelligence officer.

After much debate at Langley, and with an awareness of the high stakes should it fail, the operation was submitted to the White House for presidential approval, which came immediately.[2]

It was imperative that Sellers be able to get free and meet up with him, but the KGB knew that Sellers was CIA. That, of course, translated to Sellers dragging unrelenting surveillance teams behind him every time he stepped out of the embassy gates in the Soviet capital or left his own apartment. This meant that if he was ever going to be able to meet up with GTCOWL, we were going to have to dig deep into our bag of tricks.

Sellers lived next door to an American diplomat named Ronald Patterson, who could provide the perfect cover for an ID transfer scenario. The two men were relatively similar in builds, both around six feet three inches and slim. However, there was one significant difference: Sellers was a Caucasian, while Patterson was an African American. Jonna was part of the team assigned to this operation, working from a European location with a group from Washington who prepared an overhead mask as well as hand and arm gloves to match the skin tones. I had done a similar disguise in Vientiane, Laos, during the early 1970s, thanks to my time with Chambers out in Los Angeles.

The importance was in the details, since Sellers would have to drive past the militia guard at the gate to the apartment complex. Patterson had also helped by loaning Sellers his car, which would help to sell the disguise. In the end, it worked, and he was able to get free.

The second phase of the operation involved Sellers switching out of his ID scenario and donning a second disguise to look like a Russian man, complete with long hair and a fake mustache. The beauty of these disguises was that they had been designed to be changed in a hurry. Despite their outlandish nature, especially the Patterson disguise, they were practical.

After he had gotten free, Sellers conducted a long surveillance-detection run, until he was finally certain that he was in the black. The meeting site was in an alleyway between two Stalinist apartment blocks not far from Moscow's Lenin Hills district. However, as Sellers approached and got within twenty feet of GTCOWL, he could sense that something was wrong. The agent was thinner than Sellers remembered, and his swagger was replaced by a stammer. He was a ghost of himself, and that was when Sellers braced himself for the inevitable.

"Oh, shit," Sellers said to himself. "Here it comes."[3]

The arrest was formulaic, done at night in the blinding lights of multiple KGB vehicle high beams, like a scene out of a bad movie. Cars squealed to a stop, and men jumped out, grabbed Sellers while the suspicious agent disappeared in the melee, and threw him into the back of a KGB van. As he lay there, the Seventh Directorate officers, the jubilant watchers, talked among themselves, not knowing that Sellers could understand them. Only when one of them reached over and pulled off Sellers's false mustache did he realize who was in the back seat.

"It's Misha!" he hollered, using the Russian diminutive for Michael. The KGB men began debating in Russian how he could possibly have gotten out of his apartment and disguised himself as a Russian worker without anyone on the surveillance team noticing him.[4]

Milton Bearden later interviewed Sellers about the meeting, and specifically what happened during his interrogation, when he finally came face-to-face with Rem Krassilnikov. I'll include the episode here, which comes from *The Main Enemy*:

On the night of March 10, Sellers thought he had broken free of surveillance for his late-night run by pulling off an identity transfer with another embassy employee. Later, when he was "black" on Moscow's icy streets, he quickly changed into Russian street clothes and melted into the flow of Muscovites on their way home.

Sellers spent only a few hours in interrogation. By 2:30 AM Stuart Parker, a counselor officer in the American embassy, had arrived to take him home. But during those few hours, Sellers had sparred with Rem Krassilnikov, trying to parry each question from the KGB's gray ghost. Normally, CIA officers were told to say nothing while under arrest, except to declare diplomatic immunity and to ask to see a counselor officer from the embassy. Sellers knew the game, but he couldn't resist giving a few jabs, especially since he could speak Russian with his captors. When Krassilnikov told Sellers that his arrest would damage his career with the CIA, Sellers told him he was wrong, it wouldn't hurt his career at the agency. Perhaps to encourage Sellers to keep talking, Krassilnikov tried to switch to small talk, describing the little details of his life known to the KGB. He was the goaltender on the American embassy's broomball team—what did he think about American hockey versus Russian hockey? But in trying to keep Sellers engaged, Krassilnikov revealed some interesting facts. It became clear to Sellers that Krassilnikov didn't know how he had gotten out of his apartment for his meeting. The KGB still didn't have a good understanding of the CIA's identity transfer techniques, and finding Sellers at the arrest site had puzzled them; his watchers thought he was still in his apartment.[5]

When it was over, Sellers was declared persona non grata and was expelled from the Soviet Union. GTCOWL, whose real name was later discovered to be Vorontsov, was executed.

In the aftermath of Sellers's arrest and expulsion, the Moscow Station was left reeling and looking for answers—first Tolkachev and now this. They were staggered, like a disoriented boxer who had pulled himself up off the mat after being knocked down, only to be punched square in the jaw and sent back down again. It seemed as if the KGB knew what we were doing before we did it. And while the defections of Howard, Ames, and Hanssen had a lot to do with this new reality, there were other factors as well, including the fact that there had been a recent breach in the security of the US embassy.

★   ★   ★

When Ambassador Arthur Hartman, an American career diplomat, arrived in the Soviet Union in 1981, fresh from a two-year stint leading the US mission in Paris, he was hardly in the best of moods. Hartman was following Ambassador Thomas J. Watson Jr., a retired board chairman and son of the founder of IBM. Watson had no diplomatic experience and was the first noncareer diplomat in the post since Averell Harriman was ambassador to Moscow during World War II.[6] With Hartman's assignment to Moscow, it was becoming clear that the pool of senior Sovietologists in the Foreign Service was diminishing.

Hartman was about to lead the Moscow embassy through some tumultuous times—and the longest tenure of a US ambassador to the Soviet Union since before World War II. His authority would span the pivotal years from 1981 to 1987, from the death of Leonid Brezhnev through the leadership of Yuri Andropov and Konstantin Chernenko to the rise of Mikhail Gorbachev. He would be forced to contend with crises such as the downing of Korean Airlines Flight 007 by the Soviet military in 1983, the Chernobyl nuclear disaster in 1986, and, later that year, the detainment of US journalist Nicholas Daniloff on espionage charges. Hartman was the senior US representative in Moscow during the Soviet invasion of Afghanistan and was also just in time for the beginnings of *glasnost*, or transparency, under Michael Gorbachev in the waning years of Soviet Communism.[7] All in all, a tumultuous period of the Cold War.

Hartman had been assigned to Paris in 1977 during the Carter administration, sharing the French spotlight with the leadership of President Valéry Giscard d'Estaing and Francois Mitterrand. In France, he had made an impression on the French for his conspicuous presence at artistic events like the opera, leading to a flattering profile in a liberal newspaper catering to the Parisian intelligentsia. That the newspaper, *Le Nouvel Observateur*, a pillar of the French left, should pick the American ambassador to tell Parisian intellectuals what to go see or hear was nothing short of remarkable. "Not since Benjamin Franklin," the *New York Times* noted, "has an American envoy to France been given such public recognition for his culture."[8]

Elegant and intellectual, Hartman was the picture of the immaculate, white-haired diplomat. He was described in the *New York Times* as "silver-haired, tall, and with a slight stoop that is more purposeful—it is, after all, necessary to communicate with shorter people—than deferential." When named ambassador to Moscow, Hartman initially hesitated, as he preferred Bonn or London, where his Western European expertise could have been used. With a reputation as one of the brainiest and most professional members of the Foreign Service, the ambassador knew that the cultural opportunities would be poorer in the Soviet Union. He knew, according to the *New York Times*, that in the current climate of affairs it was unlikely that a Moscow weekly would portray him meditating on a line by Pushkin.[9]

During Hartman's tenure, he dealt with four Soviet leaders and the beginnings of *glasnost* under Mikhail Gorbachev. His official residence in Moscow, Spaso House, became a gathering place for intellectuals, dissidents, and artists. As in his tenure in Paris, Hartman was considered to be the epitome of the erudite diplomat; from the opera to the Bolshoi, he was enmeshed in the cultural affairs of his country of assignment.[10]

With Hartman's arrival, the climate of security at the embassy was about to change, not necessarily in a good way. Looming ahead of him, more troublesome than any of the other crises he would face during his tenure, lay the security woes at the American embassy itself: the building, the employees, and the forces of the KGB. This would test his mettle in ways he had not been tested before in Europe. While many of the difficulties were in play when Hartman arrived, his lax attitude toward the security issues he would deal with only exacerbated an already problematic situation.

The Moscow embassy was an island of American interests surrounded by a sea of hostile Soviet intrigue and intrusions. The embassy and its captive population were under attack constantly, from all sides and in all guises. Physical surveillance, electronic intercepts, microwave emanations bombarding its windows, bugged typewriters, known Soviet KGB plants working among the Americans and Soviet workers building a new American embassy just next door, the chemical called Spy Dust marking any Soviets who had had contact with an American—all these issues had to be countered. The work of the embassy had to prevail. And this new ambassador, with a not-unusual State Department disdain for the nuts and bolts of security considerations, was in a position to possibly embolden the opposition forces.

And then there were the Soviet women working in the embassy who were allowed by Ambassador Hartman to attend the weekly TGIF parties at the Marine House. There was a total of twenty-eight marine guards assigned to the embassy compound in Moscow, and they were all healthy, young, single men. They stood guard at Post One; Post Two; Post Two-A, a roving guard for the secure floors only; and Post Three. They were no different than other young men in their demographic, and the rules forbidding fraternization with local, Soviet-bloc women resulted in a lot of frustrated guards. And because all the Soviets working in the embassy were handpicked by the infamous UPDK, or *Upravlenie obsluzhivaniya diplomaticheskogo korpusa*, a department of the KGB, the Soviet women were invariably attractive and single.[11]

At the time of Hartman's arrival, a number of marines were seeing Soviet women, despite the rules against fraternization. The ambassador even softened the rules to allow the marines to dance with Yugoslavian girls at Uncle Sam's, the café and bar located in a small shack at the rear of the embassy complex. If Hartman thought he was trying to make some obscure political point by distinguishing Yugoslavians from other communists, it was lost on the marines, who only knew that the girls were extremely pretty. Marine guards were bringing Soviet dates to the Marine Corps Ball held every year on November 10. In fact, the Soviet's use of "swallows," or female agents, to sexually entrap our marine guards far exceeded the incidents reported by the press.[12]

In addition to these young women working in the embassy, there were others who had been there for years and were assumed to be KGB. Gayla, who cooked for the marines, was thought to be KGB. Valentina, a Soviet hairdresser who worked in the beauty parlor in the basement of the north wing, was believed to be a spy for the Soviets. And there was Violetta Seina, an attractive young woman who worked first for Ambassador Hartman and then was transferred to a post only ten feet from Post One.[13]

One US Marine, in particular, epitomized this problem. Clayton Lonetree had noticed Violetta working in the embassy for months before they had a "chance" encounter in the Moscow subway. Away from work, they had an initial conversation that got the ball rolling. Weeks later, there was another casual encounter in the subway. This time Violetta "allowed" Clayton to recognize her first. They walked and talked for some hours, and eventually he visited her at home. All this activity violated the embassy's rules against any and all kinds of fraternization.

When she was fired from the American embassy some months later for doing very little work, it was too late. Unknown to the embassy, Violetta had performed her work exceedingly well. The young marine guard had made the mistake of falling in love with a swallow, a seductive Russian KGB spy.[14]

Her initial task accomplished, Violetta would eventually introduce Clayton Lonetree to her "uncle" Sasha—a man who evinced considerable personal interest in Clayton. Lonetree was an American Indian from the Winnebago tribe, a loner, and a proverbial outsider, and he was flattered by Uncle Sasha's attention. What ensued caused an international brouhaha both inside and outside the US government. Accused of passing secret blueprints and documents to the KGB, Lonetree was arrested for also admitting Soviet KGB officers into classified portions of the US embassy after hours. The embassy had been penetrated and its communication unit compromised. The Soviets were now reading classified American correspondence.

When Hartman stepped down as ambassador to the Soviet Union in 1987, he said that he believed a more mature force, less susceptible to temptation, should replace the young, single marine guards at the embassy in Moscow. This was due to the arrest and sentencing of Sergeant Clayton J. Lonetree in 1987. In that same year, all twenty-eight marines at the embassy in Moscow were recalled to Washington, DC, and were replaced by others from posts around the world. The State Department commented that the recall was precautionary in nature and made a point of emphasizing that none of the marines being moved were involved in the espionage case. Ambassador Hartman said the embassy had been vigilant about security, adding, "But something bad has happened here and we have got to find out what happened."[15]

Several officials disputed Hartman's characterization of the embassy's attitude toward security. One said that the problem had been identified in several reports, including a 1985 study by a State Department advisory commission that attributed significant intelligence breaches to the employment of Soviet nationals at the embassy.[16]

When Lonetree was reassigned from Moscow to Vienna, Austria, in 1986, Uncle Sasha had trailed after him, trying to convince him to provide information on the CIA office in the Austrian capital. The Lonetree security case began in earnest when Lonetree asked Violetta's uncle to identify the CIA's Austrian chief of station to him. Then at the embassy Christmas party in Vienna that year, Lonetree approached our COS and confessed that he had been in a forbidden and undocumented relationship with a KGB officer in Moscow.[17] The chief of station at that time was my old friend James Olson, the same officer who had made the first entry into the CKTAW manhole in Moscow while using Disguise-on-the-Run.

Eventually, in August 1987, Lonetree was court-martialed in Quantico, Virginia, and sentenced to thirty-five years in prison. He was the only US Marine ever convicted of espionage. His sentence was later reduced due to good behavior, and he actually served only eight years.

While measures were taken to deal with the spying case, administration and congressional officials said that the embassy in Moscow, and Hartman by inference, had been slow to respond to warnings that it was vulnerable. One official described the embassy itself as "porous," while Hartman said that they had been vigilant about security. These officials said that they were shocked to learn that despite all the reports on security, the marine guards in Moscow were violating one of the most basic regulations: the ban on social contacts with Soviet citizens.[18] If the Department of State had any Moscow Rules, the rule against fraternization would have been their rule number one. *Never fraternize with the enemy.*

The embassy in Moscow had been repeatedly penetrated by Soviet intelligence. According to officials, a 1985 advisory commission, headed by Admiral Bobby R. Inman, found that the embassy's cars carried electronic listening devices planted by Soviet agents. In a more serious breach, embassy typewriters, particularly IBM Selectric typewriters, were bugged with devices that would monitor what had been typed and transmit it to listening posts.

"For years, the Soviets were reading some of our most sensitive diplomatic correspondence, economic and political analyses and other communications," said a 1986 report on counterintelligence by the Senate Select Committee on Intelligence. The secretary to the deputy chief of mission in Moscow, an official said, used one of the typewriters involved. However, it subsequently was proven that no CIA typewriters were involved in this penetration; the station had maintained control of its IBM typewriters from purchase, through shipment, storage, and final issuance at the embassy.[19]

The US embassy in Moscow had utilized Foreign Service Nationals in a variety of positions, asking them to undertake jobs that Americans could not or would not do. The embassy knew that the KGB had its way with the FSNs, planting its own people among them. The embassy had to assume that all FSNs were in the employ of the host-country intelligence service, but in some instances, that suspicion was more of a certainty. There was a particular KGB colonel, a woman, whose precise identity and military rank were confirmed. The embassy staff knew her as Big Raya, a very tall and voluptuous woman with a commanding presence. Raya was the FSN who forwarded the passports of American diplomats to the Soviet Ministry of Foreign Affairs to be officially registered in their system. She also served as the focal point for local hiring of FSNs.[20]

Raya was the primary contact between the American staff and the UPDK, the Soviet bureau that was in charge, administratively, of foreign embassies. The UPDK had a lot to say about the daily lives of all the Americans working in the embassy. It provided and assigned living quarters and gave out work assignments to Soviet employees. The UPDK was pivotal to everything, from tickets to the Bolshoi to travel outside of Moscow to restaurant reservations to vehicle maintenance. It was involved intimately in the lives of the diplomats and other Americans assigned to the mission.[21]

Although embassy security officials argued against this arrangement, the State Department found it convenient, because the FSNs both spoke Russian and knew how to deal with the Soviet government machinery. So the risks were tolerated. The number of FSNs working for the American embassy in Moscow at this time almost equaled the number of Americans.

Some officials in Washington, including the secretary of the navy, alleged that Ambassador Hartman had permitted an environment at the American embassy that was too lax, and a 1987 commission led by former defense secretary Melvin Laird found that Hartman had "failed to take appropriate steps to correct the situation."[22]

Hartman vigorously defended himself against congressional charges that he blocked efforts to improve security at his embassy. Jim Courter, a Republican from New Jersey, told a cable news network that Hartman should be investigated for resisting security improvements. Furthermore, Courter said that Hartman had come to his office in 1985 to lobby *against* an amendment to a bill that would have prohibited Soviet personnel from walking inside any part of the embassy compound.[23]

Courter also accused Hartman of making the "outrageous statement" that working at the embassy often gave Soviet workers increased appreciation of the United States, democracy, and liberty. Hartman said he could not recall whether he said those words but noted the sentiment may in fact be true.[24]

Hartman's tenure also involved the fiasco that resulted over the construction of the new US embassy in Moscow. Recall that the United States and the Soviet Union had come to an agreement in 1969; however, the materials for the project didn't begin arriving on site until 1979. Unfortunately, the US government had given the host country permission to provide the workers as well as the construction materials for all phases of the new embassy. As a result, it was later discovered that the Soviets had embedded listening devices into the precast concrete that was to be used for the building's foundation.

After the disclosure of Soviet penetration of the US embassy through built-in bugs, there was a diplomatic dustup when

Secretary of State George P. Shultz, in an attempt to avoid the microphones in the US embassy, prepared to meet in a trailer with top US officials in Moscow. A congressman charged that blueprints for the high-security vehicle were displayed on the embassy wall for days in advance of the visit.

"The blueprints for the van being constructed for Secretary Shultz were still taped to the wall—the actual architectural drawings," Representative Daniel Mica (D-FL), chairman of the House Foreign Affairs subcommittee on International Operations, described on ABC's *This Week with David Brinkley*. "Somebody could easily photograph them," Congresswoman Olympia Snowe said. "We were really perplexed." Congress was determined to fix individual blame for the security fiasco, not only for sloppy administration inside the building but also for permitting Soviet contractors to prefabricate elements of the new embassy building away from the site, a process that enabled Soviet builders to incorporate the bugging devices into the new structure.[25]

Mica and Snowe opposed Shultz's visit to Moscow after the disclosure of these security breaches. In 1982, a uniquely trained team of security experts, which included a member of OTS's Special Surveillance Team, was dispatched to Moscow, along with scanning machines that could inspect construction elements for the new embassy. The surveillance team had trained as rock climbers, and they worked through Moscow's winter nights in temperatures that fell to forty degrees below zero, hanging off the side of the building to get from floor to floor. They were removing and inspecting at night what the Soviet workers were installing during the day.[26]

Finally, in August of 1985, six years after work had begun on the new embassy, the assistant secretary of state for diplomatic security sent a secret cable to Ambassador Hartman recommending that he shut down the job. The building had been compromised to such an extent that the only solution was to tear it down and rebuild it from the ground floor up.

Former ambassador Hartman, appearing on Brinkley's show, admitted failure in only two areas during his four years in

Moscow. "We clearly failed in the case of the marines," he said of the guards who had confessed to admitting Soviet women to restricted areas of the embassy. "I think I failed in terms of lack of imagination as to whether, you know, from the point of view of whether a marine would get into difficulties, or whether he would actually go to the extreme of committing treason." He also admitted failure to stop off-site prefabrication of parts of the new embassy building. Hartman concurred with Mica and Snowe that the embassy building now under construction in Moscow would have to be demolished and rebuilt with greater care to eliminate security breaches.[27]

It was that February when the notorious Lonetree marine guard scandal broke, one of the embassy's worst episodes. One consequence of the scandal was a shutdown of all secure electronic communication between Moscow and Washington. Another was confiscation of all electric typewriters; they, too, were presumed compromised.[28]

An American investigation was critical of Hartman for security lapses under his watch, which included allowing the bugging of typewriters and the various sexual scandals of the marine guards stationed in Moscow. It was during his tenure that Clayton Lonetree was sent to prison. Hartman stressed that he was unaware that marines assigned to guard the embassy were involved in treasonable acts. A congressional charge, however, stated that the ambassador blocked efforts to improve security at the US embassy. Representative Courter (R-NJ) stated that Hartman should be investigated for resisting security improvements.[29] "At that time," Courter said, "Ambassador Hartman had a known KGB colonel as his chauffeur."

Hartman, speaking in a telephone interview, said that all Soviet citizens who worked at the embassy, including his own chauffeur, were KGB agents or reported to the KGB. "No big deal," Hartman said. "Everybody who has been in Moscow knows that." Hartman said he opposed the measure to prohibit Soviets inside the embassy because he felt it would not improve security. He said he knew that his chauffeur worked for the KGB but kept him on because "he knows how to drive." "I couldn't get any-body who was not KGB," Hartman said. "If it was an American driver, the car still would not be secure and he wouldn't know where he was going."[30]

Unbeknownst to Hartman, however, another kind of diplo-matic scandal was about to break that would resolve the problem of the FSN employees once and for all.

During the late summer of 1986, the FBI unintentionally touched off an international incident when it arrested a Soviet scientist by the name of Gennady Zakharov. Zakharov was a physicist attached to the UN Secretariat in New York. The Rus-sians quickly responded by rounding up Nicholas Daniloff for his involvement with the Father Roman Potemkin affair. While Zakharov had most definitely been a spy, Daniloff had basically been in the wrong place at the wrong time. Even so, the Soviets insisted that the two cases were tied together, which incensed the US government.[31]

In the ever-familiar tit for tat of diplomacy, America responded on September 17 by declaring twenty-five Soviet diplomats per-sona non grata, accusing them of espionage, and requiring them to leave the country within twenty-four hours. The Soviets responded by expelling five US diplomats, in what became known as the PNG War. America called their hand and raised the bet, expelling five more Soviets as a direct response and then adding fifty KGB and GRU officers from DC and San Francisco, declaring that they were bringing Soviet staffing in the United States to the same level as the American levels in Moscow and Leningrad: 251 total.

But in a dramatic, all-in, flourish, Moscow withdrew the 260 Soviet nationals working in the US embassy in Moscow and the consulate in Leningrad, comprised of 183 FSNs plus another 77 personal maids, teachers, and other private staff. Overnight, the US diplomatic mission in the Soviet Union became the only embassy in a foreign country with no FSN employees running the administrative and logistics operations.[32]

The expulsion of the US diplomats came as no surprise. How-ever, the astounding withdrawal of the Russian employees, likely intended as a coup de grâce, accomplished for the United States what it had been unwilling or unable to do for itself.

In America, Soviet intelligence was severely damaged. The list of those affected did not include all the Soviet intelligence personnel in the United States, but it did include the entire leadership of the KGB and GRU. Estimates are that the KGB and GRU were on, essentially, an operational stand-down for at least two years in the United States.

★ ★ ★

The American embassy in Moscow has never been an easy place to work. Although the CIA always expected that the political climate in Moscow was going to be hostile, many other considerations also played into the day-to-day stress of an assignment there. The climate, third-world economy, and isolation from friends and family all contributed to an environment that wreaked havoc on the diplomatic community. Both the State Department and the CIA provided hardship pay to those assigned to the Soviet Union.

The KGB-controlled UPDK provided the embassy with Soviet employees as maintenance and administrative personnel, as well as maids in American apartments. Soviets serviced and chauffeured our embassy vehicles, typed our correspondence with Soviet entities, made transportation and accommodation arrangements for us when we traveled, reserved seats and acquired tickets for us to attend cultural events around the city, made reservations at restaurants, and even operated our switchboard. In addition to the Soviets working in the embassy and our homes, the KGB used thousands of cooperative informers around the city: hotel registration clerks, restaurant managers, taxi drivers, Intourist guides, and, of course, the police (militia) who guarded the embassies and private residences.[33]

Almost all consumer goods were shipped in by rail from Helsinki, most often from a large department store in Finland called Stockmann. The embassy in Moscow received weekly shipments of consumables from Stockmann, a highlight in an otherwise dreary shopper's experience. Many of the children in the embassy community mistakenly believed that Stockmann was the capital of Finland.[34]

A number of the ordinary consumer goods taken for granted in the West were imports in the Soviet Union. Food, paper goods, and medical and office supplies all were shipped into the embassy by rail. This included a metric ton of milk each week, as Soviet milk had to be boiled prior to use. Air shipments of fruits and vegetables came in to Sheremetyevo Airport via an American airline, Pan Am. All this, plus equipment and general supplies, needed to be cleared through customs. Navigating the Soviet bureaucracy demanded both patience and finesse—all in Russian, please. And the embassy's Foreign Service Nationals had managed all of it.[35]

On the day that the news of the expulsion of the FSNs was announced, the embassy was hosting Nobel Peace Prize winner Elie Wiesel and had scheduled a banquet and reception in his honor at Spaso House. In the aftermath of the announcement, with the sudden absence of Soviet maids and chefs, Donna Hartman, the ambassador's wife, cooked a kosher banquet for seventeen guests and assembled hors d'oeuvres for a reception for one hundred.

A slim woman with graying hair, Mrs. Hartman was up to the crisis. Later visitors to Spaso House were likely to find this former State Department style-setter weeding her garden in rubber boots, an old green parka, and a man's brown felt hat. Without her two gardeners and nine other Soviet servants, she now tended the residence grounds herself and dressed the part. This was in stark contrast to her previous role in Paris, where she was a darling of the fashion set and hostess of lavish trunk shows of American haute couture.

Now, at embassy receptions, Mrs. Hartman and the marines served popcorn, since there was no house staff. But when leading a visitor on a tour of the Moscow mansion, with its massive freestanding ionic columns and glittering cut-crystal chandeliers, she waxed diplomatic over the departure of her Soviet servants. "I miss them," Mrs. Hartman said. "Some of them were lovely, but I do find the house wonderfully calm now."[36]

In a frenzy of nationalistic glee during the banishments, there was a PNG party at the US dacha outside Moscow, where the American diplomats waited for the announcement of the names of the soon-to-be-departed. After the names were called out, fueled by beer and indignation, they carried cake outside to put on top of the KGB surveillance car stationed outside the dacha.[37]

The American diplomats quickly responded to the Kremlin's attempted death blow by dividing into All-Purpose Duty teams, alphabetically, with names like the Killer Bs and the High Cs, rotating the work, as it seemed the only fair way to cover for the absence of 183 Soviet employees. There were weekly train shipments to be met and cleared through customs, congressional delegations arriving at the airport, construction materials coming in by truck and needing to be unloaded, and housekeeping in the embassy and in Spaso House, not to mention the driving of trucks and cars through the clogged Moscow traffic.

The weather held through December, then the thermometer plunged. Records revealed that the winter of 1986/1987 was the worst in 54 years, second worst in 105 years and colder than the winter that defeated Napoleon's army. The temperature hovered below minus 35 Celsius for weeks at a time. There were no typewriters for several weeks. The embassy personnel drafted classified messages on yellow legal pads using ballpoint pens, a courier flew them to Frankfurt, Germany each day, and a secretary there typed them up and transmitted them. At 30 below zero, ballpoint pen ink freezes in about five minutes. They learned to keep three ballpoint pens inside their down jackets, where body heat could thaw the ink. They wrote with one pen until it froze, put it back next to their body and continued drafting with the second pen, and so on, rotating them. Just after Christmas, the mission sent a cable to Washington titled "New Year's Greetings from the Titanic"![38]

Just like the *Titanic*, the Moscow Station was sinking fast. With the setbacks connected to the Year of the Spy as well as the expulsion of the FSN employees from the embassy, it was basically impossible to conduct operations inside the Soviet capital.

In order to rectify the situation, Burton Gerber asked Jack Downing to return to Moscow in the fall of 1986 as the new chief of station. Downing's appointment came smack-dab in the middle of the PNG War and so had to be delayed by several months because headquarters didn't want him to arrive only to be immediately expelled. When he finally got to the embassy, he was shocked by just how far things had fallen since the late 1970s, when he'd been deputy chief of station. With the majority of its agents rolled up, Moscow Station was essentially back at square one. Looking around at the rubble that remained, Jack realized that the only way the station could pull itself out of the mess was to change things up.

It was time for the Moscow Rules to evolve yet again.

CHAPTER 11

"Build in opportunity, but use it sparingly."

The roar of the engines deepened as the airplane began its sharp descent. Sitting near the window, Josh took one last look at the impossibly blue sky before the vision was abruptly obscured by a tumbling mass of gray clouds. He gripped the armrests as the cabin bucked and rocked through the rolling mist. It wasn't the turbulence that made him nervous but the thought of what awaited below. And then, as if it had been conjured before him, the clouds vanished, and the city appeared. A dark and claustrophobic landscape, it seemed to sag under the pressing weight of the thick overcast. Gray and more gray—not even the snow was white.

Josh felt a lump in his throat as the plane banked for final approach and the Fasten Seat Belts sign came on. He had the feeling of being in a protective bubble, but soon he would be out there, among the shadows. He was a magician, not a spy, but for some reason, he'd been asked to come to Moscow. It was February 1988.

Josh had met with Jack Downing the previous year out in Washington, DC, and had been instantly impressed. Jack seemed in absolute control at all times and mentioned that he had just recently been assigned to be chief of station in Moscow. Josh had read the news about the Year of the Spy, but the picture that Jack painted for him was even bleaker. The embassy had basically been gutted, and there was concern that many of the techniques that had been created over the previous decade were now obsolete.

"I need a fresh set of eyes," Jack told him. "You have a unique perspective. Would you come?"

Tall and rangy with a shock of blond hair, Josh bore a glancing resemblance to the actor Peter Graves. In the beginning, he thought that heading out to Moscow sounded fun. They had issued him an official passport, which made him feel important. He'd stared at it several times after it had arrived, like a Boy Scout who had just received a shiny new merit badge. In Josh's mind, it was akin to a get-out-of-jail-free card. Then, just days before he was scheduled to depart, he'd spoken to somebody from the Agency who had told him in an offhand way, "Oh, they can still put you in jail." But by that point, it was too late to back out. *Besides*, he thought, *they wouldn't do anything to put me in danger, right?*

Ever since he'd worked on the JIB, Josh had become a valued consultant on a variety of projects, sometimes modifying or creating devices, at other times sharing the techniques he had come to perfect over the years. Josh was highly regarded in his field, a true professional who understood that there were many similarities between his chosen profession and ours. The more time I spent alongside our friends in the magic community, the more I came to respect their gifts.

Jonna told me a tale of deception and illusion some years ago that showed me just how effective some of these techniques could be when done properly. Chief of the Disguise Branch at the time, she was in Los Angeles visiting a contractor with some administrative officers and her boss. There were five of them in all. They had an appointment with one of the magicians in the city who was rehearsing with a pair of performers at the time: a well-known couple who occupied center stage at the largest magic shows in Vegas and often appeared on TV.

Jonna and her group were watching the couple try out a new piece of equipment that allowed the female half of the couple to fly. Or to appear to fly. Once they were satisfied with their progress, the couple walked over to Jonna and her circle, along with the contractor. They introduced themselves to the visitors from

Washington and stood and chatted briefly, and then they walked back to the equipment.

The contractor turned to the group. "Check your pockets," he said with a wry smile. Two of the men discovered to their horror that their wallets were gone.

"Watches?" the contractor continued. Two watches were gone. They all looked at each other in amazement.

"Belts?" the contractor added with a laugh as he took Jonna by the arm and led her back to the equipment for a closer examination. Looking over her shoulder, Jonna saw her boss, Chuck, fumbling under his suit coat. His belt was missing! Like child pickpockets in a Charles Dickens story, they had stripped the group of their valuables, and nobody had felt a thing or heard a bell. It was an alarming and humbling lesson of the power of sleight of hand.

After perfecting the JIB, Josh had been brought out to Washington a few years later in order to put on a magic show at headquarters. It may seem humorous to think of the CIA putting on a magic show for staff members inside Langley, but that is exactly what happened. The Headquarters Building has a small theater known as the Bubble, and Josh took center stage to demonstrate a trick called the Origami Illusion. It was the perfect way for Josh to illustrate the power of concealment. After all, if he could make a person disappear right in front of an audience trying hard to spot the illusion, then we could certainly do something very similar on the streets of Moscow while being hounded by a KGB surveillance team.

The trick involved Josh wheeling out a long table upon which sat a small box, about two feet by two feet. Josh then proceeded to unfold the box in sections until it was long enough and high enough for his assistant, his girlfriend at the time, to climb in. The box was only just big enough to conceal her, making what followed seem impossible. After spinning the table in a circle to establish that there was no hidden trap door, Josh then proceeded to fold the box back up until it reached its original two-foot-by-two-foot dimensions. He completed the illusion by sticking three swords through the top and sides of the box.

The audience, consisting of case officers, OTS techs, and a host of other CIA personnel, sat in hushed silence as they waited to see what was going to happen next. Josh removed the swords and reopened the box by flipping out the various sections so that the box became large enough again to fit a person. Then his assistant magically popped up out of the box, and as if that weren't enough, she had changed from a simple dress into an Asian floral print and was now wearing a Japanese-style mask. The two of them took a bow, and the theater erupted into applause.

A little later, Josh built another device known as the Knife Board for one of our TOPS officers to illustrate the power of misdirection. Josh would stand about twenty feet away from a large wooden backdrop with a balloon attached to it. Using his upstage hand, the one away from the audience, he would then proceed to toss three throwing knives at the balloon. The first one would miss entirely. The second would appear to graze the balloon and make it move, and then, finally, the third would pop the balloon.

The trick was in the fact that Josh never actually threw any of the knives, even though it looked and sounded as if he had. Instead he would pretend to throw the blades horizontally, while in actuality he was embedding them into a piece of wood on the floor near his feet. At the same time, using a small button, he would electronically pop the fake knives out from the base of the board with the balloon.

When the trick was done right, the audience would never know, because their eyes would naturally follow the imaginary flight of the blades. All that was needed was the thunk of the knives hitting the wood, and their minds would fill in the rest. Essentially the trick depended on the magician being able to anticipate what the audience would be thinking so that he or she could then manipulate their expectation. It was the perfect kind of trick because it could be performed by a relative novice, and it showed how people's minds could be used against them.

Josh's career in magic began back in the 1950s. He had grown up in Kansas, the son of a schoolteacher. As a kid, Josh spent his time hanging around the local magic shop. One day he happened to meet the star of a magic show on local TV and discovered that the magician was looking for an assistant. Josh had a mechanical mind and often enjoyed messing around in the garage, putting things together and taking them apart. The idea of apprenticing to a "famous" magician seemed too good to pass up, so he volunteered to help out on weekends. As he was only fourteen at the time, the magician's wife had to pick him up from school and drive him to the workshop. The magician had a little kit of tricks that he sold to department stores, and Josh quickly became adept at putting it together.

Eventually, the magician got a contract with a major network, and Josh followed him out to Los Angeles in the early 1960s, when he was just twenty-one years old. In the beginning, he worked alongside a team of other assistants, but eventually, as he grew more experienced, Josh was given more freedom to work on his own. Each week the show would have one big illusion as a final act, and the first thing Josh ever built was one of these tricks in which he had to figure out a way to make a full-size elephant disappear. He came up with the concept of putting the cage on the back of a truck and then designed it so that the elephant could walk in the back and then "disappear" by walking unseen out the side. It worked perfectly and was a huge hit with the audience.

Josh stayed with the magician for about ten years before he branched out on his own. By the time Chambers approached him during the 1970s, Josh had become a leading figure in the industry, working on films and TV shows, for a variety of professional magicians, and even for rock stars anxious to up their theatrical performances. He was extremely successful, which made the fact that he had agreed to help us out all the more incredible. He didn't do it for the fame or the money; in fact, he knew that none of the things he built would ever be used on a stage before an adoring public, but he did it anyway out of a sense of duty and devotion to his country. And now here he was, about to enter the belly of the beast itself: Moscow.

After his plane had finally touched down at Sheremetyevo Airport, Josh followed the disembarking passengers as they made their way across the frigid tarmac and toward the terminal. Inside, a series of lines snaked their way through passport control, and Josh took his place among them. The mood was solemn, the room lit by dim overhead lights that buzzed like bug zappers. It suddenly occurred to him that having an official passport might not be such a good thing. Would they single him out? He told himself to remain calm; after all, he had only just arrived and so hadn't done anything yet. When his turn came, he slid his passport over to the stern-looking guard who sat perched inside his Plexiglas cubicle. The guard gave him an icy stare, and all Josh could think to do was to smile politely. The moment seemed to last forever, until finally the guard stamped his passport and waved him through.

One of our TOPS officers, Luke Swisher, was waiting for Josh out by the curb. Luke fit the mold of the younger crowd that had joined the CIA at that time—longer hair, a bit of a dreamer, anxious to push the limits, but operationally sound. Jack had personally requested that Luke join him in Moscow for just that reason. What the station needed now were innovators, men and women who were not afraid to think outside the box.

Josh had met Luke back in Washington, and he was relieved to see a familiar face. The magician had been given an apartment at the old US embassy, but rather than bring him straight there, Luke took him on a little tour of Moscow first. The two went to see Red Square and then to a department store. Of course, it wasn't just a sightseeing tour but an opportunity for Josh to witness the KGB surveillance teams in action. Several cars slid in behind them as they drove away from the airport, and Josh was amazed by how clumsily they attempted to keep pace. The cars didn't even try to hide the fact that they were following them. It was the same when he and Luke stepped foot inside the GUM department store. *Good god*, Josh thought, *they're everywhere*.

When they got to the embassy, Luke took Josh up to the Bubble so that he could meet with the chief of station. Jack was delighted to see the magician and thanked him for coming out. Since the two of them had talked in Washington a year earlier, it seemed that problems at the embassy had only gotten worse. By this time, the Lonetree scandal had broken, and headquarters was concerned that the KGB had been able to penetrate the Moscow Station. As a result, Jack had been forced to pack everything up, even the furniture, and send it back to Langley. The KGB had also seemed to step up their surveillance, and several officers at the station were getting nervous and aborting missions because they couldn't get black. It was almost as if the surveillance teams knew ahead of time where we were going to be.

Jack reiterated the fact that he was hoping Josh might be able to work out new scenarios for getting out of the embassy without alerting the surveillance teams. Jack said, "Maybe some magic is exactly what we need."

The following day, Josh took a tour of the embassy and was shocked by what he found. Normally a building had security to keep people out, but in this case, the security was there to keep tabs on the people living inside, like Big Brother. Josh was amazed to see that there were even cameras in the parking garage. In addition, there were any number of areas that might be used by a KGB agent to try to sneak in, such as air ducts and other crawl spaces. As an expert in concealment, Josh was able to explain that the human body was small enough to fit into a space as small as nine inches.

At this point, the NOB was still in the process of being built, and Josh took note of the construction equipment lying around, all of which could be used to set up a potential illusion. The key, he knew, was to find something that the Soviets were familiar with, an object that they would see day in and day out. He could build the most beautiful device in the world, but if it stood out, it would only serve to draw attention. And then, as he entered the garage, he saw what he was looking for: a pile of nearly thirty dollies lying in the corner. They were the two-wheeled and four-wheeled kind that were typically used to unload goods off a delivery van. The KGB wouldn't think twice about seeing them;

however, if configured properly, they could be modified in such a way as to conceal a person who might then be wheeled out.

This was a variation on a trick that Josh had learned early on as an apprentice. The trick involved a glass box—two feet wide, two feet deep, and four feet high—that sat on a table. The magician began the illusion by rolling the table out onto the stage to show that the box was empty and would then spin it around and cover the cube with a cloth. After a few seconds, the cloth would then be pulled away, revealing a woman inside the cube. In reality, the woman had been hiding in the table the whole time. Even though it seemed as if there wasn't enough space for her to fit, the table had been built in such a way as to make it appear thin, when it actually contained a hidden compartment. The compartment wasn't huge, but it was just large enough to conceal the woman and so allow her to stay hidden.

Josh had thought about building a device of some kind that could conceal a person in a similar way, but since this wouldn't be for a magic trick but an operation, the item would have to be believable, something that had a real-world purpose. The dollies were also perfect because they could be loaded up with any number of different items. You could even put a refrigerator on them or pieces of luggage or boxes, even crates of soft drinks or beer. You would only need to find a moment in which the individual could be placed within the hidden compartment and wheeled out. If done right, you could even use real cans of soda so that if the dolly was inspected, it would pass muster. It was an ingenious idea, really, and something that only an expert in concealment would think of.

Josh would spend nearly two weeks in the Soviet capital. After touring the inside of the embassy, he was asked to examine the antennae on the roof to see if he could come up with a way to camouflage them so that the Russians wouldn't be able to discern their purpose. At our request, Luke also took him out to the American dacha just outside of Moscow. We had floated an idea of using the dacha as a launching point for an operational outing, so we asked him to examine every nook and cranny of the facility, including the playground equipment. We wanted to know if it might be possible to construct something that could allow an officer to hide among the equipment so that he or she could sneak away later once everyone else had gone back into the city. Since we were certain that the grounds were swept by Soviet militia, it was thought that it might be possible to modify the playground equipment in such a way as to create a hidden cavity.

During his time in Moscow, Josh was given a map and told to see as much of the city as he could. At first, the prospect of wandering the streets of Moscow alone terrified him; however, he soon found that the Soviet citizens were wary of foreigners and kept to themselves. If anything, he was shocked at the amount of despair he saw in the people around him, who were expected to stand in line for hours just to buy basic goods. The air was heavy, and it seemed that everywhere you went, there were eyes prying into your business. It felt oppressive, like being covered by a thick blanket on a warm day.

There was also the KGB surveillance to contend with, but over time, they seemed to lose interest in Josh—that is, until the very last day of his trip. Just before he was scheduled to leave, Josh went to a consignment store with Luke. Josh knew a lot about clocks, and Luke was hoping to get advice about purchasing one. Josh recalls that a surveillance team followed them into the store and that any time he picked up a clock to examine it, the KGB would pounce on the object the moment he placed it back on the shelf. It would have been humorous if the looks on the men's faces hadn't been so deadly serious. After that, Josh figured it might be better just to point and not actually touch anything.

When Luke dropped him off at the airport the next day, Josh was expecting to be jumped at any moment. By this point, he was exhausted; he hadn't seen the sun once on his trip and was anxious to get back to his workshop in Southern California. That was, of course, if the Soviets let him leave. All throughout the drive, he had been fretting about what might happen to him at the airport. Surely the KGB would have seen him poking around the embassy and would single him out. Would they haul him out of line or throw him into a cell to interrogate him?

As it turned out, the answer to both of those questions was no. However, even after he had made it through the passport controls, Josh still expected to be machine-gunned down on the tarmac. And it wasn't until the plane actually began its ascent and punched through the gray to emerge once again into the brilliant blue overhead that he was finally able to breathe a sigh of relief.[1]

★   ★   ★

Around the same time that Josh was visiting Moscow, a team of individuals within OTS was also working on coming up with new strategies to get our people out of the embassy undetected.

One scenario involved an apartment escape using a contraption that would allow an individual to rapidly rappel down an apartment building and return up the rope using an ascension device, which had fondly been nicknamed the Spiderman. The device relied on a water-filled bladder in the apartment, which was used to assist the officer in rapidly descending or ascending along the outside of the building without the guards stationed at the gate to the compound being aware that anything had happened.

Another concept was a variation on the Murphy bed, except that we wanted to insert an automobile in place of the mattress and box springs, resulting in a Murphy car—one that could be folded up against a wall and hidden by the cabinetry surrounding it. It was a novel idea, but in the end, it proved to be totally impractical.

A third involved creating a "capture van," a small truck that could quickly lower a ramp so that one of our station cars could drive up into it and disappear from the roadway.

We were also looking at a van escape, which involved the use of a compartmented cavity in a van or even the ability to instantly change the color and license plates of our cars with the touch of a button.

There was also talk of having the Seabees construct a room in the parking garage of the embassy that would be designed to look square but that would actually conceal a hidden compartment. The space between the apparent wall and the real wall would be used to conceal a person or persons until we could move them out of our embassy.

By this time in my career, I'd been promoted to deputy chief of the Graphics and Identity Transformation Group, and although Moscow wasn't my only responsibility, I still took a keen interest in the city. Perhaps it had to do with the fact that I had spent so much time and energy working on the Moscow Rules, including the JIB, ID transfer, and DOTR. Or maybe it was because I considered Jack to be a friend. Either way, when I heard that Howard had sold us out to the KGB, I took it personally.

For this reason, when Jack asked me to come out to Moscow during the summer of 1988, I didn't hesitate. I had been working with Josh and a handful of techs over the past few months in order to perfect some of the techniques that the magician had come up with on his recent trip to Moscow. This included a prototype of one of the dollies, which we had tested out on the streets of Washington, and Jack was keen to see our results. Additionally, the KGB had begun to employ a new tactic that was causing considerable damage to the station's ability to run operations. I'd heard from a friend that everyone was on edge. Jack was hoping that I could come out and do another survey in order to help break the stalemate.

As I had done on my previous trip, I spent some time walking around the city to get myself reacquainted. Quite frankly, I was surprised by the changes that I saw. It took just one stroll through the Arbat pedestrian mall to see that *glasnost* was in full swing. I passed thousands of citizens decked out in Western fashions and even saw some privately owned restaurants that didn't require any Party connections to get a table. The most surprising thing, however, was the number of subversive journals and magazines that were available, a lot of them highlighting the corrosive nature of the Soviet regime. They could be picked up from vendors selling them right on the street, something that would have been unheard of during the mid-1970s.

Granted, it was still a long way off from Paris or London, but I found it hard to believe that the regime would still be able to bottle up the Muscovites as it had done in the past. And if it still could, it wouldn't be able to do so for much longer. It made me wonder about this new tactic that the KGB was using to frustrate the station. In a more open society, wouldn't the KGB be less effective? I was about to find out.

Jack would explain everything the following day, when the two of us finally had a chance to sit down in the Bubble and talk. As it turned out, the KGB hadn't tried to fight the new openness that was making headway through Russia at that time but instead used it to their advantage by flooding the Moscow Station with double agents. It was a rather ingenious strategy that tied up the case officers and had them chasing ghosts. Jack had gotten wind of the tactic when he had run into a KGB officer on the *Red Arrow* express during the spring of the previous year.

The *Red Arrow* was a popular overnight train from Moscow to Leningrad. Jack had been on the train with his family when he had left their compartment to grab a smoke. He had decided to walk back to the caboose when a dark-haired Russian man with a military bearing approached him. Jack could instantly tell that the man was KGB. The man said nothing, however, as he handed Jack an envelope and then walked quickly away.[2]

Jack waited until he was safely inside the CIA's Leningrad office before opening the envelope. As it turned out, not only had he been right that the man was a member of the KGB, but the young Russian was actually Jack's KGB case officer. And in order to prove it, the man had included a surveillance photo of Jack and his wife taken on the day that Jack had arrived in Russia to take charge of the station. In addition to the photo, the KGB officer had included a note saying that he was unhappy with the Soviet government and that he hoped to one day defect to the United States; however, for the time being, he would be happy to spy on behalf of America.[3]

Jack was beyond thrilled by this information. Ever since he'd returned to Moscow, he'd been forced to deal with one setback after another, and morale was running dangerously low at the station. But if Jack could show some positive results, that might help to turn things around.

Jack's initial excitement began to wane, however, after he met with the KGB officer a second time and heard what he had to say. As it turned out, the KGB had decided to employ a new strategy that would involve using a series of double agents with the sole purpose of trying to confuse the station. The concept was simple: overwhelm the CIA with so many new volunteers that they couldn't possibly have enough time to properly vet them all, let alone run them. This would also have the added effect of prompting the CIA to turn away legitimate volunteers. The KGB officer, who would eventually be given the code name GTPROLOGUE, had even provided a list that contained the names of the first double agents.[4]

Headquarters had initially been skeptical about the validity of GTPROLOGUE's story. It seemed almost too fantastical to believe. Did the KGB have the resources to pull off such an operation? However, a few weeks before I was to come out to Moscow, the first man on the list, a Soviet engineer whom GTPROLOGUE had indicated was a KGB double agent, had dutifully appeared, as if on cue.

This immediately put Jack in a quandary. Thanks to the information passed along by GTPROLOGUE, Jack was certain that the engineer was a dangle. However, if he turned the man away out of hand, it might alert the KGB that he knew about their plans. This meant that he would have to act as if the man were a legitimate agent and assign a case officer to run him, meaning that he would have less time to dedicate to other cases. It was the exact scenario that the KGB had hoped to create.

By the time I had arrived for my survey, the Moscow Station was running nearly half a dozen of these double agents, and Jack was getting frustrated. To make matters worse, the latest version of the SRR-100 had been seemingly picking up signals every time one of our case officers went out on an operation, lending credence to the belief that the KGB was now using some kind of ultrasecret ghost surveillance that was allowing them to remain unseen. It was clear that Jack was tired of playing the KGB's game. He wanted to be aggressive, to go on the attack. But the question was, how?

I spent the next few days talking to various case officers while taking excursions around the city. I also gave a lot of thought to Jack's predicament. In the past, Jack and I had been able to hone the technique of ID transfer to the level of a fine art. So much so that even after case officers like Mike Sellers had been rolled up, the KGB still had no idea how they'd been able to get black. The ingeniousness of the tactic rested on the fact that we'd been able to create a group of persons of little interest who could be used as cover for our more covert officers. But if the KGB had caught on to our little trick, the tactic would be worthless. Had the KGB somehow been able to identify these persons of little interest? If so, it might be able to explain why our case officers were having trouble getting black.

On the Fourth of July, everybody headed out to the embassy dacha for the traditional American Independence Day celebration. We drove out in a sort of convoy to Serebryani Bor, along the well-marked roads, with Soviet militiamen positioned occasionally along the route and at the gatehouse to ensure that nobody got lost or strayed too far off the prescribed path. There were guards at the dacha itself; security was foremost in the KGB's mind. Once we were present and accounted for, the afternoon began with a short talk by a senior embassy staffer and a promise of a picnic lunch to follow.

About twenty miles outside of Moscow, the embassy dacha, a two-story country house, or bungalow, as the Russians preferred to call their dachas, seemed like another place in time. Nestled on several acres in stands of pine and birch, the compound contained both a small cottage and a larger house. In the summer, it was the site of Camp Wocsom, "Moscow" spelled backward, and served as a summer day camp for American children. The Moskva River was only about two minutes away.

It was during the talk that I first noticed the noise coming from the river. I moved to the back of the crowd in order to get a better view. And what I saw changed everything.

Prior to the PNG War, there were more than 260 Soviet Nationals working in the US embassy in Moscow providing support. When these FSN employees were kicked out during the fall and winter of 1986, it had caused a massive logjam at the embassy. At first, it was thought that after the diplomatic crisis had passed, the FSNs would come back to the embassy and things would return to the way they once were. However, after the events of the Marine Corps guard scandals, coming as they did during the same time period as the Moscow embassy construction scandal, Congress decided that the matter was closed and no Soviet employees would work at our missions in Moscow and Leningrad. It was also around this time that Ambassador Hartman departed his post, to be replaced by Ambassador Matlock, who brought with him a new point of view regarding security.[5]

And so rather than welcome the Soviets back into the US embassy, a firm was hired in Los Angeles to help "Americanize" the workforce at our embassy, which it did by launching a unique nationwide recruiting campaign for employees, ranging from car mechanics and plumbers to electricians and food service workers. The first batch of US citizens began to arrive in Moscow in mid-January 1987, and by March, the new staffing was complete. A California firm, Pacific Architects and Engineers Inc. (PA&E), said that there was no lack of interest in these jobs; the number of applicants had run into the thousands. These PA&E employees were young, adventurous, and, as it turned out, totally unpredictable.[6]

In fact, the noise that had caught my attention at the dacha was coming from a group of new PA&E employees who had just arrived at the party. However, in true iconoclast style, these young Americans hadn't taken the highway like proper diplomats would. They arrived at the dacha by paddling a boat down the river. Loud and raucous, they were singing and laughing as they made their way to shore. The Soviet guards were as startled as I was. It was as if the rules had been broken. This group, approximately ten newly arrived American civilian employees, had simply stepped out of the security perimeter and had not been challenged.

But that was not all.

One of the new people approaching the dacha was a young woman with a head of hair the likes of which I had never seen. It was curly—frizzy, in fact—and red with an orange cast. It was shoulder length, and the effect when you first saw her was that the sun might be setting behind her. It was a halo and quite remarkable.

It was then, as I looked at that beautiful head of hair while this young group of Americans came charging up from the river hoisting cans of beer, that it hit me. If the KGB was going to try to overwhelm us, then we could do the same thing right back at them. Thanks to the PA&E employees, the Moscow Station would now have hundreds of new scenarios to use for potential ID transfers. A smile lit my face as I thought about how we were going to be able to overwhelm the KGB's senses with an army of young Americans marching through the streets of Moscow. I knew my good friend John Chambers would appreciate the irony. I turned back to the party to find Jack. The Moscow Rules were about to evolve once again, and the KGB didn't stand a chance.

EPILOGUE

Years later, we can view the devastation of the Year of the Spy in 1985 and the aftermath it wreaked on the CIA station in Moscow. The majority of Soviet citizens working for us had been arrested and executed, most of them betrayed by Americans inside the intelligence community. It would seem, on the face of it, that our Moscow office had little more to lose. The trail of classified rubble left by Sergeant Clayton Lonetree and Ambassador Arthur Hartman, allowing the KGB access into our embassy premises and protecting a KGB presence working in our facilities, respectively, had resulted in shattering the infrastructure within which we worked.

However, just four years later, 1989 was the year that changed the world. By then, Russia's borders had been pushed back, undoing more than three hundred years of czarist and Soviet advances toward the West. America's euphoria over détente had initially turned sour, creating doubt about Gorbachev's intentions, but as events unfolded, skepticism turned to hope. The Berlin Wall, the paramount symbol of the Cold War and the division of Europe, fell in 1989. Communism had collapsed in Eastern Europe, and the USSR withdrew its last soldier from Afghanistan.

The war, the Cold War, was over. Once Gorbachev began undermining the Soviet system, a bureaucracy that could exist only by watching its opponents through the cross hairs of a gunsight, only by digging deeper and stronger defenses, only by feverishly competing for military superiority, the Soviet Union's days were finished.[1] It was to be the last great drama of the Cold War: the collapse of communism in the Soviet Union and Eastern

Europe. And you can argue that the intelligence provided by CIA's stellar agents in Moscow paved the way, cosseted and protected by the CIA's ever-changing, ever-evolving Moscow Rules.

TRIGON's window into the machinations of the Soviet *nomenklatura* provided insights into Soviet intentions and capabilities, which were at the heart of the CIA's mission. It gave us insight into policy decisions and political processes that enabled America to anticipate negotiating positions on a range of arms-limitation talks that were taking place in the 1980s. Understanding the Soviets' bargaining tools and getting a peek at the cards in their hand during the 1970s and 1980s, when SALT I and SALT II were being negotiated, was invaluable.

Tolkachev's contribution to the end of the Cold War was wide and deep. His amazing haul of documents, blueprints, and diagrams was made available to a very few strategically positioned people in Washington. It was used to terminate or reorient our US military research and development programs. Tolkachev was providing the United States with a road map for compromising and defeating critical Soviet weapons systems, primarily their radar on the ground, which defended them from attack, and the radar on warplanes, which gave them the ability to attack others.[2]

TRIGON and Tolkachev and their handlers were never detected by the KGB. Moscow Station's painstaking tradecraft and the careful use of the Moscow Rules—ID transfer, street disguises, surveillance detection runs, the SRR-100 radio monitors, the JIB, subminiature cameras, working in the gap, and deep-cover case officers—all were in support of collecting the intelligence that helped win the Cold War.

Gina Haspel, CIA director, said recently, "Within the Intelligence Community, CIA is the keeper of the human intelligence mission. Technical forms of collection are vital, but a good human source is unique and can deliver decisive intelligence on our adversaries' secrets—even their intent."[3]

Human-source intelligence was then and is now indispensable to national security. As long as it is necessary to know an adversary—to steal secrets, uncover intentions, and crack open safes—it will be essential to recruit agents who can conquer their fear and cross over to the other side. It will be necessary to look them in the eye, earn their trust, calm their anxiety, and share their peril.[4]

As Jim Steinmeyer, one of my favorite illusionists and magical thinkers in that amazing magical community in Los Angeles, said:

> In Moscow the CIA found the ultimate challenge, the spotlight that magicians dread. Moscow's constant surveillance, listening, watching and trailing left barely any room for intelligence gathering. Parts of CIA's . . . operations in Moscow were the ultimate example of understanding the audience. KGB officers were in trouble if they lost track of a CIA operative. By giving the impression that the tail was successful, by "keeping them comfortable," operatives gained precious moments to accomplish their goals. If the KGB was burning them, they had to deceive them into thinking they were doing their job perfectly—just as a magician concedes, "you got me buddy," and then waits for the audience to drop its guard.[5]

★   ★   ★

As we look back through these chapters, we are struck by the threads that run through the stories and the techniques and technologies intertwined within the Moscow Rules and their evolution. The stories are not new, but spelling out the hard work behind them, the care and precision and the innovation that went into finding solutions, was not unlike untying a cord that is fastened into hundreds of gnarled knots. The case officers of SE Division and the technical arm of the CIA, as embodied by OTS and its sister offices in the Directorate of Science and Technology, came together to understand the problems and to implement or, more often, invent the solution.

My approach, and that of my friends and colleagues in Los Angeles, was based on my grounding in the magical performances that I enjoyed so much on the various stages around the world, be they in a theater or on the streets of some foreign capital. The constant coaching and the mentoring in the magician's tools that I first found in Mulholland's book and later through Haviland Smith were the stepping-stones to the new, ever-evolving Moscow Rules.

Bob Wallace, a DO case officer and a former director of OTS, recounts in his book *Spycraft,* coauthored with Keith Melton, a conversation with an old hand in SE Division, John Aalto. "Do you have any concept of what OTS and its predecessor, the Technical Services Division, accomplished for operations? I tell you," Aalto began, "it is because of the techs and TSD that we in Soviet operations eventually won the intelligence war against the KGB in Moscow. And to my knowledge, no one has ever recorded that story, officially or unofficially."[6]

Writing this book gave us an opportunity to look more broadly at the CIA's history in Moscow and in Russia as seen through the lens of the Moscow Rules. We saw how the CIA was able to rise to the occasion, tackling each new operational situation with innovation and positive energy, with officers who didn't back down, even though they were confronted by nearly impossible conditions and a determined enemy. We could almost visualize it as a game, the Great Game, with each side playing both offense and defense. The CIA was always able to respond with imagination and technological improvisation, fashioning solutions to any challenges that came our way. Desperation is the mother of invention? Well, we were certainly desperate on occasion.

The game has changed. It has become more of a contact sport, rougher, the rules more elastic, the prize more precious. Vladimir Putin's attempts to manipulate the US government have broadened the playing field and taken the game into new territory—the US political arena. His goal of destabilizing the West has unleashed a new cadre of Russian intelligence officers with tools we could not have imagined. We are wading into a new and dangerous territory.

The history of the Moscow Rules gives us confidence that no matter what threat the Russians present to our intelligence community today, no matter how those challenges are packaged, the CIA will be ready. They have at their disposal the ability to innovate, to devise countermeasures, and to retaliate in kind. This new Cold War 2.0 is predicated on the same goals that we know so well. We have prevailed in the past, and we see no reason to think that the intelligence community will not be ready for whatever may come their way.

To quote William Faulkner, who is a favorite of mine: "The past is never dead. It's not even past."

ACKNOWLEDGMENTS

This book, which began as a straightforward tale of espionage, took many paths in order to reach publication, not the least of which was passing through the hurdles of the CIA's own Publication Review Board (PRB). The pleasure we take in its publication is difficult to put into words. This is Tony Mendez's fourth book, and his last, as the Parkinson's disease that has been shadowing him for the last ten years moves into a more pronounced phase. The race was joined with the PRB one more time, but in the final instance, they helped us over the finish line. For that we offer our thanks.

As with most books, there were many helping hands along the way. Our longtime agent, Christy Fletcher, was invaluable in the process, as was her assistant Alyssa Taylor, always on the other end of the line or on the screen, offering advice when needed. We have always considered ourselves lucky to have Christy representing us, and she proved once again that she is worth her weight in gold.

Our editor, Ben Adams, and the rest of the team at PublicAffairs—Kristina Fazzalaro, Lindsay Fradkoff, Miguel Cervantes, and Clive Priddle—provided the backing and support that helped us bring the book in on time and in good order. The jacket design, copyediting, and indexing were areas as foreign to us as another language and were handled with aplomb by a team including Melissa Raymond, Megan Schindele, and Pete Garceau.

Every book we have written has relied on tens if not hundreds of inputs from our friends and colleagues in the intelligence community. Rather than try to call them out with pseudonyms or clever rearrangements of their names or initials, we would like very much to simply give them a group nod, as they are rather well represented in the text, where they can find themselves without guidance and point out their accomplishments to their families and friends. If their covers allow, that is. Their help indeed flowed into our endeavor in an endless stream. Nobody said no. For that we thank you all.

We did not call out in the book what a group of stars we were writing about. Tony Mendez was one of three CIA Trailblazers from the Office of Technical Service in 1997 when the CIA chose fifty officers from the Agency's first fifty years who, by their actions, example, innovations, or initiative, took the CIA in important new directions and helped the shape the Agency's history. The two other OTS officers were David Coffey and Paul Howe. Paul engineered the CIA's single greatest advance in operational photography: the Tropel camera, which plays a pivotal role in our tale.

The Trailblazer award was not given every year, but it has continued to be awarded to those CIA officers who fit the criteria. And so in 2006, George Methlie, the OTS battery engineer mentioned in this book, was presented with the award. Methlie also has one of three prestigious CIA schools named after him.

In 2009, John Guilsher, the DO case officer who handled Tolkachev, was selected as a Trailblazer.

And in 2010, Jack Downing, the former deputy chief and the chief of station, Moscow, received the Trailblazer award. Jack Downing retired from the CIA in 1995, and at that time, he was presented with a lasting memory of his time in Moscow: a coffee table book that had been printed just for him by the Russians. This very small, private edition (you would have to assume that there were a few others handed out, possibly one for Rem Krassilnikov and perhaps the current head of the KGB Seventh Directorate) with a print run of less than a dozen, consisted entirely of photographs of Jack under surveillance on the streets of Moscow—in his car and on foot—while he was first deputy chief and then chief of station, Moscow.

Over the years only seventy-three Trailblazer awards have been given out of what must have been hundreds of thousands of people who were eligible. Five of them are important to our story. Over those same twenty-one years, three more OTS officers have been so honored. They were stars, every one of them, as were Penkovsky, Ogorodnik, and Tolkachev. It was an honor to tell their stories.

Disclaimer

This does not constitute an official release of CIA information. All statements of fact, opinion, or analysis expressed are those of the author(s) and do not reflect the official positions or views of the Central Intelligence Agency (CIA) or any other US government agency. Nothing in the contents should be construed as asserting or implying US government authentication of information or CIA endorsement of the authors' views. This material has been reviewed solely for classification.

NOTES

Introduction

1. Alec Luhn, "US Protests over Russian 'Harassment' as Diplomats Allegedly Given Date Rape Drug," *Guardian*, October 4, 2016.

2. Office of the Director of National Intelligence, "Background to 'Assessing Russian Activities and Intentions in Recent US Elections': The Analytic Process and Cyber Incident Attribution," January 6, 2017, www.dni.gov/files/documents/ICA_2017_01.pdf.

3. Phillip Rucker, Carol Morello, and John Hudson, "Trump Administration Expels 60 Russian Officers, Shuts Seattle Consulate in Response to Attack on Former Spy in Britain," *Washington Post*, March 26, 2018.

Chapter 1

1. Robert Wallace and H. Keith Melton, *Spycraft: The Secret History of the CIA's Spytechs, from Communism to Al-Qaeda* (New York: Dutton, 2008), 29.

2. Ibid., 34.

3. Jerold L. Schecter and Peter S. Deriabin, *The Spy Who Saved the World: How a Soviet Colonel Changed the Course of the Cold War* (New York: Scribner, 1992).

4. Ibid., 262.

5. "The Capture and Execution of Colonel Penkovsky, 1963," News and Information, Central Intelligence Agency, last modified April 30, 2013, www.cia.gov/news-information/featured-story-archive/2010 -featured-story-archive/colonel-penkovsky.html.

6. Charles E. Lathrop, *The Literary Spy: The Ultimate Source for Quotations on Espionage and Intelligence* (New Haven, CT: Yale University Press, 2004), 177.

7. Oleg Kalugin with Fen Montaigne, *The First Directorate* (New York: St. Martin's Press), Chapter 6.

8. Robert Gates, *From the Shadows: The Ultimate Insider's Story of Five Presidents and How They Won the Cold War* (New York: Simon & Schuster, 1996), 97.

9. Oleg Penkovsky, *The Penkovsky Papers,* trans. Peter Deriabin (New York: Doubleday, 1965), 12.

10. Ibid., 14.

Chapter 2

1. Robert Wallace and H. Keith Melton, *Spycraft: The Secret History of the CIA's Spytechs, from Communism to Al-Qaeda* (New York: Dutton, 2008), 12.

2. Tom Mangold, *Cold Warrior: James Jesus Angleton, the CIA's Master Spy Hunter* (New York: Simon & Schuster, 1991), 43.

3. Ibid., 54.

4. Ibid., 76.

5. Jonathan Haslam, *Near and Distant Neighbors: A New History of Soviet Intelligence* (New York: Farrar, Straus and Giroux, 2015), 50.

6. Milton Bearden and James Risen, *The Main Enemy: The Inside Story of the CIA's Final Showdown with the KGB* (New York: Random House, 2003), 35.

7. Ibid.

8. Hayden Peake, "Intelligence Officer's Bookshelf," *Studies in Intelligence* 55, no. 4 (December 2011): 43.

9. Ibid., 38.

10. Ibid., 37.

11. Sandra Grimes and Jeanne Vertefeuille, *Circle of Treason: A CIA Account of Traitor Aldrich Ames and the Men He Betrayed* (Annapolis, MD: Naval Institute Press, 2012), 24.

12. David E. Hoffman, *The Billion Dollar Spy: A True Story of Cold War Espionage and Betrayal* (New York: Doubleday, 2015), 33.

13. Ibid., 21.

14. Ibid., 35.

15. Ibid.

16. Ibid.

Chapter 3

1. Milton Bearden and James Risen, *The Main Enemy: The Inside Story of the CIA's Final Showdown with the KGB* (New York: Random House, 2003), 16.

2. Martha Peterson, *The Widow Spy: My CIA Journey from the Jungles of Laos to Prison in Moscow* (Wilmington, NC: Red Canary, 2012), 119.

3. David E. Hoffman, *The Billion Dollar Spy: A True Story of Cold War Espionage and Betrayal* (New York: Doubleday, 2015), 25.

4. Bearden and Risen, *The Main Enemy,* 52.

5. Ibid.

6. Peterson, *Widow Spy,* 66.

7. Author interview with Peterson, December 28, 2017.

8. Peterson, *Widow Spy*, 125.

9. Ibid., 135.

10. Bearden and Risen, *The Main Enemy*, 52.

11. Peterson, *Widow Spy*, 164.

12. Ibid., 175.

13. Ibid., 174.

14. "TRIGON—Spies Passing in the Night," News and Information, Central Intelligence Agency, June 20, 2016, www.cia.gov/news-information/featured-story-archive/2016-featured-story-archive/trigon-spies-passing-in-the-night.html.

Chapter 4

1. Author interview with TOPS officer Ron, August 4, 2017.

2. Ron Kessler, "Revealing the CIA's Secrets," Newsmax, July 30, 2008, https://www.newsmax.com/ronaldkessler/revealing-cia-secrets/2009/12/12/id/341610.

Chapter 5

1. Gina Haspel, "The Missions and Ethos of CIA (Based on Selected Portions of the Official Remarks by CIA Director Gina Haspel at McConnell Center at the University of Louisville on 24 September 2018)," *Intelligencer: Journal of US Intelligence Studies* 24, no. 2 (Fall 2018): 23.

2. Jerold L. Schecter and Peter S. Deriabin, *The Spy Who Saved the World: How a Soviet Colonel Changed the Course of the Cold War* (New York: Scribner, 1992), 351.

3. Ibid., 20.

4. Sandra Grimes and Jeanne Vertefeuille, *Circle of Treason: A CIA Account of Traitor Aldrich Ames and the Men He Betrayed* (Annapolis, MD: Naval Institute Press, 2012), 45.

5. Martha Peterson, *The Widow Spy: My CIA Journey from the Jungles of Laos to Prison in Moscow* (Wilmington, NC: Red Canary, 2012), 184.

6. Ibid., 203.

7. Ibid., 206.

8. Ibid., 211.

9. Ibid., 214.

10. Ibid., 224.

11. Ibid., 241.

Chapter 6

1. Ben Macintyre, *A Spy Among Friends: Kim Philby and the Great Betrayal* (New York: Broadway Books, 2014), 123.

2. Katherine L. Herbig and Martin F. Wiskoff, "Espionage Against the United States by American Citizens 1947–2001," TRW Systems, July 2002.

3. Barry Royden, "Tolkachev: A Worthy Successor to Penkovsky," *Studies in Intelligence* 47, no. 3 (2003): 5.

4. David E. Hoffman, *The Billion Dollar Spy: A True Story of Cold War Espionage and Betrayal* (New York: Doubleday, 2015), 46.

5. Stansfield Turner, *Secrecy and Democracy: The CIA in Transition* (Boston: Houghton Mifflin, 1985), 104.

6. Christopher Moran, *Company Confessions, Secrets, Memoirs, and the CIA* (New York: Thomas Dunne Books, 2015).

7. Ibid., 169.

8. "The Embassy Moscow Fire of 1977," Moments in US Diplomatic History, https://adst.org/2014/08/the-embassy-moscow-fire-of-1977/.

9. "The US Embassy Moscow Fire of 1977," *Huffington Post* Blog, last modified December 6, 2017, https://www.huffingtonpost.com/adst/the-us-embassy-moscow-fir_b_8078818.html.

10. Ibid.

11. Steve Vogel, "Gardner R. Hathaway, CIA Chief of Counterintelligence, Dies at 88," *Washington Post*, November 26, 2013.

12. Author interview with TOPS officer Ron.

13. James Schumaker, "Moments in U.S. Diplomatic History: The Embassy Moscow Fire of 1977," Association for Diplomatic Studies & Training, August 2014, https://adst.org/2014/08/the-embassy-moscow-fire-of-1977/.

14. Ibid., 4.

15. T. Rees Shapiro, "Adm. Stansfield Turner, Who Led Major CIA Overhaul as Director of Central Intelligence, Dies at 94," *Washington Post*, January 18, 2018, https://www.washingtonpost.com/local/obituaries/adm-stansfield-turner-who-led-major-cia-overhaul-as-director-of-central-intelligence-dies-94/2018/01/18/eac46390-fc99-11e7-ad8c-ecbb62019393_story.html?utm_term=.44f16a0f815c.

16. Edward Jay Epstein, "Who Killed the CIA?: The Confessions of Stansfield Turner," October 1985, http://www.edwardjayepstein.com/archived/whokilled_print.htm.

17. Vogel, "Gardner R. Hathaway."

18. Royden, "Tolkachev: A Worthy Successor," 10.

Chapter 7

1. Barry Royden, "Tolkachev: A Worthy Successor to Penkovsky," *Studies in Intelligence* 47, no. 3 (2003): 18.

2. David E. Hoffman, *The Billion Dollar Spy: A True Story of Cold War Espionage and Betrayal* (New York: Doubleday, 2015), 188.

3. Ibid., 189.

4. Ibid., 54.

5. Ibid., 71.

6. Ibid., 67.

7. Royden, "Tolkachev: A Worthy Successor," 10.

8. Ibid., 12.

9. Ibid., 9.

10. Ibid., 10.

11. Ibid., 24.

12. Ibid., 19.

13. Hoffman, *Billion Dollar Spy*, 74.

14. Ibid., 78.

15. Ibid., 95.

16. Royden, "Tolkachev: A Worthy Successor," 22.

17. Ibid., 25.

18. Hoffman, *Billion Dollar Spy*, 156.

19. Ibid., 162–163.

20. Ibid., 149.

21. Ibid., 183.

22. Royden, "Tolkachev: A Worthy Successor," 26.

23. Ibid., 24.

Chapter 8

1. Robert Wallace and H. Keith Melton, *Spycraft: The Secret History of the CIA's Spytechs, from Communism to Al-Qaeda* (New York: Dutton, 2008), 139.

2. Ibid., 141.

3. James M. Olson, *Fair Play: The Moral Dilemmas of Spying* (Washington, DC: Potomac Books), 2.

4. Ibid., 10.

5. Wallace and Melton, *Spycraft*, 151.

6. Ibid.

7. David E. Hoffman, *The Billion Dollar Spy: A True Story of Cold War Espionage and Betrayal* (New York: Doubleday, 2015), 236.

8. Barry Royden, "Tolkachev: A Worthy Successor to Penkovsky," *Studies in Intelligence* 47, no. 3 (2003): 28.

9. Ibid., 27.

10. Ibid., 30.

11. Hoffman, *Billion Dollar Spy*, 235.

12. Ibid.

13. Royden, "Tolkachev: A Worthy Successor," 30.

14. Ibid., 18–19.

15. Milton Bearden and James Risen, *The Main Enemy: The Inside Story of the CIA's Final Showdown with the KGB* (New York: Random House, 2003), 45.

Chapter 9

1. David Wise, *The Spy Who Got Away: The Inside Story of Edward Lee Howard, the CIA Agent Who Betrayed His Country's Secrets and Escaped to Moscow* (New York: Random House, 1988), 199.

2. Ibid., 24.

3. Ibid., 23.

4. Ibid., 35.

5. Milton Bearden and James Risen, *The Main Enemy: The Inside Story of the CIA's Final Showdown with the KGB* (New York: Random House, 2003), 108–109.

6. Ibid., 110.

7. Wise, *The Spy Who Got Away*, 88.

8. David E. Hoffman, *The Billion Dollar Spy: A True Story of Cold War Espionage and Betrayal* (New York: Doubleday, 2015), 213.

9. Ibid., 133.

10. Ibid., 227.

11. Senate Select Committee on Intelligence, "An Assessment of the Aldrich H. Ames Espionage Case and Its Implications for US Intelligence, Part 1," November 1, 1994: 4.

12. Duane R. Clarridge, *A Spy for All Seasons: My Life in the CIA* (New York: Scribner, 1997).

13. Sandra Grimes and Jeanne Vertefeuille, *Circle of Treason: A CIA Account of Traitor Aldrich Ames and the Men He Betrayed* (Annapolis, MD: Naval Institute Press, 2012), 178.

14. SSC Committee, *Assessment*, 7.

15. Ibid., 10.

16. David Wise, *Nightmover: How Aldrich Ames Sold the CIA to the KGB for $4.6 Million* (New York: HarperCollins, 1995), 115.

17. Ibid., 118.

18. Ibid., 285.

19. Ibid., 297–298.

20. Bearden and Risen, *The Main Enemy*, 427.

21. Elaine Shannon, "Death of the Perfect Spy," *TIME*, June 24, 2001.

22. Bearden and Risen, *The Main Enemy*, 430.

23. Ibid., 435.

24. Victor Cherkashin and Gregory Feifer, *Spy Handler: Memoir of a KGB Officer—The True Story of the Man Who Recruited Robert Hanssen and Aldrich Ames* (New York: Basic Books, 2004), 230.

25. Ibid., 234.

26. Ibid., 247.

27. David Vise, "From Russia with Love," *Washington Post*, January 6, 2002.

Chapter 10

1. Milton Bearden and James Risen, *The Main Enemy: The Inside Story of the CIA's Final Showdown with the KGB* (New York: Random House, 2003), 128.

2. "Moscow, USSR (1984–1986)," Michael D. Sellers, John Carter Files website, accessed January 2019, http://mdsauthor.thejohncarter files.com/moscow-ussr-1984-1986.

3. Bearden and Risen, *The Main Enemy*, 210.

4. Ibid.

5. Ibid, 209–211.

6. Kevin Klose, "Ex-IBM Chairman Watson Chosen as Envoy to Moscow," *Washington Post*, June 18, 1979.

7. Emily Langer, "Arthur A. Hartman, US Ambassador to France and Soviet Union, Dies at 89," *Washington Post*, March 17, 2015.

8. Stephen Engelberg, "Departing US Envoy Criticizes Use of Young Marine Guards in Moscow," *New York Times*, March 31, 1987.

9. Richard Eder, "Man in the News: From Opera to Bolshoi: Arthur A Hartman," *New York Times*, August 22, 1981.

10. Sam Roberts, "Arthur A. Hartman, US Ambassador to Soviet Union, Dies at 89," *New York Times*, March 18, 2015.

11. Ron Kessler, *Moscow Station: How the KGB Penetrated the American Embassy* (New York: Charles Scribner's Sons, 1989), 11.

12. Ibid., 47.

13. Ibid., 112.

14. Ibid.

15. Engelberg, "Departing US Envoy Criticizes."

16. Maura Dolan, "Didn't Oppose Better Security, Ex-Envoy Says," *Los Angeles Times*, April 12, 1987.

17. Kessler, *Moscow Station*, 187.

18. Ibid., 47.

19. Ibid., 5

20. Ibid., 149.

21. Ibid., 43.

22. Langer, "Arthur A. Hartman."

23. Dolan, "Didn't Oppose Better Security."

24. Ibid.

25. Don Shannon, "Rep. Mica Says Blueprints Could Have Been Photographed: Breach Involving Shultz's Moscow Van Is Feared," *Los Angeles Times*, April 13, 1987.

26. Ibid.

27. Ibid.

28. Allan Mustard, "Recalling All-Purpose Duty in Russia," *Foreign Service Journal* 84, no. 5 (May 2007): 35–41.

29. Dolan, "Didn't Oppose Better Security."

30. Ibid.

31. Bearden and Risen, *The Main Enemy*, 616.

32. Mustard, "All Purpose Duty."

33. James R. Holbrook, *Moscow Memoir: An American Military Attaché in the USSR 1979–1981* (Bloomington, IN: AuthorHouse, 2018).

34. Mustard, "All Purpose Duty," 4.

35. Ibid.

36. David Grogan, "In Moscow, Donna Hartman—the US Ambassador's Wife—Proves a Good and Faithful Servant," *People*, November 17, 1986.

37. Mustard, "All Purpose Duty," 1.

38. Ibid., 2.

Chapter 11

1. Author interview with Josh, August 2017.

2. Milton Bearden and James Risen, *The Main Enemy: The Inside Story of the CIA's Final Showdown with the KGB* (New York: Random House, 2003), 1002.

3. Ibid., 1004.

4. Ibid., 1019.

5. Ron Kessler, *Moscow Station: How the KGB Penetrated the American Embassy* (New York: Charles Scribner's Sons, 1989), 262.

6. Jerry Cohen, "L.A. Firm Recruiting for Posts in Moscow: Americans Take Over Embassy Jobs," *Los Angeles Times*, December 28, 1986.

Epilogue

1. Benjamin B. Fischer, *At Cold War's End: US Intelligence on the Soviet Union and Eastern Europe, 1989–1991* (Washington, DC: CIA, 1999).

2. David E. Hoffman, *The Billion Dollar Spy: A True Story of Cold War Espionage and Betrayal* (New York: Doubleday, 2015), 120.

3. Gina Haspel, "The Missions and Ethos of CIA," *Intelligencer: Journal of US Intelligence Studies* 24, no. 2 (Fall 2018): 4.

4. Hoffman, *Billion Dollar Spy*, 255.

5. Jim Steinmeyer, review of *The Master of Disguise: My Secret Life in the CIA*, by Antonio Mendez, *Studies in Intelligence* 46, no. 1 (2002): 67–70, https://www.cia.gov/library/center-for-the-study-of-intelligence/csi-publications/csi-studies/studies/vol46no1/article09.html.

6. Robert Wallace and H. Keith Melton, *Spycraft: The Secret History of the CIA's Spytechs, from Communism to Al-Qaeda* (New York: Dutton, 2008), xix.

INDEX

ABOUT THE AUTHORS

Courtesy of the Authors

Jonna Mendez is a former chief of disguise with over twenty-five years of experience as a CIA officer working in Moscow and other denied areas. She participated in a number of training exercises, along with Tony, which ultimately led to the codification of the rules. She cowrote *Spy Dust* with her husband about their shared experience in Moscow during the twilight of the Cold War. Her work has been featured in the *Washington Post*, WIRED, NPR, the *New York Times*, and other places. Often cited for her expertise in the field, Jonna is a much-sought-after speaker and consultant.

Antonio (Tony) Mendez served in the CIA for twenty-five years and was a highly decorated CIA officer, one of the top fifty officers in its first fifty years. He received the Intelligence Star for Valor for the ARGO operation, the story of which was told in the 2013 movie of the same name. He is the author of the *New York Times* best-sellers *Argo*, *The Master of Disguise*, and *Spy Dust*.

Matt Baglio is the best-selling author who previously worked with Tony on *Argo* and is also the author of *The Rite*.

PublicAffairs is a publishing house founded in 1997. It is a tribute to the standards, values, and flair of three persons who have served as mentors to countless reporters, writers, editors, and book people of all kinds, including me.

I. F. STONE, proprietor of *I. F. Stone's Weekly*, combined a commitment to the First Amendment with entrepreneurial zeal and reporting skill and became one of the great independent journalists in American history. At the age of eighty, Izzy published *The Trial of Socrates*, which was a national bestseller. He wrote the book after he taught himself ancient Greek.

BENJAMIN C. BRADLEE was for nearly thirty years the charismatic editorial leader of *The Washington Post*. It was Ben who gave the *Post* the range and courage to pursue such historic issues as Watergate. He supported his reporters with a tenacity that made them fearless and it is no accident that so many became authors of influential, best-selling books.

ROBERT L. BERNSTEIN, the chief executive of Random House for more than a quarter century, guided one of the nation's premier publishing houses. Bob was personally responsible for many books of political dissent and argument that challenged tyranny around the globe. He is also the founder and longtime chair of Human Rights Watch, one of the most respected human rights organizations in the world.

·   ·   ·

For fifty years, the banner of Public Affairs Press was carried by its owner Morris B. Schnapper, who published Gandhi, Nasser, Toynbee, Truman, and about 1,500 other authors. In 1983, Schnapper was described by *The Washington Post* as "a redoubtable gadfly." His legacy will endure in the books to come.

Peter Osnos, *Founder*